Murder in the Heart

Murder in the Heart

A True-Life Psychological Thriller

Alexandra Artley

HAMISH HAMILTON • LONDON

HAMISH HAMILTON LTD

Published by the Penguin Group
Penguin Books Ltd, 27 Wrights Lane, London W8 5TZ, England
Penguin Books USA Inc., 375 Hudson Street, New York, 10014, USA
Penguin Books Australia Ltd, Ringwood, Victoria, Australia
Penguin Books Canada Ltd, 10 Alcorn Avenue, Toronto, Ontario, Canada M4V 3B2
Penguin Books (NZ) Ltd, 182–190 Wairau Road, Auckland 10, New Zealand

Penguin Books Ltd, Registered Offices: Harmondsworth, Middlesex, England

First published in Great Britain by Hamish Hamilton Ltd 1993
10 9 8 7 6 5 4 3 2 1

Typeset by Datix International Limited, Bungay, Suffolk
Filmset in 11/13.5 pt Ehrhardt
Printed in England by Clays, St Ives plc

A CIP catalogue record for this book is available from the British Library

ISBN 0-241-13150-2

For my parents

Contents

Foreword

At Liverpool's Crown Court in November 1988, June and Hilda Thompson, both in their late thirties, were convicted of murdering their father with a shotgun. The verdict was never seriously in doubt, but the sentence was frankly surprising. Having listened to some of the most astonishing and revolting evidence ever to be presented in a courtroom, Mr Justice Boreham decided that the sisters merited no more than a token two years' imprisonment, to be suspended. "I accept that in many ways your life has been a form of torment," he said, "and in a sense you have taken your punishment before the event." June and Hilda burst into tears.

Alexandra Artley has undertaken the task of revealing just how deep was that torment. It is a distressing tale of "one small, ordinary family gone completely mad", and the catalogue of cruelties inflicted by Tommy Thompson upon his wife and daughters over a period of nearly forty years is at times painful to read. So, too, it should be. It is not enough that these three devastated women have been given an opportunity to recover from their intolerable ordeal. It also matters that we, the public, should be made aware of what they suffered at the hands of a malign sadist, for there are other Tommy Thompsons in our midst, and the sooner we abandon that complicity of good manners which prevents our intervening to stop such men, the better it will be for who knows how many other wretched wives and children cowering in dark corners to escape their poisonous attention.

This story contains scarcely credible details of incest sandwiched between television programmes, of daily humiliations refined to a point which would bewilder a seasoned psychiatrist, of beatings, manic regulations, tyrannical restrictions and systematic degradation. The most appalling image in the chronicle is also the simplest: June and Hilda standing either side of their mother to prevent her falling when their father put his boots on to kick her in the shin or punch her in the face. The burden of destructive tension endured by both girls since birth makes it clear that no prison could possibly be worse than the one which had always been their home.

This book might additionally help to educate our legislators. The legal understanding of 'provocation' is hopelessly narrow, as the defence is required to prove that the accused was provoked more or less immediately before the offence. It does not encompass the notion that provocation may be cumulative, and thereby more severe. It is time that we recognize that the kind of life led by the Thompson women was not just a mitigating factor but the cause and source of their collapse.

The jury is enjoined to deliver a verdict according to facts and the law. The writer has the liberty to address wider issues in an attempt to discover why normality should so disintegrate as to render a terrible crime inevitable or, as in this case, serve as the alleviation of something demonstrably worse. As Alexandra Artley points out, it is banal to point the finger and call Tommy Thompson 'evil'; one has to show how and why such evil came to flourish. But even explanation is insufficient, except perhaps in a case history to be studied in a journal of criminology. The writer may expand beyond bald chronicle to engage the reader in an exercise of imaginative empathy, to do that which is forbidden in the courtroom – namely, to make the audience *feel* what it was like to live under the same roof as Tommy Thompson.

This Alexandra Artley has done triumphantly. It cannot have been easy, and it is important that it has been done by a woman. At the end of her book, the reader is bound to agree with her that Mrs Thompson and her unfortunate daughters are heroic characters just as visibly they are tragic ones.

Brian Masters

Acknowledgements

I would like to thank Mrs Hilda Thompson and her daughters, June and Hilda Thompson, for their courage and co-operation in helping me to uncover a very harrowing family story which they hope "will be of use to others". I would also like to thank Jacintha Alexander for persuading me to undertake the book and my patient and supportive editor Kate Jones of Hamish Hamilton.

I depended greatly on the time and personal generosity of many people in central Lancashire. I am particularly grateful to Detective Chief Inspector Donald Biscombe of the Lancashire Constabulary; Michael Leach of Dorothy Heaton Solicitors for making legal files available to me and to Mr Barry Hitchin, Office Manager of Dorothy Heaton; Mr Arnold Thompson; George Birtill OBE, Chorley's Honorary Town Historian; Andrew Schofield of the North-West Sound Archive, Clitheroe; the Lancashire dialect poet Joan Pomfret; Mr A. P. Danischewsky and Mr C. R. Effendowicz of Droyt Products, Chorley (manufacturers of excellent soap); Albert and Phyllis Entwistle of the Entwistle School of Dancing, Chorley; Maureen and Dennis Preston, craft weavers; Richard Swift of the Initial (UK) Laundry Ltd, Chorley; and Brian Atkinson, landlord of the County Arms, Preston.

Grateful thanks are also given to Catherine Tite, librarian of the NSPCC Headley Library, London, and to the staff of Chorley Central Library; the Harris Library, Preston, and the Mitchell Library, Glasgow (the biggest public reference library in Europe); to Alison Andrew of the Lansdowne Clinic, Glasgow; Pat and Roddy Stafford for quick bursts of domestic help; Anthea Madden for a spell of secretarial assistance and, of course, to my husband and family and dear friends near and far.

Introduction

On a spring night in 1988, a Lancashire woman dialled 999 and was switched through to the Lawson Street police station in Preston. Her speech seemed slurred, as if she had been drinking, and she said quite simply, "Someone has shot my husband in the head and I think he is dead."

The first policemen to arrive at the house found three women reeking of whisky and weeping quietly beside the body of a murdered man. When it came to sorting out who had made the emergency telephone call, there seemed to be some confusion as to which woman actually was the dead man's 'wife'. There were three survivors in the house – an elderly woman, whose delicate face seemed slightly contorted, and her two middle-aged daughters. They were all accustomed to wearing gold wedding rings and initially they seemed to be rather uncertain themselves about the 'wife' in the telephone call.

That evening, Detective Chief Inspector Donald Biscombe of the Preston Division of the CID had been at home on a weekend off when a call from his office suggested that he should get down to Skeffington Road, in the old industrial Ribbleton neighbourhood of Preston to take a look at what, even to less experienced eyes, already seemed like a rather odd case, because of its strange neatness, even serenity.

Allowing for my inexperience in police matters, Mr Biscombe had been trying to explain in the nicest possible way how in this case the murder scene had been different. We were sitting in his new office on the outskirts of Preston and he had just refreshed his memory from the file.

"When you go to a house with a murder, to put it bluntly, Alexandra, it usually stinks. Poor people in depressed areas – I hate to say this – often council estates, high-rise flats. There's usually been drink involved. But this house was very neat and clean – as murders go, clinical almost. It was not the 'violent' murder done in a fit of temper. There was no stabbing or bludgeoning in this case, of course. But no signs of a struggle or furniture upturned either."

He paused to see if I had grasped the point he was making.

"Unusually calm . . ." I said.

"It was an *execution* really."

At twenty minutes to ten that evening, Mr Biscombe, accompanied by Detective Inspector Ronald Hooper, had drawn up in the usual unmarked CID car outside 193 Skeffington Road – "It was the typical terraced house you find in the mill towns of Lancashire: two-up, two-down, with a back gate" – and entered the principal downstairs room, which had two neatly made-up beds in it. A dead man, perhaps in his sixties, was lying on the bed beneath the window. He was fully dressed, with what looked like one big gunshot wound to the chest now oozing through layers of clothing. The television set was still on and, rather eerily propped up on pillows, the dead man, his eyes opened wide, appeared to be continuing to watch it.

Out in the kitchen, Donald Biscombe found the back door securely fastened on the inside by two bolts and, on the floor, a 12-bore single-barrel Baikel shotgun. Very precisely, two spent cartridges had been placed directly side by side on a shelf in the pantry. Upstairs in the house, the same chilly order prevailed in a bedroom which had one three-quarters bed in it. Next door, on the tiny landing, he discovered some kind of family storeroom or boxroom.

By this time, the women had already been removed from the house for interview and Donald Biscombe did not see them until he was back in the office on Monday morning. Then, like his colleagues and all who later met the Thompsons, he was rather taken aback by their quiet presence – three acting rather remotely as one.

"They were very composed – not hysterical. They looked odd. Not being disrespectful, but they do look odd, don't they?

The mother, Mrs Thompson, perhaps because of the operation to her face . . .? The girls because there's something not quite *compos mentis* about them . . .?"

"I suppose all people seem strange when taken in extremity," I said.

But Mr Biscombe went on, newly intrigued after three years by the women's remoteness and calm, perhaps even by their 'lady-like' quality. "I don't want to be disrespectful, but they *are* very strange people."

By 11.30 that night, with his examination of the house completed, Donald Biscombe stood with other colleagues in the mortuary of the Preston Royal Hospital while a Home Office pathologist began the first of two post-mortems on the murder victim.

Because Tommy Thompson would not be watching it any more, Detective Chief Inspector Donald Biscombe had paused before leaving the house in Skeffington Road to finally switch off the television set.

God would take us 3 because we
couldn't carry on with life living like
this, because if Dad shot us all he
always said he would shoot us in the
legs & that we would suffer dieing
slowly. He wasn't a big man but he
was very strong when he was in a
temper, he thought nothing of thumping
you, head butting, kicking, dragging you
round the room with your hair. It
was bad enough him hitting Hilda & I
but to have to stand & watch him hitting
Mum was unbearable at times I couldn't
watch I had to turn my head away, if
Hilda or I had to speak while he was
hitting Mum he would hit her more.
Mum has had to go to Hospital so
many times because of him hitting her,
there was one time he broke her nose
there was blood everywere he said to
Hilda & I stop her nose from bleeding
or I'll put you both in hospital we
we tried everything to stop it bleeding

A Page from one of June Thompson's notebooks.

I

Getting to Know You

To the casual eye, Tommy Thompson seemed to be an ordinary man. If one looked into his history, it at first appeared to be rather ordinary too – army conscript, textile worker, building labourer and then, chronic invalid. But more unusually for such a man, Tommy Thompson had not only enjoyed playing tricks with photography for almost forty years, he had gambled with appearances: on most people believing that everyday life is the way it looks.

For his own last appearance before the camera lens Tommy Thompson lay in the mortuary of the Royal Preston Hospital, Lancashire, as a police photographer's shutter (clicking in the clinical echo) recorded each stage of this murdered man's post-mortem. When glossily printed up, these colour photographs were destined for the police Blue Books, which are kept in Britain as a visual record of every murder inquiry. Each murder victim gets two: one Blue Book shows in detail the 'scene' of the murder, while the other records each stage in the murder victim's post-mortem. I had travelled 250 miles from Glasgow that day to sit in a policeman's office and look at these last photographs of an ordinary man and a Blue Book was opened before me.

The first time I had full sight of Tommy Thompson he was lying on a metal post-mortem table which was pierced with circular holes. In the manner of a cook triumphantly dealing with a whole poached salmon, it was as if the pathologist had lifted him dripping out of obscurity on the drainer of a giant fish-kettle. Standing to the back of the photograph (and only visible from the waist down) was the pathologist, Dr Edmund Tap, amply swathed in green. Having drawn on fine flesh-coloured rubber gloves, his hands exuded a degree of professional impatience and were hanging ready to start.

Shot dead at the age of fifty-seven while in the middle of an epileptic fit, Tommy Thompson lay flat on his back, chin sharply raised, on the pierced-metal pathology table. Bright with surprise, his dark eyes still seemed to catch the moment of extinction. His mouth was also open in a kind of hardened gasp, revealing either decayed teeth or old metal fillings. It was a brown desiccated mouth, like that of an animal petrified in the outrage of taxidermy. Above finely checked beige trousers, a leather belt perhaps had been loosened to give him greater ease during his last fit and a red sports shirt fell open at the throat. Shades of red abounded. There was red on red – a huge red dent on the red shirt and, immediately beneath it, the darker red pool of a second, deeper shotgun wound.

I had never seen a post-mortem in any form before and this first picture in the Blue Book turned out to be the pleasant one. After that, Dr Tap had begun to undress the corpse for the camera, taking off one layer at a time in a kind of pathological strip-tease. In the next picture Tommy Thompson's red shirt was off, revealing a white sleeved vest with a shocking soak of red. Personal idiosyncrasies also began to appear: on the murdered man's left arm was the tattooed face of a panther, its stiff whiskers spraying out like wire brushes. Tilting the body to remove the red shirt seemed to have smeared a trail of new blood round Thompson's throat and now there were splotches and spatters of watery red on his forearms, and more had leaked down on to the metal pathology table. Next came the true nakedness of the man himself. Immediately over his heart, beneath a pallid nipple, the coarse, dark chest hair had been literally parted by two enormous circular wounds, so deep and cleanly formed that I could unwillingly glimpse a glistening mush of maroon organs beneath. Perfectly red, circular and livid, the top wound was still quietly draining into the second. Suddenly, darting down below all this came the long, white track of an ancient surgical scar – in the circumstances, as remotely innocent a mark as the jet trail in a summer sky.

"Shall we go on?" Detective Chief Inspector Biscombe asked

me gently (and when I failed immediately to reply, his hand lingered comfortingly on the turn of the next page).

Cooks are advised always to buy beef on which the fat is a rich yellow and, as we tentatively went on, I was surprised to see that the internal fat on this human being was also a bright yellow, in contrast to the red glare of internal flesh. Now the pathologist's beige-gloved hand was stained like a butcher's as it held back one half of Tommy Thompson's rib-cage to show the hundreds of tiny black lead pellets which had spewed out of each cartridge and into the chest cavity. For visibility, Dr Tap had neatly sawn off the rib-bones on one side, as if some horrid kind of chops were in the making. Quite involuntarily, Rembrandt's famous still life of the hanging ox carcass came to mind, along with totally unsuitable Meat Marketing Board slogans like slam in the lamb. With relief I noted that in Detective Chief Inspector Biscombe's last picture Tommy Thompson was recognizably human again. Here was the side view that in happier circumstances a wife or mistress might cherish from a bed – a long, secretly white male body and, resting beside it, a tough sinewy forearm covered in light-brown hair. Another drift of hair on the thigh led down to what, on this man, had done so much damage to his own daughters. Tactfully, this secret part of the man was out of frame.

"The jury don't usually see this book," said Mr Biscombe, with an eye on its proper place in the steel-grey filing cabinet behind his arid desk. And closing it, he put his big hand over the cover, as if to blot out shock.

The Thompson murder case glided to public notice in the *Lancashire Evening Post* in March 1988, when a local reporter, Philip Widdows, whacked together a short item on the death of a disabled man from shotgun wounds in a terraced house in Skeffington Road, Preston ("Three held in death probe").

Skeffington Road is a slightly grander version of the famous plasterboard set for *Coronation Street* and is built of harsh red machine-pressed bricks, called technically in the building trade

'Accrington bloods'. But even in supposedly simple British terraces, the design inspiration varies wildly. Here, square-headed 'portcullis-style' doorcases pop up as an industrial echo of the ancient medieval doorways at Lancaster Castle and give a hint, in a Victorian mill town, of Lancashire's heraldic red-rose past. The scene of the murder, 193 Skeffington Road, turned out to be the last house in the terrace, with a small brick electricity substation stuck on one side like a shed.

All was sharply conservative and respectable, and yielded up precious little to a reporter in a hurry. The Thompsons' front door had been painted bright red with the precision of scarlet varnish applied to a fingernail, and cleanliness shone out from the windows crisply hung with bridal nets. By doorstepping neighbours in the usual way of journalists, Philip Widdows eventually extracted the fact that the occupants of the house were 'very insular'. Later, across the bar of the nearby County Arms, the local publican, Brian Atkinson, juggled professional expansiveness with local prudence and was guarded on behalf of all concerned, implying that Tommy Thompson might have had reason to take his own life. Perhaps sensing the deluge of grotesque suffering which violent death might release from this house, he affably confined himself to remarking that Thompson (a regular at the pub) was a registered epileptic who "seemed to be a very worried man, as if something was playing on his mind".

By the time these simple inquiries were completed, Thompson's widow and daughters had left 193 Skeffington Road and were already in the hospital wing of the Risley Remand Centre near Warrington, Cheshire. Ten days later, the neighbours again caught up with them in print when the three women were charged at a magistrate's court in Preston with murder and with conspiracy to murder. Unlike most fictional murder stories, the mystery of Skeffington Road was no longer Who Did It, but how murder in this particular family had been averted for so long.

Like the neighbours in Skeffington Road, this was a story I was initially keen to avoid. Everything about it seemed forbidding and, in any case, my thoughts at the time were scattered elsewhere. After living in central London for twenty years, I had recently removed to Glasgow and was digging a family into a new (albeit welcoming) city. As well as this painful uprooting from a city I love, in other ways my life was changing too. It was time to fully accept that my thirties had vanished and, as with most people in early middle life, I was emotionally in turmoil. It was then I realized that in age the two daughters in the Thompson murder story were roughly my contemporaries and that, in infinitely more harrowing circumstances, they too must have been suddenly drawn into this emotional foundry in which the submerged child in us suddenly and resoundingly rises up to shape us for new maturity.

From what I had already casually read of the life patterns of sexually victimized children, most finally break away from the abuser in adolescence. Usually, they run away from home (a factor now beginning to be appreciated in teenage homelessness), blow the whistle or, in small conservative societies, dive into an early and often destructive marriage. But the Thompsons' situation was quite unlike any aspect of this recognized pattern. June Thompson, in particular, had been used for sexual intercourse by her father up to six weeks before his death, when she had been thirty-six and he fifty-seven. In other words, when two sisters wait until their thirties to murder a father who had never ceased to brutalize them since birth, some kind of particularly violent 'mid-life' crisis must have taken place.

The *age* of the women when they murdered Tommy Thompson continued to tempt me forward. Reports of their insularity and reticence of speech also began to present something of a technical challenge, as well as fuelling my new curiosity about the emotional possibilities of middle life. Eventually, after spreading out a handful of Press Association newspaper cuttings on the plastic table of a 7.00 a.m. fast train from Glasgow to Preston, I did a bit of journalistic origami.

*

Like McDonald's versus Burger King, the *Daily Mirror* and the *Sun* had sizzled a Preston murder-trial aftermath and slapped on a house brand of garnish. Sharply tarted up with typographical sesame bun and picture pickle was the yarn of two middle-aged Lancashire women called June and Hilda Thompson, who had rather remarkably shot their father together at point-blank range while he had been seized by an epileptic fit in a downstairs room of their tiny terraced house in Preston. In differing ways the tabloids accurately caught the curious combination of high banality and low horror which characterized not only the Thompson family but any family which has gone very seriously wrong in the way it is supposed to 'work'.

"Just about everything in that drab little house holds some awful memory for those two tormented sisters," wrote Christina Appleyard in the *Daily Mirror*. "Even the Hoover."

> "Dad used to make us hold the Hoover lead in a particular way when we were using it," Hilda Thompson, 35, says.
>
> "If we didn't, he'd head-butt us on the back of the head where he knew the bruises wouldn't show. Or he'd put his shoes on and kick us hard in the stomach."
>
> The fact these two women still call the monster they have been describing 'Dad' takes a little getting used to. And so does the fact that two such helpless-looking women could actually take a shotgun and cold-bloodedly shoot their father, Tommy, while he was temporarily in the throes of a fit.

She went on:

> After drinking a large amount of whisky, the shaken pair then telephoned the police in Preston, Lancashire, and confessed to what they had done.
>
> "We were sent to Risley Remand Centre – and those were some of the happiest days of our lives," June, 36, recalls . . .
>
> Sitting listening to all this and occasionally joining in is their

mother, Hilda senior, who's 57. Now she is a wrecked shell of a woman, kept awake at night by lurid nightmares in which her husband comes back from the dead and blames her for allowing the girls to kill him.

"You might ask why we didn't just run away," she says. "It must seem strange to everyone from the outside. But remember, we grew up being scared of him. We didn't know anything else. He used to say that if we did anything he would kill us. And we had reason to believe him. He did everything else he threatened to do."

As for the freedom the sisters can look forward to . . . "Well, we go to bingo now," Hilda says, her eyes lighting up. "And we buy ourselves *Woman* and *Woman's Own*. He'd never let us have those in the house."

With heart-breaking childish glee she adds: "Oh . . . and we have Shredded Wheat for breakfast every day."

Straight down to sex, violence and freshly ground screw of the grotesque, the *Sun* simply printed a most unflattering photograph of the Thompson sisters in its News Special: THE FAMILY THEY CALLED THE MUNSTERS:

> Evil dad Thomas Thompson and the two daughters who shot him dead were known by neighbours as The Munsters after the weird TV clan.
>
> Locals watched in amazement as Thompson marched his wife and daughters military-fashion up and down the street . . .
>
> Thompson first forced June to have sex with him when she was 14 – and later made her go on the Pill . . .

After a very po-faced account of the court proceedings, the *Daily Telegraph* then typically electrified its readers by supplying one extremely harrowing detail that the tabloids had mercifully omitted to print (and which does not appear in this book).

By Christmas 1988, the three women were left without a rag of private or public dignity between them, the Press moved on and, with the help of Preston social services department, the family disposed of the house they owned and attempted to begin life afresh in a quiet council maisonette about half a mile away from Skeffington Road. Even after murder, in the old-fashioned working-class way of 'staying put', to move away from the neighbourhood entirely seemed quite unthinkable.

After the Highlands of Scotland, the Lake District is rather like passing through a pleasing rockery. As the railway stations, which were to become as familiar as stops on a local bus route, glided into reality – Carlisle, Penrith, Oxenholme-in-the-Lake-District, Lancaster and then on to Preston – I looked again at the face of Detective Chief Inspector Donald Biscombe, who had been in charge of the Thompson murder inquiry and whose photograph in a newspaper rather appealed to me. Shortly, I hoped to able to match the picture with the reality of the man.

Approaching Preston station from the north, the railway passes close to a vast red-brick palace with a campanile effect at one end. Glowing in the haze of industrial summer, the building blazed with huge letters set into the terracotta wall in white brick: TULKETH MILL. Then I arrived in the airy Gothic sprawl of Preston station, which feels in summer as if trains are being announced among the hanging baskets in a Victorian conservatory.

"How will I know you?" Mr Biscombe had said.

"Well, I'm five feet two, with dark hair with reddish bits in it, and green eyes. But don't worry, I'll look out for you. I've already seen your picture in the *Lancashire Evening Post*."

Tanned and slightly balding, the Detective Chief Inspector was not at all dissimilar in height and bearing to Mr Gorbachev in his powerful, virile days. Soused like a herring in Diorissimo, I felt sorry to have the momentary advantage of him, as I watched him near the station newspaper stand shyly checking the whiteness of his cuffs, the shine on his shoes and the smoothness of the lapels on his smart grey suit in the lightning way that some men seem to prepare themselves for a dubious business meeting in which appearances may be of particular account.

"Alexandra?"

"Mr Biscombe?"

He was a very reliable man, and his handshake was so enfolding that it was like putting my own hand into a warm duvet. Mr Biscombe drove in the fast, absolutely expert police way and soon we were whizzing to his out-of-town office through the leafy summer lanes of Lancashire. Not having met before, it was curious that we immediately had the intimate lives of so many complete strangers in common – Tommy Thompson, his wife Hilda, 'young Hilda', June, and Tommy's macho brother Cyril. Through them, it was as if we had known each other for years.

"You see, Mr Biscombe, it's not enough just to say that Tommy Thompson was a monster, a villain, a tyrant. He was all those things, but I need to know *why* he was like that. I can't just write a book about a child abuser saying he was an 'evil man'. These people don't just spring out of the ground like dragon's teeth. There has to be a reason for what he did."

Mr Biscombe kept his eyes firmly on the minor road which was now parting the shaking, glittering green of the noon-day countryside before us.

"He was abused in some way as a child, you know."

"What evidence do you have for that?"

"Oh, nothing . . . It's said these men usually have been. But whatever happened to Tommy Thompson as a child, it wasn't police business – more of a social-work side, like you're doing, Alexandra."

Mr Biscombe's car swept firmly into a vast, landscaped complex – a sort of police university with blocks of 1950s brick-built students' flats, a firearms range, a rugby pitch and strong-legged young men distantly bopping tennis balls over a shimmering July net. Up in his office, which had the austerity of public duties taken seriously, Detective Chief Inspector Biscombe hung up his jacket, rolled up his shirt-sleeves and temporarily set aside the demands of his new job as head of the Lancashire Police Complaints Department in order to help me with my work.

We had lunched together and relations were cordial, but these were days in which even a strikingly honest high-ranking policeman had reason to fear the undertow of treachery in a writer. Child abuse is a subject which flays people open to the soul and perhaps seeing me in his own office made him once more professionally cautious about my motives.

"Look, Mr Biscombe," I said, "I'm not here to trap the police. All the professionals involved in this case were exemplary – the police, the legal representatives, the social workers, even the judge, when he gave the unfortunate sisters only two years' probation for murder and said, 'Go home and look after your mother.' For once, the whole thing was a triumph of British justice."

I hate using tape-recorders. They can be the technology of lying writing (conveying what was said, but not always what was *meant*) and they can be pretty blunt instruments for truthfully recalling events. Mr Biscombe flinched too, as the stupid tape in mine kept leaping and gasping like something slippery making its way upstream.

"If I were here to trap you, don't you think I'd know how to set up a tape-recorder properly? I think the children must have put some My Little Pony thing in this."

Patiently, Mr Biscombe appraised the black box, sorted it out and then reached for the police file I had come to discuss.

The Thompson home at No 193 Skeffington Road had fallen into the category of 'notorious houses' (buildings where a murder or a suicide has taken place) which are difficult to dispose of immediately on the open market. As is usual in such cases, the Thompson women had eventually sold it to a professional builder who had then totally revamped it to expunge the unpleasant associations of the past. Internally, its present form was now useless to me, and to understand the exact details of the family's lives I desperately needed to see the place as it had been at the time of the murder. The first Blue Book (the photographic record a jury always sees) had very usefully recorded the Thompsons' home within hours of the murder and, after we had talked about the case for some while, Mr Biscombe set it before me.

As if flying with an all-encompassing eye, the police photographer had passed like a spirit behind the very proper red front door of 193 Skeffington Road to record the most astonishing domestic interior I have ever seen. This 'home' was not the warm and comforting place that, with social crenellations of 'hearth' and 'children', is supposed to distinguish the Englishman's castle. It was a house organized on the ground floor almost entirely as an NHS hospital and on the upper as a military barracks. It was an eerie amateur museum of one small, ordinary family gone completely mad.

Downstairs (in what estate agents call the 'one recep'), there were no comfortable chairs, no sofa, nor any general table for the entertaining of outsiders or for use by the family itself. Instead, this 'living' rather than 'sitting' room was fitted up as a kind of twin-bedded hospital ward with two single beds projecting from each side of a fireplace.

The whole house had been neatly decorated in a kind of bleak Modernism of the 1960s with earlier echoes. In some 'contemporary' fashion, the fireplace wall was painted chocolate brown (to contrast with the three other plain white walls) and a big electric fire was set into a teak surround with strong horizontal lines. Above the fireplace was a photographic mural of three fluffy white kittens looking up against sprays of pink spring blossom to an irresponsibly blue sky.

Around each bed were signs of His 'n' Hers chronic invalidity. Mr Thompson had a blue plastic waste-bin beside his bed, and at its foot he had squarely hogged the TV set for his own convenience. Beside Mrs Thompson's bed the plastic waste-bin was pink, and among the endless pill-boxes, jars and bottles of medicine (quite separately set out for each patient on the fiddly little decorative shelves of the teak fire-surround) she had personalized her part of the room with a small plastic duck.

The spirit hand of the photographer then seemed to pull out drawer after drawer in this room to reveal a veritable chemist's stock of medicines – pills, tablets, ointments, dressings, pessaries, suppositories and gels – for epilepsy, diabetes, cancer, back pain, skin disorders, contraception and toothache. Inside the door of one cupboard in this 'living-room' literally dozens of biro-written notices had been posted up in the manner of a ward sister's dispensing notes.

"You see these bits of paper . . ." said Mr Biscombe, like me inwardly marvelling as we pored over the Blue Book together. "One, two, three, four, five, six – there are twenty-two or twenty-three there!"

Even without the magnification he offered, the bigger notices in the small photograph were reasonably easy to read because of the clarity of a childlike hand:

MORN TABLETS

DAD

DAD (Fits)
4 Phenytion
1 Sun
1 Royal Jelly
1 Vitamin

JUNE
1 Epelim
1 Sun
1 Royal Jelly

HILDA
1 Epelim
1 Sun
2 Vitamins
1 Nortriptyline

MAMS
1 Sun
1 Royal Jelly
1 Vitamin
1 Blood Pressure
1 Anti-Sickness

Referring to the pet bird whose cage was suspended a few yards away above a bullet-pocked pink bath in the kitchen, a further notice pinned up inside the door of the same cupboard read: BUDGIES LOSE THEIR FEATHERS (MOULTING) IN SEPTEMBER. And then, as a bizarre pointer to the way I was later to discover that this family documented every banal commercial detail of its forty-year existence, another notice read: STARTED TO USE NEW SOAP DISH (FROM 'CHOICE') ON 26.11.87. £3.99.

"Choice!" I exclaimed. "I don't think there was much 'choice' in this family."

"Aye, 'Choice'," said Mr Biscombe ruminatively. "It was some kind of supermarket place on Preston high street."

As his hand again turned the page, my eyes flew up steep, dark, narrow stairs, in fear of what might lie above. On the landing was a small, white, wrought-iron table, bearing a vase of plastic roses such as one might find in depressingly spotless, night-before-the-Cherbourg-ferry boarding-houses in Portsmouth. Then, behind one dark-blue door lay what seemed to be a *warehouse*, with endless rows of carefully labelled 'supplies' thrust up on metal industrial racking. Banged up on austere shelving for rapid recall, such things as tinned and dried food, medical items, clothes, torches, emergency cooking utensils and tools gave the room the distinct air of a military stores. Next door, the room beside the 'stores' was the one I feared. It seemed that even as adults, June and Hilda Thompson had shared a bed in a room as narrow and bleak as a coffin. In terms of what it contained and displayed, no soldier could have been so stripped of personal identity. Apart from the bed, curtains and a box for storing clothes, the only personal item in the room was one small, tinny alarm clock which doubtless rang across the icy-looking lino to say, Go To The Factory. This was the room to which Tommy Thompson had casually gone up week after week to rape his daughters.

I had seen enough and, sensing that matters were drawing to a close, Mr Biscombe sent out in his kindly way for tea.

The entire Thompson family had been born in the neighbouring town of Chorley and had lived there until 1970, when June and Hilda were teenagers. Getting to know Chorley seemed the most sensible thing to do next and, to get me there, Mr Biscombe was at the wheel in a flash.

Reopening the police file on this case had brought back to him the sheer horror of what had happened to the women in the Thompson family, the acute details of which had become naturally submerged in his memory during a deluge of subsequent work. Having seen the very rooms in which the events had taken place, I was in a state of mild shock. I realized that we were both experiencing the emotional conflict which affects all professionals, both legal and therapeutic, who have to deal with the incest perpetrator. There is an urge to revile and harm the man while, at the same time, we are rationally aware that he himself is often the victim of childhood circumstances submerged from our view and, if we can manage it, equally needful of understanding. That week, Britain's youngest rape victim had been announced in the Press – a little girl of three subjected to full sexual intercourse by a male 'babysitter' of twenty-six in whose care she had been left by some all too casual mother. How many parents have not clenched their fists in violent feeling at such cases and thought, *Leave me alone in a room with him for ten minutes and whatever human pulp crawls out can go free*? Perhaps thinking more precisely of the two vast shotgun wounds in the chest of Tommy Thompson, Mr Biscombe defused our sombre mood with a curt laugh.

"I reckon those two lasses did us all a favour."

We had reached Chorley and he seemed concerned that, once I got out of his car, I would be alone in a strange town.

"Don't worry, Mr Biscombe," I said. "Chorley is on the railway network. When I've had a look round, I'll be able to connect up somehow to get back to Glasgow."

"You're quite sure you'll be all right?"

"Of *course* I will!"

Then again, perhaps fearing the kinds of things that are sometimes written about silent sexual victims like June and Hilda Thompson, he added, as he leaned across me to open the car door, "You'll be kind to them – won't you?"

When Mr Biscombe's car had slowly negotiated an exit from the crowded shopping street in Chorley and then disappeared, I was on my own in Tommy Thompson's home town for the first time. Unlike many modern women, I have no sense of direction whatsoever and usually rely on ephemeral landmarks like shops and more reliable buildings like churches or pretty houses to vaguely remember where I am. As if offering the hand of friendship, a large coloured tourist map in the market place said ambiguously, 'You Are Here', and soon I was able to pick up a handful of cheerful-looking tourist literature extolling the attractions of this part of Lancashire.

Perhaps such a beautiful summer's afternoon in any central Lancashire town would have produced the same effect, but Chorley almost immediately struck me as particularly open and charming. At first glance it seemed to be an ancient and pleasantly hilly market town set beneath the jutting blue of Anglezarke Moor. Despite a blustery bus station and a fair amount of commercial activity (including two vast open-air markets still in full swing), Chorley had magically retained a semi-rural air – hilliness and the promise of moors, modest Georgian houses with a glimpse of Gothick window, a medieval parish church, a couple of country-looking pastel-washed pubs, a fringe of steeply shelving bluebell woods and everywhere the tense, pleasurable feeling of trapped water longing to burst out beneath one's feet in typically Lancastrian 'flashy' streams. Lively tourist literature featured the little town at the centre of the Lancashire Heritage Trail ('Discover the Charms of Chorley') and happily mentioned that this was the home town of Sir Henry Tate (1819–99), sugar magnate, philanthropist and founder of the Tate Gallery, London.

Tommy Thompson had been born in Chorley on 29 March 1931 and, perhaps foolishly, I was surprised at the apparent sweetness of a little semi-rural town that could also claim him as a son. But as I walked on in search of Buchanan Street, where he had spent his childhood and youth, I soon discovered that Chorley is sliced very oddly in two by a humming blade of railway line and that immediately on each side of these tracks there were two very differing Chorleys. My place of passage was a solidly built, green-tiled Victorian subway beneath the railway, vigorously marked at street level by big cast-iron railings topped with lumpy fleurs-de-lis. Dart like a rabbit into a burrow on one side of the railway and one left behind a pleasing medieval market town genteelly engaged in the heritage trade. Pop up a few yards away on the other side and, in a fusty orange glow of Accrington brick subdued by purplish soot, lay a Victorian industrial townscape caught in amber, a cotton mill (or the hole where a cotton mill had once been) at the end of each small street. I was drawn in and soon, as if to add a transcendental note to my confusion about how to establish time, place and reality in the birthplace of Tommy Thompson, Lancastrian Catholicism suddenly rose high at the entrance to Buchanan Street in the shape of a bulky orange-brick church called the Sacred Heart.

With a population of only 25,000, Chorley has no fewer than five big Roman Catholic churches. Like the Sacred Heart itself, they were the Victorian continuation of the powerful current of ancient Catholicism which had caused the people here both inwardly to resist the Reformation and, during the Dissolution of the Monasteries, physically to reinstate places like Cartmell Priory, a great abbey of the Lancastrian coast, so that its bells and beacons would continue to give warning to seafarers blinded by walls of wintry water off Morecambe Bay. Nowadays, only a few bomb sites opposite this particular Catholic church suggested that any kind of violent past, either national or personal, had ever happened here at all. Instead, Buchanan Street, running off from the church, was an oasis of 1980s gentility. Both cast down and amused, I walked along the street in which this sadistic man had once played.

Buchanan Street is a small, desirable terrace on which estate agents' boards hang densely like a forest of dropped signals on a short, old-fashioned railway journey. The individuality of Britain's home-owners is bold and convincing. So-called 'Kentucky Fried Georgian' front doors now replace earlier, plainer ones. One house has startling white Swiss shutters and hanging baskets cascading with pink geraniums; another boasts panes of 'bull's-eye' glass to give a cosy, goggle-eyed look, while, further on, another tiny house with picture windows almost as big as itself reveals posh mauve puffs of Austrian blind. This glossy New Brit-scape ends in a small cobbled zone of municipal saplings and a corner pub called the Cotton Tree – as coolly whitewashed, spotless and inwardly reserved as if it lay in the remotest part of Norfolk.

Sitting rather disconsolately in the Cotton Tree while working out which train from Chorley might possibly connect that evening with Glasgow, I began to realize that the lives of Tommy Thompson and his family would not be yielded up easily, because appearances had been kept up for too long. Forty years of sadism, supplication and silent endurance had already passed by, and behind all that lay Tommy himself – as a child. In any case, there are no certainties in family history. As if to compensate for being inevitably locked into the past, the English above all other nations tend to remain silent while fiercely seeking to expunge it.

Finishing a glass of appalling white wine, I reluctantly recognized that every type of research method I had ever heard of would now have to be brought to bear on a mystery so rarely attempted in detail – what had really happened in one particular family sunk among the masses of Britain's truly obscure.

*

Despite the now-sagging flesh of a man in his sixth decade, Tommy Thompson's face in all the tabloid newspaper cuttings was not without refinement. Propped up in my little private room, the pictures showed a high, intelligent forehead, a small, bony Roman nose like an eagle's beak and a hardened, dry mouth whose thin upper lip suggested a practical interest in control or power rather than sensuality. His eyes, however, were as striking as those in a portrait by Ribera. Set quite openly, beneath bushy black brows, they were the kind of very dark, piercing eyes in which it is impossible to distinguish the pupil from the iris. Unlike lighter-coloured eyes, behind which one can sometimes see thoughts passing like clouds, or feelings wavering like a candle-flame in a draught, these eyes seemed to offer only a limited range of communication with others – compulsion, perhaps, and decision, occasionally charged with the yellowish flash of anger.

Tommy Thompson was the youngest of four illegitimate sons born to Mary Ann Thompson and her common-law husband, James, a heavy drinker who worked somewhat reluctantly as an all-purpose day labourer. Tommy's elder brothers (in birth order), Arnold, James and Cyril, still lived in Chorley and my hope was to speak to them first to try to establish what had really happened to Tommy in childhood. Above anything else, I wanted a first-hand glimpse into that childhood terraced house in Buchanan Street before the fancy ruched blinds spoke of a new era to passers-by. But Arnold was a recluse and James may as well have been vapour for all the contact I could establish with him. That left Cyril, a window-cleaner and Judo black-belt, who was known locally as a very macho type. Cyril had been called as a defence witness in the Thompson sisters' trial to describe his brother's violent, tyrannical character and, as he was contactable by telephone, I started with him first.

I was terribly apprehensive as I dialled Cyril Thompson's telephone number from Glasgow, because in his situation I too might feel that the whole affair was really none of my business. Cyril Thompson turned out to be one of those men who find high, light women's voices as irritating as summer gnats. When attempting to communicate verbally with rather tough men, a woman is supposed to pitch her voice lower and to be very direct in speech, with no lateral meandering to the point of a conversation. But, alas, I seemed to jangle him from the start and I could feel his irritation mounting at a voice apparently issuing from some far-distant twingle-twangling fairy off the top of a Christmas tree.

In the first place, Cyril seemed to resent the fact that the Thompson women might get involved in a written account of their lives at all. Now that several years had passed since the murder and they had settled down in their council maisonette to try to start a new life, Cyril felt they should be "glad to live quiet".

"Are they getting money for it?" he asked sharply. "Are *you* getting money for it?"

The bright-blue logo of the Royal Bank of Scotland shone almost tangibly before my eyes as I instantly thought of overdrafts, statements, letters, credit-card demands, time running out, train fares back and forth from Glasgow to Lancashire, hotel bills, part-time childcare at just under £400 a month and the latest American child-abuse reference books specially ordered at £25 a time.

"Well, yes. But you see, trying to write very carefully about June, Hilda and Mrs Thompson is my *work* for about eighteen months . . . And, anyway, they say they *want* to tell their side of the story."

Cyril Thompson clearly did not regard time spent looking into the lives of his nieces as "work" and suddenly yelled in anger, "If I hadn't spoken up in court as I did, those two lasses would be in gaol!"

Like his brother, he seemed to be no stranger to shows of violent temper.

"I want nowt to do wi'it and if you mention my name in the book I'll sue you!"

Following his banged-down telephone receiver, a clear singing line was left uselessly in my hand.

A week or two passed. I was now utterly determined to get to Arnold Thompson, because his very reclusiveness led me to suppose he was a man with something interesting to say. Another fortnight of telephone calls and tentative letters eventually led me to an elderly woman who knew Arnold and was prepared to take me to him, provided she could remain anonymous. The best she could suggest was that she would lead me to Arnold's house and hope that he would eventually agree to let me in. The method of approach troubled me but I could see no other way.

Although it was a great relief at least to have a go at meeting Tommy Thompson's reclusive elder brother, the purely practical part of me resented having to make a journey from Glasgow to Chorley purely on spec. To get in something like a working day in Lancashire, every trip meant rising at 5.30 a.m. to bung a slow-cooking casserole in the oven for family supper later that day and remembering a myriad of things, like cutting school sandwiches, setting out clean clothes on each sleeping daughter's chair, scribbling spouse-instruction notes ('Deliver to ballet, Marywood Square, 5.00 p.m. Collect 6.00 p.m. sharp'), and not forgetting to leave a hairbrush and ribbons on the hall table so that a good neighbour could come in at 8.00 a.m. to plait the girls' hair before they went to school. Then came the stupid tape-recorder, papers and panic rammed into a plastic carrier bag. But by the time I managed to flee the house around 6.20, early-morning taxi drivers, rail men and newspaper sellers would always manage to sweeten the day with the camaraderie which exists between all people who find themselves working at odd hours of the night and semi-day.

Even in Glasgow, Scottish midsummer nights carry a faintly Scandinavian feeling in the sky, which never turns completely black at that time of the year but reserves a rich, royal-blue light even at midnight. By 8.30 a.m. that particular morning, the royal blue had been long dispelled by another perfect day rounding itself out of the Cumbrian fells, and by the time I was led to Arnold Thompson's front door by my helpful contact, northern English daylight, like an oven turned up, blazed in full July.

Arnold Thompson occupied a whole house in a distinguished-looking council estate full of mellow brick semi-detached houses built during the 1930s. With rather smeary windows, drooping colourless curtains and a battered front door, his was one of the few houses on the estate which was not now in private ownership. Around it, cascading gardens, hanging baskets, elegant patches of white trellis and estate agents' boards proclaimed the privatization of council estates during the 1980s. My guide knocked timidly on the door and soon, to our delight, it opened a crack.

"Arnold, are you all right, love? It's only me and I've brought my friend Alex with me. Can we talk to you for a minute?"

Not only was Arnold Thompson at home, but he was actually letting us in, and I was in a state approximating to joy, not untinged with guilt.

Unlike Cyril Thompson, whose rudeness and aggression I had been partly expecting, Arnold Thompson turned out to be a man not only of charm but of a rather sophisticated humour. He was in his late sixties, tall and broadly built, with a craggy, romantic head from which smiled two large, pale-blue eyes.

Nervously, I sat down on the proffered sofa in his sitting-room, marvelling that neither in coloration nor temperament did he seem to bear the least resemblance to his notorious younger brother. Feeling a complete fraud and intruder (and wondering how on earth I was ever going to introduce the subject of Tommy's possible abuse as a child), I just smiled in an all-purpose way and left it to Mrs X to open the batting.

Arnold Thompson was an English type I had long ago recognized – a charming old Filth Packet who lives in that easy-going twilight state between never quite getting up but never quite getting ready for bed. With long grey hair worn strongly back in the manner of the elderly Liszt, he had on a shirt loosely open in a dégagé way that smarter young men might take five minutes to achieve and a pair of washed (but not pressed) grey flannel trousers over no underpants.

In deference to a sore leg which he kept sticking out firmly in front of him, he wore one slipper and one shoe (sock on shoe foot only). His sitting room was a palace of nicotine, with a ceiling coloured pub amber. Darting with sharp triangles and squares, the 'contemporary' wall paper had now reached that dark-orange stage where, if one felt inclined to lick it, it would be smoky-bacon flavour and on it was hung a tremendous number of ancient Catholic wall calendars dating back to 1971. The main furnishings in the room were a huge black-and-white television set (kept because it did not need a licence and "everything on telly is black and white anyway") and a coarse, green-hide three-piece suite designed in the 1930s with big rounded arms. Arnold Thompson seemed solitary but not lonely – he was a man with spiritual or inner resources of his own. Beside his telly-watching chair sat forty more cigarettes, a bottle of tomato ketchup and a jar of yellow piccalilli for instant application on fireside takeaways. As Mrs X began to speak, I looked down to the floor, which was a mosaic of lino offcuts in 3-D pebble and marble effects.

Mrs X is a slight, prettily faded and very intelligent woman in her sixties who had known Arnold off and on since youth. She had been a factory worker and, if she had come from a different background, her brightness and social aplomb might well have marked her out as a television interviewer, such was her calm and surprising grip on the entire situation: I needed to know something rather delicate and, properly approached, Arnold Thompson well might be persuaded to tell me.

Gaining the confidence of 'intimate' interviewees by carefully establishing past association with them is the first rule, and she understood it instinctively. Putting her knees together in a rather winsome way which he instantly noticed, Mrs X laid one small hand on the broad, rounded arm of the green-hide armchair and said:

"This suite's done champion, hasn't it, Arnold?"

"Aye. It has that. We had it in mother's time in the old house."

"You looked after your mother when she got old, didn't you, Arnold?" I quietly interjected and, after partly explaining my objectives, we somehow moved on from there.

Mary Ann Thompson, Arnold's mother, had been powerfully attracted to a big, heavily built man called James, with whom she had lived and eventually had four sons. Of her precise origins, Arnold either knew nothing or could remember very little. In Lancashire in the 1920s, as the cotton industry declined, work of any kind was increasingly hard to find and James was not particularly committed to finding it anyway. Whatever money he did manage to come by was increasingly spent on drink in the violent local pubs off Lyons Lane.

Mary Ann and James had the kind of domestic relationship in which both partners are dangerously similar in temperament and strength of personality. Neither was prepared to swallow suffering in the interests of another day. Like many working-class women who eventually find themselves with a big, young family, an unreliable partner and no regular income, Mary Ann's own powerful temperament was gradually and fiercely transmuted into the kind of hard maternal will which somehow drives an ignorant and penurious family back from the very brink of physical extinction. When money for it could be found, the house was lit by paraffin lamps. Gradually, in the shadows of that house, infinitely danker and gloomier than anything now visible in modern Buchanan Street, Mary Ann became locked into the role of violent matriarch, dealing out blows, yells and curses to keep the irritation and raucousness of four young sons in check, attempting to drag her partner out of pubs and being reduced to pence to buy the things that would stave off hunger in the children for another day – potatoes, margarine and tea.

At that very moment in history, this type of domestic thraldom was being assessed by Eleanor Rathbone, the Family Allowances campaigner, with painstaking door-to-door inquiries in her own home town of Liverpool. It was a common situation in which women had the moral and practical responsibility for bringing up children but were so rarely given the adequate financial means even to buy a bar of soap or basic food. The stings of poverty vary from time to time and from subclass to subclass, but cold and damp are particularly dispiriting. Here, motherhood often meant being woken on a freezing winter's morning by three or four children staggering about, their legs bowed with the soiled rags lashed between them, and without as much as warm water, a bag of coal to light the fire or a loaf of bread to palatably grease for them.

In Chorley, as elsewhere in the North, a primitive attempt to redistribute income between working husbands and dependent wives was occasionally made by socially conscious pub landlords. At the end of a week's physical labour, many men went straight to the pub and set their money on the bar to pay for oblivion from Friday night until Sunday afternoon. When a pub closed at night, each man's remaining money was then set aside for the next day in separate Toby jugs, sometimes marked with a differently coloured pigeon-identification ring. When drink had taken hold on Friday night, a good landlord would "do a little Robin Hood, robbing the rich to give to the poor – the men's own wives and children". With the appropriated money, a landlord's wife would make a big pan of soup which was then applied for by women running with jugs to the back door. That way, in what some old people in Chorley still call "the barefoot days", total starvation in some families was averted and the thin, maddening whine of ravenous children was temporarily staunched.

Mary Ann Thompson was a woman of initiative. To supplement James Thompson's halting income as a reluctant day-labourer, and with four small sons round her feet, she began to take in washing. Standing in clogs in all weathers in the back yard to thump at other people's laundry in a dolly-tub with a long, four-legged pole called 'dolly-legs', she then desperately tried to dry the washing in front of a tiny coal range on a wooden stand called a 'maiden'. As he grew to be three or four, little Tommy hated the upheaval of permanent wash-day, when the house was turned upside down by the need to dry other people's clothes and, for the first time, he matched his mother's violence of will with his own, kicking over the maiden and yelling, "Get it out o't me way!"

"Do you think perhaps Tommy was the way he was because he was hit a lot as a little boy?" I asked Arnold.

Arnold's large blue eyes shone with humour.

"No . . . you allus got a clout if you needed it in them days."

Birth order in a family (an only child, an elder or eldest child, a second child uncomfortably 'floating' between two, or the 'baby' of a family) quite differingly colours our attitude to our parents and, in adult life, to other forms of authority. Like many eldest children who closely identify with the striving of parents, Arnold Thompson seemed to have sympathized with his mother's struggle to bring them up and, never marrying, he had ultimately looked after her. In the house we now sat in, he had continued to do so until even he could no longer cope with her senility, and she had been taken into geriatric care in her eighties. The spartan messiness of an unwell elderly man nursing a difficult old woman was still evident in the house. Arnold's sitting room was now as smoky as a kipper-curing shed and beyond it sliding doors painted tango orange sat open to reveal his unmade bed, on which a grubby cable of sheets had been cast adrift on the striped ticking of a bare mattress. Beside the bed, night after night, some kind of upturned industrial storage bin served as a bedside table and bore only a bicycle lamp and a big grey metal watch on a chain. Sitting close to the sliding doors, Mrs X was mortified by the sight of the yellow plastic bucket, which suggested some difficulty in getting upstairs to the loo at night.

Even at the age of eighty-six, it seemed that Mary Ann Thompson's violence had reasserted itself.

"When she were going senile," Arnold explained, "she would sit over there and drum her fingers so hard on the edge of that chair that one day she broke the bones in her hand."

Then she had scratched him on the arm, uttered some curse and yelled, "*You did that*!"

Two nurses had arrived on a house call and she had still accused him, as they examined her broken hand, "*He's done that!*" But the nice nurse had said to Arnold, "Don't worry, love. Sometimes that's the road they go. They always turn on the one they love."

Arnold's gentle face bore neither acrimony nor sorrow, just plain acceptance, and above his chaotic mantelpiece hung a round china plaque decorated with roses and sweetly lettered in gilt:

> You can only have one Mother,
> Patient, kind and true.
> No other friend in all the world
> Will be as true to you.

Although resisting glib classification, the way families are internally organized seems to fall into three main categories: there is the 'chaotic' family (in which there is no regular domestic routine and little consistency in parental behaviour); the 'rigid' family (in which suppression of feeling and behaviour in the interests of domestic order can be equally nighmarish for children); and 'normal' families in which parents dispense love, disapproval and physical care with reasonable skill. In some ways, Tommy Thompson's early childhood seemed to have taken place within the chaotic-family type, in which arbitrary violence was the norm. I asked Arnold again if he thought Tommy had been particularly badly treated.

"Naw . . ." but he nevertheless remembered another brother, James, being ordered to give Tommy's head a good banging on the floor in punishment for some misdemeanour.

Throughout his entire married life, Tommy Thompson had a horror of sleeping upstairs and would always insist on siting his bed in the sitting room.

"You – you don't think there is any possibility that Tommy might have been . . . interfered with as a child?"

Arnold looked at me with round humorous blue eyes of absolute steadiness.

"Oh, no. No."

Arnold Thompson was (I have not seen him since) a man of extraordinary charm and courtesy. He was particularly kind to me as one who had just arrived on his doorstep unannounced. But that afternoon, beneath the easy-going flow, I sensed a quite proper determination that, as regards his younger brother's childhood, Arnold had reached a point beyond which he either could not or would not go. After that, to reconstruct the obscure childhood of a dead man with, it seems, no surviving boyhood friends, it was down to me to piece his early life together from other sources and I can only say that I believe I have done the job accurately.

To begin with, among a collection of 85,000 oral-history tapes, I found just one lucky, long and vivid testimony of a Chorley man who had spent his own childhood during the Depression in a neighbouring street to Tommy Thompson's. As northern children, particularly boys, roamed together outdoors at that time, I think the contents of that tape are a sound reflection of Tommy Thompson's childhood circumstances on the streets just off the once-notorious Lyons Lane.

My principal source for life in pre-war Chorley was a very detailed local history, *The Changing Years: Chorley and District Between the Two Wars*, by George Birtill, OBE, Chorley's town historian and a former long-serving editor of the *Chorley Guardian*. Through all this, I began to thread any other bits of personal information about Tommy Thompson that I could find.

Tommy Thompson was about seven years old when his violent, drunken natural father went blind. With the utter ruthlessness of the female animal hell-bent on survival, and in any case presumably despising the crippled male, Mary Ann rapidly detached herself from him and soon afterwards married Jack Topping, a gentle, dreaming man who worked as a spinner in Rhodes Mill, set on the incongruously named Pall Mall in Chorley.

Even at its height (around 1913), the textile industry in Lancashire was notoriously subject to market fluctuations. Like all pioneering industries of world class, it inevitably subjected its workers, like gentle Jack Topping, to mini-booms and then precipitous fall-backs after sudden technological advances. The industry ran, as in the physical process of spinning itself, with heady periods of vicious freedom, then suddenly snapped to be frantically married up again. In one boom of cotton confidence, parts of Victorian Chorley had been given spanking new metropolitan names to attract even more capital, leaving simple streets of Accrington brick with bizarre London names like Pall Mall, Chancery Road, Fleet Street, Holborn Street, Cheapside and Russell Square (at the top of Stump Lane). Jack Topping turned out to be the perfect husband for Mary Ann, with her four small sons to support. Returning from a day in the fierce humidity and clamour of Rhodes Mill on Pall Mall, he turned over his pay packet to her at the end of each week without demur and she then doled him back some pocket-money. In the main, he kept his mouth shut and did as he was bidden, becoming her fifth and most economically useful son.

Never trusting cotton for a moment, Mary Ann continued to take in washing. But now, in the best manner of country-house laundry servants, she confined the actual wash-day to Monday. A more stable income also enabled her to establish better domestic order and to do what, with all her faults, she was noted for in the family – that she was a very good cook and baked a lot, always seeing to it that "the men got their food".

But when things seem reasonably safe economically at last, a woman in her thirties cannot live by baking alone. In her own way, Mary Ann seems to have realized that in everyday life the needs of body and spirit can be so rarely brought together. Decent, quiet Jack Topping had presented her with the means of bodily support for herself and her sons, but, if she could so easily direct him in life, he was not what she would have called a man. There was no sparkling clash of sexual wills here – just reasonable day-to-day safety – and it seems that her talk both to neighbours and within the family, increasingly concerned *men* – what men ought to be, what one needed to do with men and to think about them. Although fiercely possessive of all her sons, Mary Ann's particular regard was already for Tommy, whose innate violence of will seemed to match her own and that of his natural father. "Wolves love lambs as lovers love their loves," said Socrates, and from the age of three or four when, at the height of her domestic desperation, Tommy had first kicked over the wooden maiden ("*Get it out o't me way*!") she seems to have lavished on him a particularly loving and cruel regard which now increasingly set him apart.

It was time for a cup of tea and, with Mrs X moving swiftly before him, Arnold Thompson limped stiffly out of the stale sitting room to a kitchen where the increasingly bright pitch of Mrs X's voice indicated that, even for an elderly reclusive bachelor, the scene was more than usually spectacular. The sole feature in Arnold's entrance hall was a lonely bottle of sterilized milk with a tight metal cap, and this was now sought out. As cups were rinsed and rattled and an ancient kettle was grinding slowly to the boil, out in the kitchen Arnold and Mrs X considered Tommy Thompson's behaviour towards his wife and daughters.

"Why does it happen?" said Mrs X.

"You do nowt to nobody your whole life and then it all starts happening," said Arnold, thinking of victims everywhere.

"Why does God let it happen?"

"Well," said Arnold, in what I now realized was a hard-won, serenely accepting state, "I just take each day as it comes."

Settling down again with cups of tea, we all then considered a new and different strand in Tommy Thompson's childhood – the strange inner life of his gentle new stepfather, Jack.

By day, when industrial times were reasonably good, Jack Topping worked as a spinner in Rhodes Mill, Chorley. In the spinning-room, fragile yarn had to be worked in a humid atmosphere (of at least 90 degrees Fahrenheit) produced by vast, open water-tanks which steamed all day, even at the height of summer. To keep going physically, spinners drank literally gallons of water and both sexes stripped off for work – men to vests and trousers, women down to petticoats. Running and jumping in a kind of industrial *la voltà* to keep pace with the relentless activity of the machines, spinners worked barefoot to get a better grip on the wet, oily floor, picking up coarse wooden splinters under their toe-nails on the way. On hot July afternoons – like this one when I was sitting in the stale shade of Arnold Thompson's living-room – buckets of water were also cast over the spinning-room floor in an effort to keep up the humidity. I later found out that when the high summer sun blazed on the front side of Tulketh Mill – the mill I had seen from the train near Preston railway station – cotton spinners like Jack Topping worked in 108 degrees Fahrenheit.

Caught between hell's kitchen by day and Mary Ann's kitchen at night, Jack Topping retained his dignity and power as a man through spiritualism. Although thin and of little physical account, his soul was a kind of grey vapour which still had the agility to slip between the pincers of day-to-day humiliation. He was not only a spiritualist but a medium, and he truly dwelt in inner twilight, attuned to footfalls on the boundaries of another world.

Arnold Thompson's revelation that his stepfather had been a spiritualist caused an involuntary chill in me. I have always associated spiritualism, perhaps wrongly, with a kind of petit-bourgeois female chicanery in which yards of fine grey chiffon were concealed in a middle-aged vagina to be suddenly and moistly produced as 'ectoplasm'. But spiritualism, I eventually learned, is now acknowledged to be the first 'industrial religion' through which sensitive factory workers like Jack Topping (cut off several generations before in harsh new circumstances from the conventional Christianity of rural towns and villages) asserted that there is more to human life than can be seen, touched and physically endured. We cannot live by cotton alone. In Lancashire particularly, where underlying Roman

Catholicism was given new Victorian life by waves of wretched Irish immigrants and also from vigorous Liverpool-based missionary work by Italian priests like Father Luigi Gentili (1801–48), spiritualism rapidly developed alongside native Catholicism and Methodism as the 'modern' religion of the people.

The spiritual journey of the pioneer socialist Robert Owen shows perfectly the new arc of assertion which led from Chartism, socialism, strikes and atheism to spiritualism. Owen ultimately became a spiritualist convert and his son, Robert Dale Owen, was one of the most important exponents of the new industrial religion.

By the time Jack Topping was occasionally acting as a medium in Buchanan Street during the late 1930s, spiritualism was still seen as the elevating religion of the working man and woman. Spiritualists believe (among many other things) in God, in Christ as a great medium and healer, and in the survival of human and animal souls after death. But in philosophical terms, this religion is contradictory. While spiritualists proclaim that science and empiricism are inadequate ways of fully understanding human existence, their religion is entirely enmeshed in materialist terms, in the need to prove *physically*, through mediums summoning spirits, that we do not die. *The dead still live*, said spiritualists like Jack Topping, *and I will, this evening, in this little room, produce them for you.*

With his large, faded blue eyes rounding in recollection, Arnold Thompson stretched out his stiff left leg and, easy of belief in the English way, he did not attempt to analyse his stepfather's religious behaviour either one way or the other.

"Well . . . You've got to have some belief in something. If you didn't believe in nothing, what's the point?"

He recalled how Jack Topping's fits of mediumship usually began with him sitting in one of these green-hide armchairs by the fireside in Buchanan Street. Then, particularly if "Hymn-singing came on't radio in the evening, he went straight under".

I was curious to know in what way Jack had gone "under"

and, for the first time that afternoon, Arnold Thompson became quite animated, throwing his head back in imitation of his stepfather entering a trance.

"He would lean back, start sweating a bit and then things would start to come out of his mouth – words and voices."

"Was it his usual voice?" I asked, but Arnold could not remember.

"Something happened to him anyway. There must be something up there, you know."

It seems that Jack Topping's spiritual guide in the twilight world above had been a "Red Indian" and that sometimes Jack would threaten or cajole him to gain knowledge of the future.

"When's trade coming round?" he would demand (meaning "When will the cotton industry pick up?").

Orthodox spiritualists do not pretend to be able to predict the future, but in the back streets of industrial towns during the Depression, spiritualism readily became corrupted into fortune-telling. At other times, therefore, Jack looked into the spirit world on behalf of pregnant young women who wanted to know what might happen to them in childbirth. Shaking and staring fixedly at the ceiling (while Mary Ann doubtless watched close by with a curious mixture of awe and irritation), he declared with customary banality to one young inquirer, "You'll have a hard time, but you'll pull through."

Psychological studies of religious behaviour usually claim that people subject to spirit possession suffer inwardly from deprivation, frustration and discontent, and that so-called 'spirit ratification' (proving to others that spirits really exist) is simply a way of obtaining the attention, social standing and privileges they would be otherwise denied. With light contempt for her all-too-reliable little husband, Mary Ann guttered like a naked flame in a draught between respect for Jack Topping's contact with the world of the dead and daily suspicion that no one so unmanly could possibly compel such psychic forces. But the darker side of Jack's spiritualism seems to have proffered a new weapon in the game I felt that she was now playing with her growing son – her Real Man in the Making – the infuriating, beloved and violently willed Tommy.

On evenings when his stepfather was holding seances downstairs and the Ouija board roamed, Tommy was sometimes left out alone on the stairs in the dark and then thrust further by Mary Ann to stand in a bedroom corner for hours on end in the cold and pitch black of night. Like his once-feared natural father (also dismissed by Mary Ann to stumble sightless, alcoholic and alone round the streets of Chorley), Tommy did not dare to emit his terror in the suffocating dark and, eventually, *would not*.

"*Stand there!*" she hissed, ramming her hard laundress fists into the thin child's back. "*Stand there! Or I'll send Devil t'ye*!"

For the better part of each year, until autumn hardened into first frosts and then mushed down to the dirty, gas-lit troughs of urban winter, front doors in all the streets off Lyons Lane stood wide open in daylight hours. People were able to assess each other's domestic circumstances at a glance, and baiting vulnerable neighbours was one of the street games that Tommy's contemporaries liked to play – as he stood apart and watched.

One house in Standish Street had as its sole piece of 'decent' furniture a scavenged wooden tallboy which stood directly opposite the open street door (one missing front leg replaced by an upended brick). Bowling a purple frosty turnip hard at the tallboy was one autumnal form of cricket. When someone scored a direct hit through the open street door on the upturned brick, the entire tallboy lumbered for a moment and then crashed forward to delighted jeers. In the centre of each living room in these streets most people kept a small deal table. Boldly racing into a stranger's house to leap directly on top of the table and YELL (before instantly racing out again) was another startling game. As with most spirited and intelligent children who sense a narrow life already laid out rather too clearly before them, boyhood and early adolescence in this part of Chorley was simply a kind of driving open-air defiance.

Contempt for the police grew next. Policemen would occasionally stroll down Lyons Lane in daylight. But during Tommy Thompson's childhood in Chorley in the 1930s, the streets immediately off Lyons Lane, including his own, were something of a no-go area for the law. The police were big burly men swinging along in heavy melton-cloth cloaks who went round in twos and threes for safety, but even then, they were wary of setting foot down Standish Street, where the turnip game was played.

Chorley was always notoriously badly lit. At the top end of Standish Street was a corn mill, six storeys high, which loomed like a mountain over the poor little houses near by, and close to it was a small, secretive pub called the War Office. Local lore has it that in winter, or after dark, any young policeman who walked down Standish Street alone would never emerge again at the other end.

Around the age of nine or ten, pubs began to fascinate Tommy Thompson as places where men like his natural father seemed to have their real being. These pubs were mainly ale houses, moistly issuing with the green hiss of gaslight, and for those dying of pneumonia or tuberculosis, the landlords offered "ginger or the poker" to spice or sizzle the ale. To a child watcher, sometimes seated for hours outside on the steps, the constant batting of the pub doors carried out the warm smell of beer slops, glimpses of flag floors gritted with sand, the foul ring of chewed-tobacco spittle in cast-iron spittoons a foot in diameter and a crescendo of male brawling. Eventually, as at the Victory Inn on Lyons Lane (called locally the Red House because of its red blinds and the thin blood which flew towards the end of each evening), the voice of the landlady – in the Victory's case, Mrs Gilgum – would rise to sort things out.

Mrs Gilgum was the Lyons Lane midwife. She also laid out the dead and no one dared to lay a finger on her.

"Right, lads. Let's have you in the yard." And stumbling towards each other like clog-shod bears in the dark, two antagonists would finish the fight among the reek and flutter of pigeon lofts at the back.

Water, which in the mornings sluiced sand, spittle and blood out of pub doorways under Tommy Thompson's feet as he went to elementary school, had something of fate in it in that part of Britain, because for millions of working-class people in the North, geology – what lay literally underneath one's feet – was an almost irresistible sign of adult destiny. Whether it was coal, iron ore, water or the type of rock through which a railway had been sliced, for most people the landscape determined the nature of future work. In Lancashire, to the most unprecedented degree, that world of work was textiles.

Water, running and cascading on a westward tilt to the Irish Sea (and, beyond it, the Atlantic), had made Lancashire the most intensive site for textile manufacture the world has ever seen. As I rather reluctantly began to dig about in libraries for some kind of economic fix on the background to the Thompson family, the facts I eventually excavated about the concentration of the textile industry in Lancashire at first seemed quite unbelievable. I wrote down the statistics with a kind of pride and horror and checked them twice. Shortly before the First World War, it had been estimated that of 81 million cotton spindles then at work in the world, 42 million were operating in Britain and, of those, 41 million were in Lancashire. Oldham ('the cotton-spinning capital of the world') had 19 million spindles alone – in other words, one small English town had once produced more than the *entire* spinning capacity of the United States. Eventually, Chorley and its satellite villages of Adlington, Coppull, Euxton (pronounced Euston), Eccleston, Whittle-le-Woods and Clayton-le-Woods became the sixth-biggest weaving district in Lancashire. If you had paused, as children do, to wonder what work might come your way in Chorley when you grew up, even in Tommy Thompson's boyhood there were still twenty-three mills to choose from. Just as his contemporaries (I doubted whether he would have called them 'friends') raced into strangers' houses to leap on a kitchen table and yell, the same boys now had an urge to invade adult places of work, to see what the future might hold. Children are impelled to seize glimpses of the adult world by force. Congregating at the doors of mills, the boys at first plagued departing weavers for anything that might be left in their domed lunch cans – hardened bread or, on lucky days, a bit of broken cake. Then, later on, before the hooter went and women weavers clattered out (dressed in the same way that mill girls in Lancashire had been covered exactly 100 years before), the small, dark doorways of these huge buildings tempted them in for a dare. Drawing the boys in step by step, as if gently sucking them into a vacuum, the twilight spaces and sudden sombre roar of these places transfixed the skinny male rabbits for a moment before they escaped on jelly legs back to the sanity of the street.

Tommy Thompson was ten when the Second World War began and, suddenly, some of those early Victorian mills whose doors had been shut in Chorley during the Depression were now flung open once more and he observed exciting new life in them. In Chorley, where many of the mills were less able quickly to adapt to new wartime demands (textile manufacture became a Class B reserved occupation), the mills here suddenly acquired military importance as vast bunkers which could be commandeered by North-West Army Command as useful spaces to house ammunition dumps, army vehicle garages, warehouses for spare parts and all-purpose army stores, roughly banged up on miles of wooden racking. Soon some of the old cotton mills had been transformed into military palaces.

Hovering about the entrances to these, Tommy Thompson noted the beautiful order which the soldiers seemed able to make out of local chaos. They constructed wooden shelving inside a mill, mile upon mile of it, and everywhere soldiers and army mechanics were *rational* with each other, asking for or receiving what they wanted by exchanging and signing a piece of paper (just as Tommy struggled to do at school). Many of the soldiers came from elsewhere – London – and pronounced 'cake' 'cike'. They were cockneys who did not, he felt, easily like to dismiss him as he drew nearer to watch what they were doing to the jeeps which roared in with mud-spinning wheels at the doors of places like Progress Mill in nearby Progress Street. "'Oppit, son" was meant kindly.

Military excitement had washed into the back streets from a titanic new factory which had risen in only eighteen months in the neighbouring fields between Chorley and Euxton. This was the Royal Ordnance Factory (the ROF), which was quickly begun in 1937 to supersede the munitions output of the ancient Royal Ordnance Factory at Woolwich in London. The pubs off Lyons Lane in Chorley caught the first wash of military change as 4,000 Irish labourers arrived in the little town (a further 2,000 men were recruited locally in Chorley and Preston). The massive concrete building seemed to rise like summer grass. As a reward for the records these men broke in building it, Gracie Fields ('the feminine voice of Lancashire') agreed to open the new ROF herself at a gala held in the grounds of nearby Lisieux Hall on 20 August 1938. When such a film and radio star could visit Chorley, to entertain the builders and their families, the new military importance of Chorley was no longer rumoured but certain. As Chorley's official town historian, George Birtill, OBE, put it to me, "Chorley in the 1940s? It was like being part of the German Ruhr!"

It had rained heavily in Lancashire the night before and her train from Euston to Wigan was late, but with perfect good humour on that August day in 1938, Gracie walked across the sodden fields from Chorley to within sight of the new munitions palace, where between 50,000 and 60,000 local people were waiting. She toured a workers' funfair first and, as her arms filled up with presentations of Chorley cakes, Chorley rock and a pair of 'fancy clogs', she had a friendly word for everyone ("Ah'm laden like the juggler's assistant") before squelching on to a huge marquee. Perhaps referring to the 160-feet-high giant concrete-mixer which still stood on-site (having mixed 1,500 tons of concrete a day for this mammoth military project), Miss Fields stood on a platform in her smart, mud-spattered London shoes to sing in the famously sharp, wiry voice, "It's the biggest – *aspidistra* – in the worrrrld."

Back home in Buchanan Street in the evenings, Jack Topping increasingly looked up to the ceiling, shaking and possessed, in search of an answer to the outcome of the war (doubtless making the kind of rather hopeless pronouncements that spiritualists are on record as having made throughout the war in Britain): "Hitler has cancer of the throat and will die before the end o't war." And later: "There'll be no Hitler to defeat when 1942 comes."

Soon, the increasing activity of spiritualists in predicting the course of the war and trying, on behalf of the poor, to trace the growing numbers of missing and dead caused the British government to invoke the 1735 Witchcraft Act against spiritualists "pretending to exercise a kind of conjuration", and in the south-east of England a female medium was imprisoned.

Believing and disbelieving, Tommy Thompson caught the glimmer of a path forward out of dark, long-skirted Lancashire in the army depots which now raced and blazed with modern life in the local mills. Tank convoys occasionally tore through Chorley (once swiping down the so-called Big Lamp near Market Street), men commanded lesser men ("*Sah*!"), there was not one woman in sight and, unlike Mary Ann's steamy, chaotic kitchen in Buchanan Street, everything at all times and for good reasons had a place and was kept in it. The idea of taking orders from anyone was hateful but, like these soldiers here, it might be possible to devise a life in which he would never have to be fearful again. Women too, he was beginning to assess with his dark Ribera eyes. In future, should anyone attempt to impose their will on him, Tommy Thompson would devise ways of saying, again and again, "*I'll send Devil t'ye!*"

2

Progress Street

As they paused before them for the first time that summer, some bluebells held the magic to make her heart loop in a kind of ecstasy. Bluebells give their colour to patches of sunlight and to semi-shade, but, holding her father's hand as they plunged deeper into the bracken of Duxbury Woods, the little girl noted that as the green shade intensified, the moist live flowers turned an even deeper sapphire blue. Walking slightly behind them, her eyes always averted to some distant or inward place, her mother, Ellen, dutifully came forward at their special reach on the banks of the River Yarrow to help her frail, wobbly daughter step down into the light of the river's playful shallows.

At the age of five or six, happy children do not consciously 'love' their parents. These dark shapes – man and woman – are simply seated there with the natural permanence of rocks or trees. Secure in their presence, the little girl stood in a pair of old leather paddling sandals, absorbed in a new sepia world of rounded pebbles, the cold flick of minnows past her ankles and the slightly dizzy feeling that comes from attempting to stand firm against an onward flow of water.

From childhood onwards, Mrs Hilda Thompson was imprinted with an almost morbid love of flowers. Later on such afternoons, when rougher children filed down into the woods which closely fringed Chorley, she would pick up the bluebells they had carelessly picked and then cast down, sticking them into a jam-jar of minnows to protect their life on the homeward walk. Long before she felt able to talk fully to me, I gathered that after nearly forty years of marriage to Tommy Thompson she had a horror of real flowers in the house. ("Don't bring me flowers, love. I hate it when they die.")

For almost a year, flowers and a newspaper photograph were

the only clues I had to Hilda Thompson's background and inner life. The photograph reeked of pathos. Even at the age of fifty-seven, when charged with conspiracy to murder, it was her childlike quality which struck me. Her thin hair was still fair, her round, light eyes were almost certainly blue, and I doubted whether she stood much above a frail five feet in height. While her daughters – dressed in jumble-sale jackets, with dull cotton skirts stretched tautly across their broad knees – were aware of the scorch of public humiliation as they all three left a magistrate's court, Mrs Thompson seemed, as she held lightly on to the arm of June Thompson, to be the child of her own daughter – sickly, fragile and obedient, blown along in anxiety on a gust of events she did not fully comprehend.

Hilda Thompson was born at 44 Leigh Row, Chorley, on 19 March 1927. It was an early Victorian, four-room stone cottage lit by gas, with a block of old steep steps at the front and rear. Her father, Ernest Hartley, was a road-mender for Chorley Corporation and, from the moment he first held her while standing in his shirt-sleeves (hands carefully washed) in the light of a back-bedroom window, he seems to have regarded her with the same mixture of awe and delight that Dr Coppelius poured out on his magic doll. Without making any great fuss about it, Ernest Hartley was a naturally pious man (first a practising Anglican and later a Methodist) and I suppose he marvelled not only that this fair-headed child was partly his own creation but also that such creation was possible.

During the Depression, Chorley was classified as a 'Distressed Area' and, by the time Hilda was born (when employment opportunities in textiles had plummeted), central government had encouraged local authorities in Lancashire to create public works to alleviate economic distress, particularly building or repairing roads. Labouring outdoors in all weathers with a pick and shovel, Ernest Hartley continued to work with the more precise spade during his leisure hours, enjoying the peace and contemplative freedom of an allotment (his 'plot') on the fringes of Duxbury Woods.

Ernest Hartley's garden was half a mile away from home at a spot called Yarrow Bridge, a place so naturally beautiful that obscure local poets, writing instead of digging during their respite from day-to-day labour, had long ago dubbed it 'the Eden of Lancashire'. Chorley's own 'town poet' had been a rural postman and antiquarian called John Wilson, a thin, nervous young man who had daily trudged for miles in and around rural Chorley, with sacking over his head and shoulders in wet weather, attempting to crystallize the beauty of the place:

Oh! the wind is in the west,
All the fields with flowers are dressed,
And I've never seen my love this many a day.

Bending, digging and occasionally resting on his spade with the distant absorption of the gardener, Ernest Hartley created his own Eden within Eden, near the banks of the Yarrow, and taking his wife and daughter down to it on summer evenings, they idled up and down the rows of stiff green lettuces, marvelled at the tumbling sweet peas and runner beans curling down from stakes, and watched his fork unearth bright yellow new potatoes which would be boiled for Sunday lunch next day with a bunch of mint.

As Hilda Thompson grew and began to attend St George's Church of England Elementary School in Bolton Street, Ernest Hartley's garden contributed roses to the baskets children carried on the famous 'Walking Days'. These 'Walking Days', I discovered, were midsummer street parades in which the children carried flowers. They had been started by many Victorian churches in Lancashire as a surprisingly successful counter-attraction to the traditional mechanics' summer feasts, which had ended in extreme drunkenness and violence.

On a sultry July morning which already promised great heat, Ellen Hartley would carefully dress her daughter in the one good frock of the year, fasten the ankle-straps of her new black patent-leather shoes over sparkling white socks, and take her down to the gates of the school to meet up with the other 'scholars' who were self-consciously assembling five or six abreast. Shops in Chorley had their canvas sunshades out and by the time the church-school parades flowed together down Market Street, the pavements would be respectfully thronged with the slightly better-off people in Chorley, watching the children pass. The front row of children carried waisted baskets tumbling with flowers, and behind them the girls were arranged into separate rows of colour according to their dresses and hair ribbons – pink, yellow, white, blue and green. Dressed with all the freshness their mothers could devise, it was the little girls who carried the ritual innocence of the parade. In a blur of heat, flowers and social approval, it marked the very height of summer for families of Lancashire Primrose League (England's carefully cultivated 'little Conservatives').

At the other end of the year, Ernest Hartley went down alone to the frozen December earth of his garden, checking on it and doing a little this and that as a conscientious mother looks in on a sleeping child at night.

Mrs Thompson wanted to talk about her life and had agreed to do so, but as the months passed I began to despair that she would ever feel able to tell me even some of the things I needed to know. Apart from the most perfunctory shopping expeditions, occasional visits to hospital and her arrest, she had apparently rarely left the house or spoken freely to an outsider for almost forty years. Domestic isolation had, of course, left her verbally isolated as time had moved on. She was said to sometimes use older dialect words and speech forms, to be profoundly deaf in both ears and to have physical speech difficulties arising from surgery for cancer of the mouth. All this sounded rather daunting but as we gradually began to exchange short letters and greetings cards, I learned patiently to adjust myself to what might be formally called 'the pace of disclosure'. Not wishing to do Mrs Thompson and her daughters any further violence by unwelcome intrusion, I developed the art of waiting and, with a sense of usefully marking time, I looked about for some way of temporarily hunting out useful background facts elsewhere.

It says something about the pull of the past in Lancashire that the biggest sound archive in Britain of ordinary people's reminiscences of daily life in the mill towns is housed (and computerized for quick recall) among the ruins of Clitheroe Castle, a crumbling medieval fortress set up on a truly dizzy height above the town on a massive rock dripping with ivy and hanging moss. The prospect of 85,000 oral-history recordings drew me on a rambling bus from Chorley and, on a bright spring day, I climbed a winding path up the rock to the North-West Sound Archive. The ascent to Clitheroe Castle was so steep that eventually the little town seemed to lie about my ankles in a child's-room clutter of grey slate roofs, yellow clay chimney-pots shaped like crowns and two stubby church towers one could almost touch. As I turned every few yards to marvel at the view, the landscape beyond Clitheroe suddenly faded off into the veiled, floating grey of Pendle Hill – folklore seat of the Lancashire Witches.

That particular day, the sound archivist turned out to be a tall, warm-hearted young man called Andrew Schofield, who sat in his medieval office surrounded by instant-coffee clutter and piles of English dialect dictionaries. As we introduced ourselves, I felt instantly absorbed into this pleasingly remote place to work, with its ancient stone-flagged floors and the heraldic glitter of yellow diamond-shaped panes. I already knew that Mrs Thompson was profoundly deaf and, on casually mentioning this to him, I was surprised that he instantly seized on it.

"Elderly survivors of the Lancashire cotton industry are often deaf," he said. "Right up to the 1970s you could still see old people tick-tacking in sign language on the buses."

Andrew Schofield was clearly a busy man and I felt rather guilty that I had breezed into Clitheroe purely on spec for what I did not like to describe to him as an all-purpose background dredge.

"But a lot of old people are deaf," I said, rather stupidly.

"Well, round here," said Andrew, "old people are often deaf

because of the decimating noise of the weaving sheds. Even before their work diminished their hearing, most weavers became adept at lip-reading to communicate at work above the noise of the machinery."

He recalled a tape on which a weaver in a mill at Preston had described it like this: "You could have a good conversation like, 'Where did you go last night?' – 'Oh, we went to the Plaza pictures.' – 'I never saw you.' – 'Well, I was there.' You'd have a real good conversation. You couldn't actually hear anything, but you knew what everybody was saying."

"Come and hear what it was like," he said.

A door at the back of Andrew's office opened on to a steep wind of ancient stone stairs. From the top of these we entered a curious cavern in which the ceiling and walls appeared to drip with cigar-brown foam-rubber stalactites (to stabilize and contain sound). Festooned beneath them, on an eau-de-Nil board, was a mass of electric leads – mauve, royal-blue, grey and lime-green – all waiting to be disentangled and plugged into the jack-field of a long array of tape-decks.

Before he switched on the tape of a cotton-mill at work, Andrew Schofield warned me to be prepared for the noise, but I did not really take his advice seriously.

"If you want to understand the reality of the mill, you must try to imagine the tape three times louder. I can't play it at the actual volume of real sound, or the speakers will blow."

Still imagining that I was about to hear some quaint heritage triviality, like horses clip-clopping, the army of 7 a.m. clogs marching to the mill or the supposed cries of muffin men, I sat down and said I was ready to begin.

"I'm ready now."

Hesitant for a moment, Andrew Schofield then released the most terrifying mechanical sound I have ever heard. Like a stab in the face, the room was suddenly filled with the hard, vicious clatter of Lancashire Overpick looms running at full tilt in the weaving-shed of an old local mill at Harle Syke, near Burnley. Although running at a third volume, the sound was very painful indeed. With a heart involuntarily pounding in alarm, I clenched my fists under the listening-room table to stop them automatically rising to block out the sound. Even though he had known what to expect, Andrew Schofield's brow had also begun to shine a bit. Now reduced to a sound-archive curiosity, this was the authentic roar of Lancashire Past at work in good times – an alternative sound picture to the tinkling of Mendelssohn's *Lieder ohne Worte* on Broadwood pianos in the mill-owning houses of Preston's Winckley Square. I put my hands over my ears and smiling, signalled – no more.

"I think thirty-three seconds of that is enough," said Andrew as he now produced quiet as clear and merciful as cold water. Seeping out from the mullioned windows of our medieval electronic crow's nest, the peace seemed wonderful and some miles away cloud shadow passed like thought across the brow of Pendle Hill.

Andrew Schofield had the gift of emotional intimacy and, as the afternoon passed by, he produced not only recordings but photographs, dictionaries and old textile directories which eventually became invaluable in quickening my understanding of the Thompson family when the moment came to meet them. Andrew was very intuitive and, towards the end of the afternoon, he suddenly produced a tape which he felt might be of 'interior use' to me. It was a recording I would otherwise probably never have heard of the celebrated living Lancashire dialect poet Joan Pomfret reading her strange and commanding poem 'Untilled Land'.

"It's a very sinister poem," said Andrew. "Something about women's nameless fears for their daughters . . ."

"Think on, our Kath . . ." began a calm, well-rooted woman's voice, reading in a mode which southerners, ignorant of the north, might be tempted to call *Dalesman*-speak:

> Id's Untilled Land, Id's Witch Country,
> Id's dark an' drear an' chill –
> Love him i't fowd ort' bluebell wood,
> *But nod o' Pendle Hill!*

"Bluebell woods," I said rather vacantly to Andrew Schofield by way of parting thanks, thinking that Mrs Thompson had somehow wandered too far beyond her father's garden, or perhaps some bigger, invisible garden. And the lines continued to haunt me through the rest of that cold spring evening on the long return journey north, to Glasgow.

Some short time later – perhaps a week or two – the Thompson family suddenly drew me towards them in a way I had not foreseen. I have always admired the self-possession of people who can sit down in the morning at a well-ordered desk to open their mail with a paper knife, calmly slitting the top of each envelope with clean precision. Instead, my habit is to rip all mail open and instantly sit on the stairs to devour it. That morning, I was transfixed on the first flight of stairs by a strange packet which had been posted in Preston, Lancashire, the previous day. In it there was no covering letter, just three quite ordinary ruled exercise books filled from cover to cover with walls of painfully neat handwriting, going on and on and on with no paragraph breaks but lots of unusually placed capital letters, almost in the Augustan way of giving quite ordinary words a sudden Importance. The notebooks had the air of children's work but, as if I were some remote official who had demanded proof of identification, the turquoise cover on each notebook had been carefully lettered in biro with adult formalities. They read respectively: "Mrs Hilda Thompson D.O.B. 19.3.1927", "Miss June Thompson D.O.B. 15.6.52," and "Miss Hilda Thompson D.O.B. 29.9.53."

Rather thickly, it took me a few seconds to see that 'D.O.B.' stood for 'date of birth', and then the first book I happened to open began: *As far back as I can remember, Dad hit Mum a lot* . . . After that, in innocent prose with a strange life of its own, came day-to-day memories of work in textile mills and laundries, wife-beating, casual domestic cruelty to children (*he held my hand very close to the flame because I went near the fireplace*) and the contraceptives used for child sexual abuse (*he always made*

Mum buy Durex from the Chemist. He never bought them). In this household a trip to see a cancer specialist at the Christie Hospital in Manchester was *like a holiday* and the third book ended with a murder (painfully referred to as '*It*').

With a shock of admiration, I realized that despite all they had suffered and the extraordinary isolation in which they had lived for forty years, the Thompson women had written down their lives. Like the divining rods of a dowser, my hopes now began to twitch in the direction of their flat in Preston – towards the nervously anticipated meeting, more notebooks and, as it eventually turned out, fifteen years' worth of bizarre domestic diaries. But for the moment the contents of these notebooks were coldly compelling in themselves. Perhaps an hour later, when the plain-faced details of forty years of life in a series of far-away terraced houses in Lancashire had left their inward mark, I suddenly noticed that the sun had gone in, my own home had closed down in shadows and the stairs on which I sat were cold and dusty.

Mrs Thompson's mother, Ellen, had been the fifth of six Lancashire Catholic sisters (Lizzie, Mary Ann, Annie, Alice and Katy) and from the age of twelve or so she had worked as a spinner at a mill in the satellite cotton village of Adlington. By all accounts she was a handsome, pious and rather withdrawn woman, famed in the family for taking quiet pride in her thickly waving light-brown hair. Perhaps not unconnected with the stripped-down-to-petticoats humidity of the spinning room, there was some mystery or tragedy attached to her early life, and by the time of her marriage to Ernest Hartley she already had a daughter called X and never spoke of her own parents. To marry Ernest Hartley she converted to Anglicanism, returning fully to Roman Catholicism after his death.

Written at speed and with the pleasurable egocentricity of childhood reminiscences, Mrs Thompson depicted in her first notebook a childhood in 1930s Chorley of the prudent affectionate kind in which, with its fine sifting of coal dust, darkness and ceaseless manual labour, the Victorian age still flowed on. A few doors away in Bolton Street, the little girl learned to negotiate the two steep steps down into a strangely dark grocer's shop, pungent with the scent of cheese, bacon and brown paper, run by the Misses Culshaw, whose severely hair-bunned heads bent over her like two peg dolls above long snow-white aprons, dark ankle-length skirts and, to Hilda's fascination, shiny black-leather clogs which tapped neatly to and fro across a stone-flagged floor sprinkled with fine red sand. At home on decent Mondays, behind Leigh Row, the alleys billowed with a veritable Cowes of lightly drying sheets, the smoothing iron was heated in the red embers of the kitchen fire (later to be replaced by a wonderful Gas Iron) and, slightly drifting in the rising heat, the ironed clothes eventually aired on wooden pulleys overhead, while the good oven of the Yorkshire range enclosed fiercely rising bread, barm cakes and the spangled sugar crust of apple 'plate pies'.

When I was young we always had a Peg Rug in front of the Fireplace. We made them from old coats etc. and backed them with Sacking from a Sugar Sack. I liked helping to make them. They always looked nice and cosy. We used to make a Pattern on them with the Brighter Colours . . .

In the dark evenings of December, when Chorley's famously dim municipal gas-lamps glimmered greenly in the smog outside, Ellen, Ernest and little Hilda (no mention of the mysteriously floating half-sister, X) tentatively pulled apart the bale of holly that Ernest annually dragged in from Duxbury Woods and, seated in front of the Yorkshire range, they made holly wreaths to put on relatives' graves at Christmas time. Then, as the little family went on to make coloured-paper roses and chrysanthemums for themselves and neighbours to use as Christmas decorations, the coarse needle of their model gramophone with the big horn ground and hissed through 'The Beautiful Blue Danube' and 'I'll String Along with You':

You may not be an an-gel
Cos angels are so few . . .
But till the day comes that one comes along,
I'll string along with you . . .

Even after her father's death, Hilda and her mother quietly continued this handiwork every Christmas because the crêpe-paper flowers kept faith alive in glorious summer *when I went on my Dad's Plot with him.*

Mrs Thomson's apparently idyllic childhood, in which she was the petted centre of all things, abruptly ceased in the winter of 1937, when her beloved father suddenly died. As if in a theatrical transformation scene, not only did the ten-year-old girl's father seem hopelessly to descend from view in a roll of cold mist but the very walls and crannies of her old home suddenly appeared to fly up and be rapidly drawn out sideways as the next scene in her life was flown in on darkness.

From the purchase of the Gas Iron onwards, which had made Ellen's domestic life a little easier, the family in a quiet way had begun to see the possibility of material progress – it *might* be nicer to live in a house lit by electricity instead of gas, and to have a garden round the house, so that Ernest Hartley could walk out early in the morning, as gardeners love to do, just to look at the plants, perceiving minute changes in them, to scent the air and think. Sometime in 1937, the Hartley family therefore became the first eager tenants of a new semi-detached council house – well built of brick in the Dutch-gabled manner – at No. 2 Bowland Avenue, Chorley. At the front of the house, Ernest's first act was to tread in some roses, carefully transplanted from his garden at Yarrow Bridge. To Hilda, "it was all so wonderful":

My father had modernised the Piano by taking the Red Velvet and Fancy Wood Panel out and placing varnished Plywood in place of it & it looked better. We took our big Dresser with us. My Father had put new Chrome handles on all the Drawers. It looked nice. We bought a second-hand table also. We had to buy all new Curtains & New Carpets so we could not afford new furniture as well . . . It was lovely having Electric instead of old Gas Mantles. We could have Cold & Hot water heated by a back boiler in the Fireplace. It was a Black Shiny Range with an Oven on one side.

As a road-mender, Ernest Hartley was sometimes called upon to work outdoors in bad weather and he had been seriously ill several times before. But on this particular afternoon, when Hilda ran in from school up the grand new front-garden path and on into the bright warm room scented with baking, her father was already home and convulsed in a way she had never seen before. Refusing to lie down on the red velvet sofa (as if continuing to sit up might somehow arrest his illness), Ernest slumped uneasily at the side of the range, glistening behind the quiet tremors of advancing fever.

He wasn't well at all. He was shivering & yet the living-room was warm as my Mother had been using the Oven. We soon found out he had got Pneumonia. He had had it before. There were times he had worked in the rain . . . He got worse very soon & was given Oxygen from a Cylinder but didn't pull through. It was a terrible shock.

Within months of having left her old married home in Leigh Row, Ellen Hartley found herself widowed at the age of forty, and left with two daughters, the increased expense of a better home and the general uncertainties of a country approaching war. Quite mechanically taking a job at the Hygienic Laundry in Harper's Lane to supplement her widow's pension of ten shillings a week, Ellen not only took the loss of her husband "very hard", but never again emerged from grief and depression, becoming emotionally incapacitated as a mother. Almost immediately after Ernest's burial in Chorley Cemetery, little Hilda noted that the fire was often allowed to die out in the range, baking ceased and the water in the house ran cold ever after. After school the house was empty.

The following May, two roses that her father had transplanted from Yarrow Bridge to the new house put out their first tentative flowers after the move – one tree a deep red and the other pink. As she stood alone beside them, the child began to fully recognize for the first time the adult meaning of death: that she would never again see her father on earth, nor walk with him in Duxbury Woods.

In the turmoil of adult grief, it is usually forgotten what the emotional reality of losing a parent is like from a child's point of view. Children, in fact, suffer a double penalty of bereavement. Since the surviving parent cannot help being absorbed in personal grief, the child, in effect, temporarily loses both parents. At the very moment a child needs to grieve in its own way, the surviving parent is least capable of helping it through that delicate process. A period of intense domestic mourning need not warp a child's personality for ever, but a continuing unbalanced relationship with a surviving parent no longer able emotionally to 'give' is usually thought to do long-term damage. In Hilda's case, both father and mother were effectively lost to her for ever as Ellen Hartley never emerged again from depression, becoming increasingly dependent on her own older sister Mary Ann, who lived locally in Wordsworth Lane. On working days at the Hygienic Laundry, Ellen at first called at her sister's house for meals and then began to stay there until very late at night, leaving her young daughter alone in the tomb of a house which seemed to have robbed them both of the one man who had given their lives warmth and purpose:

> *Mostly I never saw her from early morning until very late at night. I don't think she actually liked coming home many a time. But I felt the same way and didn't like being on my own. She just took it for granted that I could look after myself...*

To escape the coldness of the new house in Bowland Avenue, Hilda began to fill the slow hours between the end of school and the moment when sleep was inevitable by *going to the Pictures on my own, to the first show*, where the illusion of human company and actual physical warmth could be bought for a penny or two.

> *The home and house was never the same without him. It was so quiet and Lonely. We didn't even have an Electric fire like people have now. It was all coal fires in those days. I felt It a waste of time making a fire just for myself . . .*

With a beloved father dead, a mother reduced to the ghost of maternity and, I supposed, a young teenaged half-sister maintaining a jealous distance, the young girl returned reluctantly each day from Highfield Council School to a house with blank windows, a dead fire and adolescence faced across a grate of ashes.

On the street corner which I had hunted out alone, the raised letters of a metal sign bleached white with age still mimed the name: PROGRESS STREET. In 1944, when she was aged seventeen, it seemed that Mrs Thompson's last job before her sinister marriage had been at Progress Street Mill, in whose redundant spaces a new soap factory had been recently opened by people her notebook described as "emigre Poles". Called Droyt Products and run by a man referred to as "Mr Danny", the factory seemed to remain powerfully in her mind as, *my last job before meeting the person who became my husband*. Perhaps because of its scent and colour, Mrs Thompson also vividly recalled the soap in detail:

> *Children's pale blue soap in the shape of policemen. They had black belts and boots and gold buttons. I also remember yellow soap in the shape of Lemons and big green round soaps – they called them shippers . . .*

It took me a little time to work out that by this last word she probably meant the warm, green woody scent of chypre.

In the past, textile mills seem to have had the economic lives of 'resting' actors – in bad times, moodily turning over a living doing almost anything while waiting for the chance to resume their own sublime calling. Consequently, Mrs Thompson passed as a young girl from one small business to another in the shadows of vast buildings which stood conveniently ready to house any activity that might come their way. At the age of fourteen, her first job was in the Friday Street Slipper Works which one day arrived in silent Primrose Bank Mill. Then the Droyt Soap Factory popped up in part of Progress Street Mill, also agreeably close to her empty home in Bowland Avenue.

Even in that part of Chorley (the neighbourhood on the other side of the railway lines which had already intrigued me as an old industrial townscape caught in amber), Progress Street seemed to be particularly remote from the flow of life elsewhere. The corner shop was still painted in classic 1930s maroon and custard, and in the artless window (fenced in at the back with a row of Rathbone's white sliced loaves) sat iced vanilla slices oozing confectioner's custard and a smaller tray of savoury pasties of unspecified content, all ready to catch the full sun. In front of these, on the floor of the window-display space, came the peculiar jumble of items perhaps still found in small, poor shops everywhere – bottles of pink nail-varnish remover mixed up with Mr Kipling cakes, tubs of cocktail sticks and drawing pins, and more modern boxes of 'pot noodles' ready to fluff up in boiling water. In the brown depths of the shop was the glint of a bacon-slicer silently spinning teatime slices of cooked ham. Beyond all this – a mere 14 feet away from the facing terrace of tiny brick houses – rose the massive silent walls of Progress Mill.

Before it had jointly housed a soap factory and a military garage, Progress Mill had been owned by the Mutual Manufacturing Company Ltd and had clamoured with 365 looms, producing "fine cambrics, jaconettes, lawns, mulls, poplins, voiles, casements and rayons, etc." (I had gleaned all this from a textile directory dated 1935 which Andrew Schofield had pointed out to me up at Clitheroe Castle). Now the huge peeling doors of the mill were closed against the street. Finding no bell to ring, my fists on the field of solid wooden panels were soundless and there seemed to be no way in. But heads had started to appear at windows in Progress Street and very soon a kind woman popped out of a house.

"Is it Mr Danischewsky you're wanting, love?"

"Mr Danischewsky?"

Feeling rather thrown for a moment, I then wondered if this might be Mrs Thompson's "Mr Danny". A wonderful possibility now flooded into me with the casual mention of that name – that the man who had employed Mrs Thompson in his soap factory all those years ago might still be there and surely not his business too?

"Yes," I answered. "Mr Danischewsky."

The woman's presence on the street had now produced two more heads, flowering in a cluster of nylon overalls high up above a winch over the door of a loading bay.

"We'll come down to you, love. It's a heavy door."

Shortly afterwards, in the dying clang of massive doors, we were embraced by the serene gloom of Progress Mill. As in chocolate factories or bakeries, the very walls and furniture were impregnated with deep sweetness.

At first, Mr Danischewsky was startling, springing alive and very small from the shadows of an office solid with gracefully rounded, early Victorian furniture. He was in his mid-eighties, with large expressive eyes, the greenish pallor of a chain-smoker and those pronounced slightly pointed ears of the mercurial. He turned out to be not Polish but Russian, had recently lost his beloved wife and, in the moments of fierce sanity which grief produces, he still seemed frequently to see the objects of the world wavering behind a sheet of tears.

"I am unsure as to how I can help you."

Behind a partition which screened his office from the factory floor came the regular rounded thumping of dies, presumably pressing out little blocks of soap, and the sound of women's voices came laughing lightly over a tinny drizzle of pop.

"I was just surprised that a soap factory where Mrs Thompson worked in 1944 was still going – and under the same owner. Don't you think it is remarkable that you are still here? I mean,

I love scent and the way something so romantic marries up with industrial chemistry . . . that a chemist should devote himself above *anything* to reproducing the presence of flowers . . ."

"I am an industrial chemist, yes."

Gentle with roundabout women, Mr Danischewsky pushed forward a big triangular green-glass ashtray as we lit cigarettes (his an uncompromising untipped Woodbine) and let me smell some of the scores of small brown white-labelled bottles which sat behind his desk on top of a dusty filing cabinet. Remembering from some ancient chemistry lesson how to carefully waft strange bottles from side to side on their journey to the nose (sniff an unbenign substance too hard and your nostrils scorch): there was cedryl acetate (a fiercely concentrated cedarwood smell), musty, sweet cananga oil, straightforward salty geranium ("that is just a concentrated natural essence") and hydroxy citronella (the very common lab reproduction of roses and lemons mixed). Behind me, as I sampled these, Mr Danischewsky sat at a vast rosewood drop-leaf table set on well-trodden beige lino, and smoked on.

Mr Danischewsky explained that he had bought Progress Mill in 1939 with a local politician, Mr Wooton Davies: "We looked through the windows of the mill and said, 'Yes'."

War in Britain was a great local employer as well as a long-term economic decimator (we were at war for one day out of every three from 1914 to 1945). Under the auspices of the Ministry of Food, Fats and Soap Production, they had at first manufactured tooth powder and soap for the Royal Navy, eventually, with an eye to future peace, branching off into civilian luxuries and novelties. Taken on by Mr Danischewsky at the age of seventeen, first to pack soap and then to operate a soap-punching machine, Mrs Thompson recalled again and again in her notebooks:

Children's pale blue soap pressed with a die into the shape of policemen with black belts and boots and gold buttons . . . Tommy used to laugh and say, "You only worked in a soap factory when I met you" and, knowing what he was doing, abusing us, laughed because I had once made policemen.

"I suppose you don't remember Mrs Thompson's soap policemen now?" I asked Mr Danischewsky.

Again, he sprang to a dark corner of the room, to a cupboard hidden behind some mahogany spoon-back chairs, and quickly reappeared with a large, black oblong salesman's display case. Set back, the dusty lid revealed a brilliant interior of scarlet felt divided into compartments by raised livid-green bands. In the hollow of the first compartment lay a smiling soap policeman with upright truncheon and gold buttons. Then, to my amazement, came a black dachshund with facial holes in which to set glass eyes, a monkey scratching its head, soap Easter eggs, another coy dog being given a kiss on the cheek by a kitten, a large Scottie dog whose prominent inset black-and-white china eyes were still intact, and a hen with chicks sitting on a nest containing blue, yellow and red eggs.

In design, the soaps had the crudely naturalistic life of expensive pre-war Berlin toys sold at luxury department stores like the Wertheimer on Leipzigerplatz ("The moulds we used for these were German"), and, after fifty years or so, their scent and proper colour had gone. Mr Danischewsky smiled as I carefully lifted the faded soap policeman from his nest.

"We sold millions of him, but on all the others we lost money."

Suddenly, an electric bell rang, the thumping of machinery abruptly stopped and Mr Danischewsky suggested that I might like to go behind the partition and on to the factory floor – just to see the place where Mrs Thompson had worked.

The soap works itself turned out to be a vast stone-flagged shed, thick with warm eau-de-Cologne, in which four solid-looking Victorian cast-iron punching machines had been operated by wooden treadles. Like some pastel Antarctic scene, big blocks of semi-transparent yellow and green glycerine soap (each about five feet high) stood about like scented icebergs.

Covered with a scrap of polythene sheeting, one served as a table and bore a kettle, cups and newspapers. Walking about was a delicate operation, as the handsome stone flags were slightly waxy underfoot.

The soap-workers – mainly women – were seated at a few wooden benches between racks of finished oval soaps for an afternoon intake of tea, crisps and *Woman's Own*. Politely smiled at by the seated workers, Mr Danischewsky led me onwards to a kind of soap kitchen in a distant, hazier part of the mill. This harboured sizeable cauldrons of molten soap, big storage bins of pearl caustic soda and metal drums of coconut oil. Here the walls also seemed frozen like a wintry cave with yet more scented, dripping wax, and down on us came a sweet, brooding light which seems only to filter in behind the massive walls of a mill interior.

Inwardly, I doubted whether the factory had changed one iota since Mrs Thompson had worked here, at the age of seventeen, but felt it would be rather rude to say so.

"You think you are stepping into the nineteenth century, don't you?" said Mr Danischewsky very quietly and purposefully at my elbow.

Rapidly returning to his office, we found that a teapot wearing a knitted, bobble-topped cosy and surrounded by bone-china cups had arrived on a tray beside his desk. Ignoring it, he moved with the dart of a swallow to produce from beneath a big leather-framed blotter, littered with invoices and export documentation, a small, sharp square photograph of 1940s soap-factory girls.

"Do you recognize your lady among any of these?"

Wearing flowered pinnies (some women with factory turbans), the soap-workers of that time stood on a fire-escape at the back of the mill, smiling with direct, trusting eyes.

"The small blonde one with bubbly hair and round eyes might be her . . . *is* her."

"As you see, I am over twenty-five," blandly continued Mr Danischewsky. "But when I meet women who once worked here on the street, they wave and say, 'Hello, Mr Danny.' Now you can go home and write that I am a nasty old man."

Although he was well into his eighties, I suddenly felt quite captivated by Mr Danischewsky.

"I shall do no such thing. You are a good man in a sweet-scented atmosphere and the people who work here like you."

Mr Danischewsky's late wife had been a Polish war correspondent who had apparently saved a vast Polish- and Russian-language library – including some Dostoyevsky. Oddly enough, I told him, a paperback collection of Dostoyevsky short stories I had been reading on the train lay beneath the desk in my handbag.

"I do not know Dostoyevsky short stories," purred Mr Danischewsky. "What are they called in English?"

With the pointed briskness of a man bent on urgent business while others are idling, Mr Danischewsky's great-nephew suddenly appeared, irritably to attend to a fax which had incongruously begun to chatter from the shadows of the old man's office ("I shall not tell you where we export to, but Glycerose soap is everywhere on sale in the Canaries").

"Those Dostoyevsky short stories . . ." repeated Mr Danischewsky, ignoring him.

"What are they called?"

The cover of the wretched book was amber and black and outside, through the sparse sepia light of this mill-owner's office, lay the low roofs of the red-brick terrace called Progress Street and beyond it, the childhood streets of Hilda and Tommy Thompson.

"*What are those short stories called?*"

"*P-Poor Folk.*"

Left mainly to her own devices at the end of a day's work at the Droyt soap factory in Progress Mill, Hilda Hartley went dancing. At first she went with her friend Noni Stuart, and they danced together when there was the inevitable wartime shortage of young men. Later she went by herself and, with hair restored to childhood fairness and body scented with Soir de Paris or

Californian Poppy, she crossed the railway lines to the medieval part of the town, which had a wonderful dance-hall (run by a young man called Albert) above the Arcade in Market Street. Albert not only ran the dance-hall but taught ballroom dancing. Although she could not afford lessons, Hilda was drawn to watch all that he did when, passing behind the black-out curtain on to a glorious big sprung floor, he and the young people of Chorley revolved and revolved for what seemed miles in closely observed 'feathers', 'telemarks' and 'reverse turns' before dissolving into the wildness of American big-band numbers (eagerly sought out by those very few young people with access to a personal radio set on the local AFN). *Albert was very tall and gentle . . . He was a Nice Person.*

Albert Entwistle was tall, elegant and perfectly groomed and, to Hilda, he was her first and residing idea of an English gentleman. Encouraged a bit by my accidental discovery that Mr Danischewsky still ran Mrs Thompson's former workplace in Progress Street, I now decided to pursue the *beau idéal* and, eventually, the classified ads department of the *Chorley Guardian* confirmed that although Chorley no longer had a dance-hall, the Albert and Phyllis Entwistle School of Dancing was still going strong.

Arranging over the telephone to meet Albert Entwistle, I perhaps foolishly imagined him to look rather like a society dance-band leader of the 1930s – in tails, of course, and a boiled dress-shirt with a front panel so stiff one could tap on it, and perhaps the vague agreeable scent of hay fields which used to waft on grey London days from elderly conservatively dressed men in St James's. But in Chorley, outside Progress Street, life had moved on. The Victoria Dance Hall, which Albert and his wife, Phyllis, had run over the Arcade during the war had closed after a fire in 1981 and now the dancing Entwistles continued their lives in a pretty little building in Byron Street. An oval plaque on the front read: INDEPENDENT SABBATH SCHOOL. ERECTED 1836. Instead of decorous ballroom-dancing lessons followed by the crash of youth in a wartime dance-hall, I suddenly found myself standing with Mrs Thompson's hero in a simple late Georgian schoolroom which had the remote and ascetic grace of a Bewick print.

Couples like the Entwistles who willingly hold each other every day for forty years are pretty seamlessly married. While Phyllis ran in and out to the car, unloading the lighter pieces of sound equipment and setting up several small tables with red-checked cloths and bottles of orange juice to refresh their forthcoming pupils, Albert and I stood rather shyly together, edging towards the verge of a chat.

Unusually for a professional dancer, Albert Entwistle was indeed a very tall man (looking up, I thought he might be possibly six feet three or four), soft-spoken, with high craggy cheek-bones, pale-blue eyes and, rather incongruously, the dull, careful dress of a summery Methodist lay-preacher which all ended in navy-blue socks and sandals. Phyllis (perhaps a little younger) still had darkish hair, pulled straight off the face (Spanish or ballet style) into a high bun; a necklace of jet beads and a full cotton skirt which swirled romantically from a waist surprisingly firm and slender. Exercise – in their case, the daily concentration on ballroom dancing – really did seem to be the elixir of life, and only the faint tendency in both partners for forearm flesh to hang slightly loose of the bone indicated that they were both in their sixth decade.

When he was nineteen or so, Albert Entwistle had become a police cadet in Preston and had been invited to the famous local Horwich Police Ball. Like public ballroom dancing itself, the annual Police Ball was, at that time, an event of some social significance locally and Albert was desperate to go.

"Of course, I couldn't *dance*. But they soon told me, 'If you learn, you'll be able to come along.'"

With a great desire to cut a figure on the dance floor, Albert sped along to the Hewitt School of Dance in Bolton ("It's not just *what* you do, it's *how* you do it – the expression") and he proved to be so naturally adept that he immediately abandoned the police force to teach others how to dance instead.

As he folded his great length down on to a chair to replace Christian sandals with soft leather dancing shoes, I reflected with an unfair tremor of disappointment how accurately he and Phyllis represented the intense respectability of dance-hall managers in 1940s and 1950s Britain, when 'Saturday night at the Palais' was Britain's second biggest leisure industry (the cinema came first), roughly estimated on St Valentine's Day 1953 in *The Economist* as being nationally worth £25m annually. Albert and Phyllis seemed to be absolutely typical of Britain's unusually well-organized and curriculum-minded professional teachers of dance who had standardized the waltz, foxtrot, quickstep and tango into an internationally recognized 'English style'. Apart from a few notorious wartime dance-halls in big cities, people like the Entwistles had turned dancing in public places into an 'artistic and health-giving pursuit' to which young girls like Hilda Hartley, while longing for romance, could safely entrust their reputations. With proper pride in their achievements, Phyllis bobbed back and forth with snippets of information about professional accomplishment.

"There was the Northern Counties Dance Teachers' Association, the International Dance Masters' Association *and* the British Association of Teachers of Dance. They have the nicest medals in the whole country."

She gracefully lamented how the metal that competition medals were made from was no longer quite as solid as it had been in their youth.

"In those days, the silver medal *was* silver and the gold was *real gold*."

Soon, the first pupils of the evening (a local man and his wife, both in their early thirties) arrived for a lesson and Albert Entwistle rose suavely to greet them.

"OK for the cha-cha?" as Phyllis set a record called 'Love Hit Me' on the rather tinny gramophone. The female pupil wore high-heeled black patent-leather shoes with ankle-straps and, closely watched by Albert, who seemed to come alive on the wooden schoolroom floor, she and her husband began the stiff-kneed progress of this least sensuous of Latin American dances.

"That's your trouble . . ." said Albert, watching the husband closely. "You're walking across," and, lithely taking the woman in his arms, he demonstrated with the subdued, powerful lead of the accomplished male ballroom-dancer how this jerky dance should go. Back together, the couple performed the dance seriously, with shy, down-cast eyes – a clear instance of the English taking their pleasures sadly. At that moment, I wished for two things – that someone would put on the infectiously bouncy beat of a good samba (say, to be perfectly honest, 'Brazil') and that Albert would ask *me* to dance. (All that a woman dancer had to do in these circumstances was to achieve that weightless 'float' in the man's arms and be guided by the subtle pressure of his thigh, hand and shoulder.)

Instead, Phyllis Entwistle very kindly brought me a glass of orange juice and, spreading out her flowing cotton skirt on the chair beside me, explained the principles on which she and Albert had run 'The Vic' ballroom over the Arcade in Chorley for almost forty years.

"The youngsters used to say, 'Your dancing classes are not only classes – they're *parties* as well.' We used to let the boys out at half-time to get a drink in the local pubs, but that meant they had to mix with *undesirables*. We're dancers, not publicans – we only applied for a licence in 1972 – but people always say we must have married half of Chorley!"

Gaining confidence from the Entwistles' firm and kindly management of the wonderful 'Vic' ballroom, Hilda Hartley ventured further afield, this time to a public dance-hall in Preston, where she met a young soldier from London who was stationed in the town and became secretly engaged to him:

He thought a lot about me. But I didn't want to get serious about him. I didn't love him really, but I liked him. He was a nice person.

And, aged a rather childlike nineteen, she eventually broke the engagement off.

Eventually, it was in the sweet sepia shadows of Progress Mill, where Hilda made soap policemen, Mr Danischewsky sought the perfect chemical reproduction of flowers and where (in the vast spaces of the redundant weaving-shed next door) Tommy had watched Cockney soldiers strip down jeeps for North-West Army Command, that Mrs Thompson was led to true love and happiness.

Because Hilda was such a quiet little thing – a five-foot wisp with lightened hair, always anxious to please and often at a loose end after work – a friendly soap-factory girl (called Lillian Todd) one day casually suggested above the chomping of the soap-punching machines in Mr Danny's waxy workroom that Hilda might enjoy "a blind date".

"What's a 'blind date'?" Hilda had asked, and, smiling at her simplicity, Lillian cheerfully explained the American fashion. Her own fiancé was a young man called Cyril Thompson – strong (but she knew he was just a little lad inside), and his younger brother, Tommy, was home on leave from National Service.

"They're alike as two fried eggs. We'll make up a foursome, see. I'll be with Cyril and you can sit with Tommy."

Sitting that evening in the Working Men's Club in Brooke Street, Cyril and Lillian lounged close together while, carefully dressed, Hilda found herself deeply scrutinized by a pair of the most romantic and warmly dark eyes she had ever seen.

He decided I was the Person he was going to Marry although he was only 19 and still serving his 2 year conscription in the Army . . . I was the only girl he had ever met that he wanted to get Married to right away he said.

For one so strong and physically compelling, Tommy Thompson seemed gentle and kind, and when he occasionally spoke, Hilda pitied him for the mar of a stammer which affronted him, as it would any grown man. Later, on leaving the damp fug of the club, he walked her home to Bowland Avenue – a courteous thing that had never happened before – and his voice remained hesitantly full of reassurances ("I l-love you", a difficult thing for a man to say) on the evenings when he and Hilda eventually went out alone together.

One spring evening, to get away from Chorley they went to a special place. Set high up above the little town, it was a pub called the Sea View, from which, like the promise of freedom and pleasure, the flat glitter of the Irish Sea and a hint of Blackpool could be seen across hills spiked with mill chimneys.

> *He told me he had been with many Girl Friends but he had never met anyone like me before that was quiet and trusting in every way and really Loved.*

They had no money at all, and certainly not enough for an engagement ring, but by the time the spring sky had bronzed with cold and it was time to go inside, they had decided to marry immediately. For the first time since her father had died, leaving only his roses behind, the young woman felt wanted. Just as real people did in films in the Chorley Plaza, he suddenly took her in his arms and, before kissing her very firmly, Tommy Thompson said quite fluently and with no hesitations at all, "*I'll be a good husband t'ye. I'll be like the Father and Brother you never had.*"

3

Learning to be Mrs Thompson

The Thompsons were expecting me for tea at four o'clock. Quickly dismissing the confident grandeur of the centre of the town, the taxi suddenly shot me out into the less certain terrain of the Lancashire poor – decaying mill buildings (now sometimes used, it seemed, to host sales of bright nylon carpet), small red-brick terraces hacked about by ludicrously complicated concrete flyovers and underpasses, faded Asian corner-shops, the damp purple-brick Gothic of mouldering churches, well-swilled pubs with Alsatian dogs at the door and then, in a turmoil of redevelopment, came blank new industrial acres filled with grey metal DIY warehouses catering for the British obsession with home improvement. Further still, after some backing up, U-turns and hesitant crawling about, the cab arrived in a neat oasis of council maisonettes decorated with white wooden 'ranch-style' balconies.

There was a glimpse of pale oval face at a window above me and then, up on one balcony, the front door of the Thompsons' maisonette was opened and left standing wide, as if by some ghostly hand. Seething with nervousness, I paid off the cab and began to mount the concrete stairs to meet Mrs Hilda Thompson and her daughters for the very first time.

That day, on arrival at Preston station, I had been gripped by a paralysis of apprehension. Finding my wishes granted at last – to meet the Thompson women face to face to begin the real inquiry into a story which they had so far only attempted to communicate to me in writing, I was now thoroughly alarmed. In all their simplicity and baldness of fact, the Thompson women's notebooks had been truly terrible to read and odd lines from them continued to run in my head like drummed-in verses from a psalm. By some perverse law of feeling, people whose suffering has been very great are often set apart in the world, and, I suppose, when clumsily aware of an endurance infinitely greater than our own, we are always initially fearful of approaching them. I was expected at the Thompsons' for tea, but to allow plenty of time for transport from Scotland to go wrong, I had already been in Preston for most of the day.

The towns of the North have their own hard magnificence. In Preston, Lancashire (once a winter resort of the eighteenth-century aristocracy and then the first place in the world to host a factory empire – Samuel Horrocks's cotton mills), provincial grandeur takes the shape of a vast public library and museum in the market-place. Built in 1877 to rival the far-off British Museum, Victorian philanthropy booms out a series of telegrams incised in gilt letters beneath the frieze of Bassae: THE MENTAL RICHES YOU MAY HERE ACQUIRE ABIDE WITH YOU ALWAYS, and then, rather more contentiously, on two further sides of the building: IN MAN THERE IS NOTHING GREAT BUT MIND. REVERENCE IN MAN THAT WHICH IS SUPREME. Drawn on into a great space full of rustling trees and stuccoed serenity, I then found beautiful Winckley Square.

Winckley Square was an address I had already seen on solicitors' writing-paper, because one of two legal firms which had defended the Thompson sisters at their trial has its offices here. Very big in the manner of eighteenth-century squares in Dublin, it undulates with graceful public gardens and is nowadays quietly redolent of law and finance. Very unusually for solicitors' offices in Britain, the windows of number 17 bear the name of a woman – DOROTHY HEATON, painted in round gold letters. Venturing inside in the hope of finding something – anything – to pass the time, I was eventually directed to the room of Heaton's present office manager, the affable Barry Hitchin.

Barry Hitchin was a big, friendly man in his thirties who sat sleek and jolly as a walrus in what looked like a buff cave built up from files. Like anyone who deals with nothing but the most formal kind of paperwork all day, he seemed glad of a brief diversion. In the kindly northern way of instantly absorbing strangers and their odd little inquiries like blotting-paper, he was soon able to fill me in on the background to a name that now intrigued me.

Dorothy Heaton had been the daughter of a wealthy Preston tea merchant. "It was the Belfast Tea Company, I think – and I suppose you could call her Lancashire's pioneer woman solicitor . . ."

Apparently, after qualifying some time in the 1920s, she was able to buy the practice at 17 Winckley Square quite cheaply, because the previous legal occupant had gone and hanged himself on an upper landing.

"Norman, the odd-job man, always says he's seen a foggy old figure or felt a presence up there – he believes in spiritualism – but, as you say, it's probably just a memory of what happened here all those years ago."

Unlike most modern professional women, Dorothy Heaton had begun her working day by sand-stoning the front step of her offices in the northern, house-proud way. Then, with just one steady old managing clerk, who took her mail round on a bicycle, she was among the first to try to arrange separations, divorces and maintenance orders for working women trapped in violent marriages – and this at a time when divorce was still the exclusive and scandalous bolt-hole of the rich.

"She was a lovely lady was Miss Heaton," said Barry fondly, still somewhat surprised that these days anyone should come into the office to ask after her. "I think people used to like the idea of women seeing a woman solicitor about their matrimonial problems. Of course, she was elderly and walked with a stick when I knew her, she had grey hair and some crippling illness towards the end of her life. But she had been a beautiful woman in her day – very tall and fair with blue eyes and a beautiful speaking voice."

Barry Hitchin leaned forward and invited me to look at the solid oak desk between us. "This was her desk, you know – and this was her room."

He pointed to a place on the floor.

"She had a little Boston terrier called Rocky, who always slept over there. Every day when she was coming in, her managing clerk had to put out police cones at the front of the building, because people round here were very wary of her parking. She would drive forward till she bumped the car in front and then reverse until she hit the car behind her . . . It's sad, really, what happened at the end of her life."

"And what was that?" I said, by now immensely pleased to know the origins of a firm that had dealt so well with the Thompson sisters' case.

"Well . . ." said Barry speaking carefully and not wishing to be disloyal. "It was said that she was rather unfortunate with her second husband."

"I would have thought a woman who dealt all her life with difficult matrimonial cases would have been rather good at choosing a husband."

"In her case, it turned out she wasn't."

"I don't wish to pry . . ." I said, but in fact, by now, I was absolutely burning to know.

"Well," said Barry, looking at the door and resigning himself to parting with the information, "it turned out that her second husband was a bigamist. There was quite a carry-on about her estate after her death, I gather."

I was so dumbfounded that, I am sorry to say, I let slip a disrespectful remark. "Well, you've heard the old legal saying, Barry – act for yourself and you act for a fool."

And then it struck me that if such an able and confident woman as Dorothy Heaton had been deceived in her choice of a husband, what chance did poor young Hilda Thompson have in Progress Street?

Later that afternoon, as I finally reached the open door of the Thompsons' maisonette, I no longer felt that Mrs Thompson had been quite so reckless in allowing herself to be swept off her feet by Tommy.

Mrs Thompson turned out to be a small, frail, well-dressed woman in her early sixties, with the remains, in a surgically collapsed face, of a round-eyed blonde prettiness.

"Hello, love," she said, coming forward rather gracefully to shake hands, while her daughters, June and Hilda, just stood by smiling quietly. In their presence, for the first time, I had a sense of leaving the real world behind me.

Looking back on it, my impression of this first meeting is one of almost total verbal unimportance. They had written; I had read, and, in the English way when dealing with difficult matters – poverty, grief, violence, incest, terminal illness, madness, murder and shame – we concentrated intently on such important things as my train journey, the weather in Preston, what the weather was like in Scotland and on the preparation of tea, which was gradually spread before us with porcelain tea cups and saucers set down carefully on coasters, Marks & Spencer's pink-wafer and chocolate-coated biscuits genteelly arranged on a plate, with paper napkins to hand. As with all conservative women, however disadvantaged, the instinct of the Thompson women was to rise above unpleasantness, to underplay difficulty and to be what is unfashionably called 'a lady'.

If their possessions had been pushed up a designer notch or two, the Thompsons' sitting room on this first meeting could have been described as 'minimalist'. I recollect two brown velvet armchairs, one brown velvet sofa, one small gilt mantelpiece clock, one big television set and a tiny, white flop-haired Yorkshire terrier bitch called Candy, who was endlessly fondled on young Hilda's knee. June and Hilda Thompson seemed to have visually softened a bit too since the days in Skeffington Road. Shortly after the murder, when the sisters had appeared in tabloid newspaper photographs after appearances in court, their femininity seemed to have been outwardly extinguished by the preceding decades of quite extraordinary domestic brutality and sexual abuse. Then, their hair had been severely cropped, their faces had been set square and harsh, and their clothes had been rather mannish, as if duty-bound to follow a masculine model of being and dressing like cadets from some ghastly platoon. Now, a few years later, as their father had begun to recede a little into the past, the new taste of June and Hilda had begun to visually assert itself. It was heartening to see that the supposedly trivial (but actually very important) signs of feminine health – the living flame of vanity or *amour propre* – had begun to burn again. Their thick dark hair was now a bit softer and wavier and they seemed to like neat little blouses, Acrilan cardigans in pastel colours and full skirts with a cinched waistline. They both had good, naturally pale skin and, as we talked of this and that, I wondered if one day they might go so far as to enhance it with a little make-up. A light waft of flowery scent was already on the air. But after an hour or so on that first day, when natural reticence on their part and mine might have begun to recede a little, I began to notice that what I had taken for extreme shyness on their part now seemed rather more sinister than simple natural hesitancy. Mrs Thompson and her daughters seemed to have the 'frozen watchfulness' first observed and noted in academic studies of maltreated children during the 1960s. Already too familiar with blows, emotional coldness and derision, the child with frozen watchfulness stays unnaturally still and quiet, drawing as little attention to itself as possible, and closely scrutinizes the faces of adults to anticipate the faintest signs of displeasure or physical advance. Having drunk it, tea, I suddenly realized, had been produced in the quietest way I had ever known in the confined space of a small family home. As the Thompson sisters had prepared it, they had moved about the house as little as possible and, when they had of necessity moved, not a cup had rattled in the kitchen, there had been no footfall or sound of a drawer opening or of a kettle being filled or of tea things being lightly set down with absolute precision on the teak veneer of the new coffee table. For the first time, I most unwillingly began to feel what it must be like to have absolute domestic power over other human beings. Like ideal Victorian children, June and Hilda Thompson spoke only when spoken to, smiled only when smiled at, answered a trivial question promptly but added no afterthoughts of their own. Then, as they began to show me over the little house, I finally became aware of their intense inner silence and emotional 'invisibility', as if they had no interior 'swim' of natural feeling. It was rather an eerie thing, like putting one's ear to a conch shell and hearing no sound of the sea.

The silent tour of the new maisonette took us up on broad, open, modern stairs of polished wood, rather like those of a yacht, except these were thick with deep, pink carpet. Upstairs, the bedroom and bathroom were a blur of pink – there was pink, pink and more pink. One bedroom had pale-pink walls, rose-pink curtains, rose-pink carpet and a double bed with a deeper pink velvet-buttoned headboard and a plump white duvet sprinkled with pink roses. I was very surprised to find that June appeared to share this bed with her mother, because of "bad nights". But in the bland afternoon light of this room, it seemed impossible that night could ever fall and the bedside table bore an earthenware ornament in which a sweet brown rabbit lay cutely in bed under a turquoise quilt, while a smaller rabbit snuggled up to it.

The doors of the bedrooms were left wide open at night, because that way Mrs Thompson and her daughters felt more emotionally secure. Directly opposite lay the room where 'young Hilda' seemed to sleep alone, lulled by anti-depression and relaxation tapes played through a Sony Walkman. In this little room a chest of drawers bore a clump of yellow artificial flowers, imprisoned under a modern glass dome, the duvet was again sprinkled with roses and, on the bedside table, a single wild rabbit again snuggled deep into a turquoise pottery bed, peeping with one eye over a label saying 'Wakey'.

That left Bedroom Three, on which the door was firmly closed, but after some slight hesitation it was opened for me to look inside while June stood back on the landing. Entering the third bedroom alone, I felt for a moment that somehow I had traversed the boundaries of possibility and stepped through into one of the sinister photographs of Skeffington Road which Detective Chief Inspector Biscombe had shown me so long before in one of the police Blue Books. The room happened to be painted a cold blue and even now, in this new fresh maisonette, it had been fitted out in the manner of Tommy Thompson's 'military stores', full of severe metal industrial racking, stacked with pots and pans, a pressure cooker, dried food, tools, cardboard boxes labelled with extreme neatness and all the harsh gear of life under siege.

"You – you still keep a room for 'stores', then?" I felt impelled to venture, backing out of the room and hastening to leave the upper floor altogether. "Just as you used to do at Skeffington Road . . ."

Standing out on the landing, June answered quite automatically and remotely; "We use it for spare items."

Back downstairs, as I began to gather my things together to leave, the Thompson sisters with their short wavy hair, cinched waistlines and soft Acrilan cardigans were momentarily silhouetted against the bright, neatly swagged picture windows of the sitting-room and, for some reason, I suddenly recalled the simple device of the fashion historian, the 'fashion silhouette', which, by obliterating confusing details of colour and decoration, shows in stark outline the inventive way that women's clothes and hair balloon up and in, then out and down, from one decade to the next. That afternoon, seeing them standing together against the lowering light, I suddenly realized that, both inside and out, June and Hilda Thompson had been frozen in time as two young teenage girls of the 1960s – the moment when sexual abuse had started and their emotional development had stopped. Like a silent clock which had been somehow recently wound anew without being reset to the appropriate time, the lives of the sisters had now begun to slowly beat the minutes forward in an hour which had long gone by.

In the tradition of wartime weddings which lingered on with the continued rationing of clothes and food, the marriage of

Hilda Hartley to Tommy Thompson on 22 September 1951 was civil, quick and austere. But in the three warmly rounded summer months – June, July and August – when they had seen each other as often as possible and had begun to mesh a bit with each other's families, Hilda's love affair with Tommy presented her with a new emotional experience. For the first time, she was discovering the sometimes quite frightening exhilaration of an intense sexual rivalry in which two women duel for power over a man.

At some point during the preceding decade, Mary Ann and Jack Topping and her four grown sons had removed to a small, well-built council house in Randless Avenue, Chorley – heated as before by a tiny black cast-iron Yorkshire range. On these summer evenings when the family briefly hung about in Mary Ann's stifling kitchen before going out, Hilda, primly well dressed and scented, became increasingly conscious of the regularity of the rising din of violent and futile arguments between Tommy, his mother and elder brothers, while poor Jack Topping (Tommy's spiritualist stepfather) sat to one side, silent and quite disregarded. Mary Ann had reached the stage of giving her assessment of Tommy's character in front of him, whether he liked it or not.

"If you marry our Tommy," she said, looking the little soap-factory wisp straight in the eye, "I'm warning ye. He'll put you through the eye of a needle."

For her part, Hilda seems to have thought Mary Ann was coarse, mercenary and unhealthily possessive of her sons, and discovered that one minor pleasure of her forthcoming marriage would be to deprive his mother of him.

I thought she was just trying to put me off him – if he didn't marry me he'd be at home and putting his wages up as usual.

It also crossed her mind that, rather like herself, Tommy might be keen to get married "because he was sick of bother at home".

I could quite see how, with the distanced eye of an older

woman, Mary Ann's assessment of Hilda would be long and contemptuous. Whereas she – Mary Ann – had carried and borne four sons, almost literally broken her back with hard physical work to bring them up and had lived through times before the war that even now were scarcely believed by some, this little Hilda was a lightweight thing – sharp one day, pathetic the next. She was not at all the right wife for Tommy – if any woman could be.

In complete contrast, Ellen Hartley seems scarcely to have had the will to analyse the character of her prospective son-in-law at all. Returning weary and depressed from work at the Hygienic Laundry, her summing up of Tommy was short and approving. She was relieved to see such a courteous, smartly got-up young man (physically quite good-looking too) seriously offering to provide her daughter with a purpose in life. Over the years since her husband's death, Ellen had returned to Roman Catholicism and had drifted back to Mass at the Sacred Heart church on the corner of Buchanan Street. As she looked at Hilda, now aged twenty-three, it was as if from somewhere very high up in her mind like a remote shelf of prayer that she just said one day: "I think he'll make you a grand husband."

As the simple preparations for the wedding were inevitably set in train, Mary Ann took care late one summer night also to gave Hilda a parting gift of words ("*Make your bed with him and you'll lie on it*!") and then, doubtless with the consolation that another woman's misery would be almost certain, she said no more.

Now moving as if in a dream towards the companionship she craved, children of her own and a home in which she could reproduce the golden part of her past, Hilda was less surprised than she should have been when Tommy suddenly seized control of the wedding arrangements, even down to issuing the few verbal invitations to parents. Her mother was not asked to attend the wedding; nor was Tommy's stepfather – only Mary Ann. Ellen Hartley was hurt that Tommy did not want her at the wedding, but drew comfort from the fact that Tommy's mother, although invited, had made it plain to all concerned that she would not be going either. Ellen also took comfort from the fact that many old-fashioned family ways of doing things had been disrupted by the chaos of war – perhaps youngsters running off to get married with only the legally required number of witnesses was just the strange new post-war way of doing things. Tommy Thompson, however, seems to have remained uneasy about his mother's continuing contempt for his marriage plans. Letting him swing for a while had been often the way his mother had drawn him back to her, and it was no surprise to Mary Ann when Tommy asked her again, this time quite anxiously on the morning of the big day, "You'll be coming to watch wedding, won't you?" But even on the day itself she angrily turned away.

It was a round, golden morning in September when Tommy, with his older brother Cyril as best-man, automatically bulled their shoes in the conscript way, set white carnations (stems wrapped in silver paper) into the lapels of their navy-blue serge suits and combed their hair neatly with water from the kitchen tap.

Even though it was a Saturday morning and a day she had long given up for doing laundry, Mary Ann had been also up early in the day to heat extra water. By the time the magnificent luxury of a taxi was waiting outside the front door to bear the bridegroom and his best-man to terracotta officialdom in the Gilibrand Street registry office, Mary Ann had put on the clogs that many working women in Lancashire continued to wear for rough work until well into the 1950s and was standing out in the backyard, thumping her pain and fury into a tub of hot washing, pounding and pounding with the wooden dolly-legs ("*He's – never been – no good to me*!").

But some ameliorating souls cannot allow a certain moment to pass. Although he had not been invited to Tommy's wedding, having sweated in the raging steam and clamour of Chorley's spinning rooms to help feed and clothe another man's children for almost fifteen years, Jack Topping came forward and, lightly resting his thin, shaking hands on the lowered window of the taxi, looked into the cab and said warmly to Tommy, "Make best of it, lad. You'll be all right if you pull together."

Barely acknowledging him, and with a new, different life in prospect, the occupants of the cab glided away.

No matter how the marriage eventually turns out, few women of romantic temperament will ever say a word against a wedding day, particularly their own and particularly if, on that day, they were in love. Looking back on her own wedding day in Gilibrand Street, Mrs Thompson still recorded it in her notebooks as *a lovely day . . . a very happy day . . . we were all so happy.* Within the means at her family's disposal (and, more often, just her own savings), it is one day in life when a woman, no matter how ordinary or ill-destined, momentarily tastes the sensuousness of privilege – nice clothes, scent, flowers and a sense of life's liberality.

Taut with wedding nerves and with full physical consummation a novelty in store, the young bridal couple from Chorley were photographed standing anxiously to attention *in a cheap studio on the front at Blackpool*, the place they had glimpsed across the hills only three months before from the Sea View pub above their small home town. With her blonde hair dressed in a 'pageboy' (a longish, well-turned-under bob) and dried in front of the fire that Ellen Hartley had stoked up that morning with a sense of new life coming to her widowed house in Bowland Avenue, the new Mrs Thompson wore a pale-blue dress in fine wool with a Peter Pan collar and soft pleats falling from a pin-tucked bodice. Remembered in loving detail, her coat was *a shade darker* and bore a bold 1940s-style corsage of pink carnations. Standing very upright beside her, Tommy Thompson bore in his stance the soldierly signs of recent conscription beneath a smart widely cut dark serge suit, festively frosted with the silver-paper signal of a working man on his wedding day:

> *My mother had asked us if we would be calling home to Bowland Avenue before going to Blackpool for the day. On arriving home we were surprised. My Mum and her friend had prepared a boiled ham salad for us all and made a big Trifle & had got cakes etc for us.*

Cyril's fiancée, Lillian, who had so miraculously brought Hilda and Tommy together in Mr Danischewsky's soap factory, was a joyful bridesmaid. Borne third-class on the smutty little steam train direct from Chorley to Blackpool, the wedding party of four then set off on a honeymoon trip for the day, hoping they "could clear the lot" for five pounds.

Blackpool, more so than any other English resort, is a place which, even in 1951, continued to symbolize the high moment of Edwardian gaiety rather than actually providing it. Created like a garish music-hall set at the height of the Lancashire cotton trade around 1900, it captured the spirit of industrial good times when the tens of thousands of cotton-working families, who were its *raison d'être*, poured out in summer from stifling holiday steam trains, carrying whole boiled hams and tin trunks filled with cake to last the week. It was the one week out of fifty-two when, suddenly released from the hard clamour of machinery, ceaseless physical labour and sexual prudence, vital beings burst out of their factories for the annual spree, "as if the boilers had exploded and blown them out". Sophisticated in its survival techniques, Blackpool was now mechanized and Americanized, rethought in the 1930s for newer generations of passive and listless pleasure-seekers who had been left behind spiritually to die with their industry after the North's brighter youngsters had escaped.

On her afternoon honeymoon at Blackpool, following the boiled ham salad at Bowland Avenue, the new Mrs Thompson was glad of the early autumn sun, which made the resort seem almost like summer. Now reduced in status to the merely unwed, Cyril and Lillian were respectfully in tow. In the curious state of wearing stiff, new formal clothes beside the seaside and of being technically married but not yet having fully experienced each other, Hilda and Tommy Thompson wandered about for miles on the vast three-tier promenade which seemed to shield half the Lancashire coast against the Irish Sea and was now still dotted with fortifications of a grimmer kind – clumps of huge, grey concrete cubes ringed with rusting barbed wire to impede enemy tank-landings. They took a peep inside the

Blackpool Tower, where a vast pioneering public dance-hall had been created to hold waltzing spinners and weavers by the thousand. It was the very Mecca of dancing Lancashire, with inviting acres of sprung cedar-wood floor (relaid every few years), Dubarry-style powder rooms with pink-tinted mirrors, handbag repositories, severely tiled washrooms where young men could hire safety razors, and other vaguely chintzed rooms where ladies could iron their dresses before taking the floor. On the Pleasure Beach they crashed about a bit in dodgem cars (Tommy demonstrating casual, one-handed prowess at the wheel), respectively drank bitter and Babycham when licensing hours permitted it and spun the creaking, white-painted wooden stands on which thousands of libidinous coloured postcards re-ran Edwardian mill gaiety in modern austerity dress and celebrated the sea as a shining release from workaday Lancashire.

To Hilda Thompson spinning on Babycham, ozone and happiness, immediately post-war Blackpool seemed to be a whirl of skirts naughtily whipped up by the wind, willies lost and found, hair stiffening in the salt spray and holiday-makers plunging about on Pleasure Beach rides ("We don't know where we're going but we're on our way!").

With the moon and one of Blackpool's three piers behind him, the seducer on a picture postcard murmured:

> The moon lights up the summer sea,
> The stars in heaven shine;
> And what a girl learns at her mother's knee
> She soon forgets on mine.

Wartime meant a bride sitting bolt upright in bed with a gas mask on ("Mother told me that if I was a sensible girl I should take precautions"), while the outdoor lavatories of old terraces in mill towns had helped to create the celebrated chamber-pot and honeymoon joke set in the kind of Blackpool hotel that Tommy and Hilda could not afford:

HOTEL RECEPTIONIST TO NEWLY MARRIED COUPLE: Shall I show you to the Bridal Chamber?

NEWLY MARRIED HUSBAND TO RECEPTIONIST: Nay, lad. Just show us the bedroom and we'll find *that* for ourselves!

Much later in the evening, no longer very tight on Babycham and in a nervous flutter of excitement that this was the first night – the only night – of her five-pound honeymoon, the new Mrs Thompson arrived back home with her husband to their new home in the front double-bedroom of Bowland Avenue, Chorley, where Tommy instantly made her his.

Tommy never once showed any signs of his bad temper during the day and evening at Blackpool. But when Tommy started to hit me soon after we were Married I was shocked at the change in him since our marriage.

From the start, Tommy Thompson seemed very uneasy in Bowland Avenue – quite natural, perhaps, in a young man beginning married life in his mother-in-law's house during the post-war housing shortage. But Tommy seems to have been particularly uneasy at having to sleep upstairs. He also seemed to regard the marriage not so much as a new way of going forward in life, but as a means of instantly paying back for something that Hilda did not understand and that he himself could not quite remember. The newly married couple seemed to be sidling round each other in the dark.

"F-from now on, what I say goes."

"Well, you don't need to say that to me, because that's how I want it."

As if to reinforce his point, a few days after the Blackpool honeymoon, when he had just returned from his job at the Commonbank Bleach Works, Tommy suddenly hit his new wife very hard across the side of the head and she found herself – here in her mother's quiet house – lying beside a dressing table whose mirror swam up into the light of the big bay window. People quite unused to physical violence can at first only bow their heads in a kind of accepting surprise and receive it. This kind of treatment had never happened to Hilda before. Surely it would not happen again.

Barely a week before, the shops fronting the Pleasure Beach at Blackpool had been stacked with thousands of funny postcards, including one very popular one entitled THE FIRST THREE YEARS OF MARRIAGE. Convinced that working-class couples were usually quite fatalistic about the way that marriages all too often accelerated downwards into mutual loathing and that, in any case, people traditionally expected to sacrifice themselves for the betterment of their children, the artist (Donald McGill) had lettered the card in his usual witty style: "The First Year, He talks and She listens; the Second Year, She talks and He listens and the Third Year, they both talk and the neighbours listen." Within days of the newly married couple, Hilda and Tommy Thompson, having moved into Ellen Hartley's big front bedroom, the neighbours in Bowland Avenue could not help but overhear a good deal, and, utterly bewildered by an absurd violence of voice and fist that she too had never experienced before, Ellen was reduced to tapping urgently on the bedroom door to plead timorously, "*Will* you lower your voice, Tommy. *Think* of the neighbours."

> *Once we were married I found out within days what a bad wicked temper he had. He didn't control it . . . He used to raise his voice so loud, my Mother once asked him if he would try to be a bit quieter for the sake of the neighbours who were nice people. She could hear he was hitting me as well when he got in a temper . . . It was no use telling his Mother. She knew him and his ways. She used to say to me, you've made your bed you must lie on it.*

On that autumn morning when she was quite sure that the taxi had taken her fierce son away, Mary Ann had continued with her washing and just once allowed herself the luxury of feeling deeply and inwardly: "*Tommy, I loved thee if tha had'na made me cry.*" And in Bowland Avenue, far from discovering how to give as good as she got in the supposedly comic cut and thrust of marital warfare, the new Mrs Thompson was silenced for the next forty years.

4

Nowhere to Go

Mrs Thompson had a goodish memory despite all that she had suffered – or possibly because of it. But, while focusing quite clearly (like many old people) on the incidents, impressions and pleasures of childhood and youthful working days, she seemed to have a bit of a memory dip in the harsher, greyer years which followed immediately after her marriage to Tommy.

I was rather confused too about the actual sequence of events in her later life which, for people settled in happier circumstances, tends to be divided into the periods of time spent in this house or in that; in a life's progress of marriages, love affairs and children, or in job moves from one part of the country to another.

Quite soon, I began to feel rather justified in finding the Thompsons' family history a little hard to grasp when I discovered that they had, in fact, moved house an extraordinary number of times – about thirteen or fourteen times in all throughout Mrs Thompson's married life. Eventually, using the Thompson women's notebooks and their useful but strangely bureaucratic habit of hoarding the most banal receipts, bills, letters and official forms (all carefully filed in white envelopes and wrapped in plastic for the past twenty years at least), we managed painstakingly to piece together some idea of the family's house moves from what seemed to be the beginning to the end.

First of all there was Hindley Street, Chorley, and then John Street; after that came Trafalgar Street, Moor Road, Blackburn Row, and then out to Waterhouse Green in the satellite village of Whittle-le-Woods. Next the Thompsons came back again to Chorley, to Granville Road, then Tatton Street and on once more, for the last years in that town, to Lyons Lane. A clearly remembered and certain watershed of existence had been the move in 1970 to Skeffington Road, Preston, but then came Sulby Drive (a nice semi-detached house with central heating, which Tommy instantly took out) before a quite arbitrary move back to another house in Skeffington Road, the one where Tommy was eventually murdered.

Hating to be domestically uprooted myself, I was utterly bewildered that a family could have moved house so many times within such a small geographical area. The Thompson women too, far from finding many 'memory landmarks' in any of these places, seemed to feel they had merely ridden round and round on some futile property whirligig of which the overwhelming impression was a blur of unrelenting discomfort and distress. As I would later realize, constantly moving house was one of the more laborious ways in which Tommy kept firm control over the family, emotionally as well as physically, undermining his wife and daughters. Women, particularly with young children, have an overwhelming need to 'dig in' and stay in one place. With his usual sadistic perception, Tommy Thompson seems to have realized that. It is women who deftly 'plug in' the family to a new area – the invisible but vital circuit of neighbours, schools, shops, doctors and so on. Tommy may not have been doing it consciously, but moving house so often certainly had the effect of keeping the Thompson family enclosed by disrupting any tentatively developing contact with outsiders.

Hoping that if some of these streets still existed, the actual sight of them might bring the odd but precisely telling memory to the surface, I next arranged to take Mrs Thompson back to Chorley for the first time in something like sixteen years.

On a blustery spring morning, a few days after her sixty-fifth birthday, I arrived at the Thompsons' maisonette to take Mrs Thompson off on the jaunt to Chorley to revisit the scenes of her early married life. As usual, June and her sister Hilda were shadowy, courteous and withdrawn but, on that day – apparently fired with excitement at the prospect of visiting a little town she still liked and had not seen for so long, Mrs Thompson seemed to have burst into life and, to my astonishment, positively flashed with pleasure and vivacity while standing in the centre of the room, beautifully dressed in smart new clothes. Both surprised and delighted at the change in her, it struck me that I might be witnessing a step or two in Mrs Thompson's return to emotional normality. There was something clearly *recoverable* in her personality which presumably stemmed from the mundane but great gifts of her early childhood – secure attachment, love and domestic serenity. But, as her own daughters seemed to have been denied any part of a 'normal' childhood, I now wondered, as they hovered together out of our way, whether June and Hilda themselves would ever develop what they could not regain: a spontaneous sense of the sheer pleasure of living.

Over a soft white blouse, Mrs Thompson wore a smart black and gold Chanel-style suit bought in Blackburn, and to complete her outfit big gold ear-rings gleamed like elegant shields beneath her hearing-aids and bouffant blonde hair. Her skin was soft, fine and cameo pale with powder, and, as she watched herself drawing on tightly fitting black cloth gloves with sharply tapering fingers, she lamented how she longed to wear colour make-up again but feared that her face might be now too distorted. Mrs Thompson had taken such care in turning herself out for the day-trip to Chorley that I felt rather embarrassed at having arrived as usual in the all-purpose mac and dusty (though very narrow and well-cut) ankle boots I had once bought in France and often resorted to for long days away involving unpredictable amounts of walking. Just as she had done in childhood, Mrs Thompson still loved black patent shoes and, just before we were wafted out of the house on her daughters' remote and automatic wishes for a happy day, she turned an ankle thoughtfully from side to side, worrying that the petersham bows on her black patent court shoes might not be perfectly centred.

My plan had been to take Mrs Thompson for a good lunch in Chorley and, restricted by lack of a car, I had vaguely thought of the Swan with Two Necks, a rather nice restaurant-pub set amid leafy Georgiana at the foot of Church Brow – a steep wynd with pretty views in the medieval part of the town. But cancer of the mouth (Mrs Thompson's hard palate had been removed in 1986) turned out to be the imperative guide as to where we should eat. Only very, very soft food would do and, fearing that unsuitable things might be imposed upon her, she firmly but tactfully settled in favour of a café opposite Chorley Bus Station. I followed her in some surprise. With its rustic patches of exposed brickwork, screwed-on black plastic beams and fancy plastic-lace tablecloths, the Italianate café did indeed seem to offer the usual soft pasta things, plus welcoming northern fish and chips, but again to my great surprise, as we entered it Mrs Thompson immediately approached the counter with a quick, stylish directness to inquire:

'Love, can you do me mashed potatoes and gravy? Ah've got no roof to me mouth. Ah've had cancer."

Mrs Thompson was no longer the reserved, often rather shaky, elderly woman I had been accustomed to visiting. This simple day-trip seemed to have drawn out new confidence in her and she was quite in control of our situation.

Over the lunch table, Mrs Thompson's voice bubbled like a spring and her speech fascinated me. I decided that her crisply trilling *r*s really did make her sound very like Gracie Fields (when talking rather than in the delivery distortions of high-voice singing) or like a feminine version of the contemporary Conservative politician Dr Rhodes Boyson. But the recent cancer operation had now caused her natural speech to be overlaid with what might be called 'shushiness' ("I were a poor shcholar . . . a small place near Yarrow Bridge where we uesh to go for walksh . . ."). With her speech so impaired, hearing-aids sizzling in both ears and the constant drip of water from her collapsed eye-socket and mouth, which she constantly dabbed neatly and tactfully with a succession of very clean paper tissues, I thought how brave she was, given her age and disabilities, to be bothered to wander about with a stranger on a cold and gusty spring day just in case something we saw might eventually jog her memory.

Lancashire is a county which oddly seems to express its character quite naturally in sound – the irrepressible voices, water, the corny old ring of embattled clogs on industrial streets which sound-archivists so love to play, and the equally conspicuous silences embedded in the shadows of huge factory buildings which once held back the roar of cotton. As we – or rather she – talked on that day over lunch, I was mesmerized by Mrs Thompson's very maternal way of speaking in which, while nothing much was actually said, her voice rose and fell, trilled, shushed and gurgled with pleasure in a way that provided social comfort and expressed mood, much as one croons and yums additionally to wrap a young baby in sounds of approval and emotional warmth. Bizarre though it may seem to the outside world, given all that her defenceless young daughters had later suffered at the hands of their father, I felt that somehow, in her own way, Mrs Thompson had been (or had tried to be) a very good mother and that in turn, her badly damaged daughters still recognized it – and then I was suddenly longing, quite urgently, for life beyond the brass-ringed café curtains, out on the market-day streets of Chorley.

The thing I next got to grips with that afternoon was Mrs Thompson's engaging vanity. It was not the fierce, hard self-regard sometimes found in richer women with the price of flights to high fashion in their pockets, but a simple sensuous pleasure in now being free once more to express herself in the clothes, shoes and general prettiness that she had been harshly denied by Tommy for so long. It was, too, an almost inborn passion for cloth – its colour, weight and weave. Despite her age and infirmities, I was amazed at the way Mrs Thompson suddenly darted away from me several times on our walk round Chorley, losing me in the crowds and vanishing into market stalls to hold up skirts and blouses, rapidly examining the linings and finish, and holding up a garment to try the texture of its fabric this way and that against the light ("Now, *thatsh* a well-made little shkirt . . .").

As her fragile blonde head continued to bob excitedly among the stalls of the famous Flat Iron market, I suddenly recalled a photograph which Andrew Schofield, the archivist up at Clitheroe Castle, had long ago shown me as a change, on that afternoon, from listening to a sometimes rather tedious succession of oral history tapes. He had casually explained that whereas the great industries of the North (mining, steel, ship-building and machine-tool-making) were harsh male preserves, textiles in Lancashire had become predominantly women's work and, when times were good, comparatively well-paid work too. Having spent the week making cloth for other people, mill women quite naturally wanted some of it for themselves and took particular delight in exceptionally fine dressing at weekends. Andrew had shown me a big sepia photograph entitled "Saturday Night is My Delight but What about Monday Morning?" In it an Edwardian mill girl had been captured in all her finery – level-eyed and confident in a huge hat frothing with feathers, a high-necked broderie-anglaise blouse with frilly cuffs spewing out of a tightly curved jacket, tin jewellery at throat and ears, and the glimpse of a big, furled umbrella finished with an animal's head on the handle and a flying tassel. In the adjoining picture, Monday in the weaving sheds depicted the same industrial princess now stripped down like an Irish peasant woman to a huge shawl over the head (fastened at the throat with a pin) and, for accessories, a tin lunch-can carrying her "bait". It was this possibility of earning good money that had also produced the exceptionally low birth-rate in Lancashire (presumably achieved by coitus interruptus, abstention and amateur abortion) and the famously sharp brand of young Lancashire wife who had often threatened to clear off to a well-paid job in the weaving sheds if her husband did not behave himself: "Ah con allus get four looms . . ."

And then I thought of Tommy Thompson, who had almost immediately begun to demoralize his young wife, not only by hitting her but by mocking the new kind of work that she had found to do in the redundant spaces of Progress Mill ("*You only worked in't bloody soap factory when I met ye . . .*").

Although I was personally delighted to see Mrs Thompson's quite unexpected vivacity and pleasure at our little outing to Chorley, I inwardly and professionally became increasingly glum as the day progressed at what seemed to be the now rather futile attempt to bring scenes of her immediately post-war existence to life. As I had expected, having already once before crossed the railway lines into the Victorian part of Chorley, pockets of some old neighbourhoods had been demolished and rebuilt in a rather half-hearted way, usefully keeping old street names but not always following original street lines. But, after seeking directions across a confusing 1970s council estate, gleaming with white 'ranch' boarding and where Golden Wonder crisp packets rolled vacuously on its trampled public spaces, Mrs Thompson abruptly halted our walk and stood quite still at the sight of a low, reddish building which seemed to bring back some flicker of the past.

"We musht be near Lyons Lane," she said rather hesitantly.

I knew that shortly before moving to Preston after twenty years of marriage, Mrs Thompson had lived for some while in a terraced house in Lyons Lane, but now it seemed she had been stopped quite literally by what appeared to be sheer force of recollection, at the sight of Greenfield Mill which still landmarked the old neighbourhood, like an industrial parish church. The windows of the mill were tightly shut and its massive leaf-green doors were also closed, with an imposing sense of permanence but, rather incongruously in her smart Chanel clothes and black patent shoes, Mrs Thompson quickly approached the building and, pressing an ear to the doors, excitedly cocked her head about from one side to the other.

"On Lyons Lane in shummer," she said, "When I had bedroom windows open, you could hear machinery inshide."

Intrigued, I listened too, but could hear nothing except the gusting rise and fall of the bright spring afternoon and the distant dog barks and children's yells of the council estate.

"I can hear machinery working inshide," she repeated, but I concluded that whatever it was that she could hear, it must be some aural fuzziness connected with her deafness and, with a sense that some important memory did indeed lie there but could not be quite recovered, we rather reluctantly moved on.

Some hours later, on the rattling, privatized country bus which blustered back to Preston, we began to fly once more through the green tangle of villages which still surrounds Chorley, once the sixth biggest weaving district in Lancashire. Accepting that deafness, impaired speech and the maddening rattle of the bus made talk impossible, we silently called a communications truce and began to look quietly and comfortably out of the window. Left to myself, I began to note how the little mill which had so attracted Mrs Thompson was in name, as well as in appearance, quite unlike those of bigger and harsher industrial places in Lancashire where, on a sunny day, emblazoned in huge white-brick letters, the names of industrial Empire had once spoken half a mile away: CAIRO MILL, MONARCH, ACE, DURBAN, INDIA and DELTA. In contrast, the mills of Mrs Thompson's little home town came from an earlier, but not necessarily sweeter, part of the Victorian age when the waving green fields had still tried to rise up to the very doors of the textile industry. There was the mill we had just paused outside – GREENFIELD – and now, even smaller ones, tucked away in a derelict state behind tiny rural stone terraces: ACORN MILL, BRIAR MILL, LILAC, SWAN and PRIMROSE BANK. In semi-rural towns like Chorley and its surrounding villages, these fallen-in places continued to remind passers-by that the smoke and hard pounding of machinery were only temporary things – they have come and gone – and that Mrs Thompson herself, now sitting quite happily on the bus seat beside me, was one of those elderly northern people whose inner being, despite hard industrial streets and exceptional harshness of life, still rests in a father's garden.

Suddenly, as we rounded a great curve to enter a village called Bamber Bridge, Mrs Thompson looked out on a piece of wild rising ground which bore a crumbling glimpse of old stone buildings at its foot.

"Thatsh where we uesh to get water – at lodge gatesh."

"Lodge gates?" I said, inwardly cursing the roar and clamour of the two-thirds empty bus.

"Where we – ye know – we ueshed to live in caravan on Cuerden Park."

With a horrid mixture of regret and triumph, I realized that Mrs Thompson's entire mood had plummeted and that the pain I had so guiltily sought in her memories of the past was now welling up.

"Cuerden Park is where we ueshed to live – in caravan with June and Hilda as babies."

Rather like a seismographer, sitting apprehensively beside a roll of wired-up graph paper, I had waited all day for any emotional tremor caused by one place in Chorley rather than another 'opening up' Mrs Thompson's memories. Then I might glimpse down into the molten terrors and longing of her past. I knew nothing whatever of "Cuerden Park" – this piece of wild ground we were just passing. She had never spoken of it, nor mentioned it in her notebooks or letters. It was typical of the way I was having to proceed with the Thompson women's story. They always co-operated politely, *wanted me to know* but naturally, in their circumstances especially, had rammed the past down hard.

Mrs Thompson's mood continued to be lowered for the rest of the journey, although we changed the subject and, given the rattling of the bus, chatted on. But, quickly glancing back at the grey lodge gates of Cuerden Park that afternoon, I knew it was the place where my digging would begin next.

Within a few months of marriage, Hilda Thompson became pregnant. On hearing the news, which now filled his new wife with additional anxiety rather than the romantic glow of motherhood she had once anticipated, Tommy Thompson had immediately forbidden her to continue working at Mr Danischewsky's soap factory. As this last contact with the outside world was severed, the young woman had time – day after day, in the quiet of the two makeshift rooms they still occupied at her mother's house in Bowland Avenue – to dwell not only on the strange physical changes now taking place in her body, but on the almost unbelievable calamity that seemed to have befallen her. As the baby ceased to flutter inside her like a trapped moth and began, instead, slowly to turn over and over, a bigger and weightier shape, she too turned over and over in her mind the quiet horror of finding herself irrevocably married to a man who seemed to have undergone a violent personality change in a matter of weeks. In the way that a young child is momentarily suspended in deep perplexity by a loving adult who suddenly puts on a grotesque mask at a party (You Are My Source of Love – You Are Horror), her love for Tommy and her own need for survival had now dissolved into a sharp, aching mood she had never known before – real fear. A more sinister thought also occurred to her now: that possibly what she called 'love' had never at any time entered into their relationship and that instead, in a cold and calculating way, she had been deliberately chosen and deceived into marriage as the perfect mild-natured partner for a sadist.

> *Tommy told me from the beginning that he would never be told what to do by Anyone again, now that he had married Me. It was going to be Everything that he said from now on. I could have understood him saying that if I had been the Bossy type but I was just the opposite. People still remember what a quiet person I used to be when I was younger. I got along well with people though. Tommy must have Targetted me out as his wife whom he could Domineer and Later Bully soon after being Married. Once the Wedding Ring was on my finger, he made it clear he owned me.*

A deliberate blow to the face is an insult to the soul. From the very first beating she had received in the honeymoon front-bedroom at Bowland Avenue, Hilda Thompson, like her new husband, also changed inwardly. During the long, slow, spring afternoons of first pregnancy when her mother was away as usual at the Hygienic Laundry and neighbouring children and dogs yelped normality in the street, Hilda Thompson tried to regain a degree of rationality about her situation. This man was her husband. He had said, and sometimes still continued to say, that he loved her. Was the sudden change in his behaviour therefore caused by some intolerable fault in her? She had never had much to do with men before and perhaps was some sort of blundering amateur in the art of intimacy. Sometimes she would resolve to make matters better by being more alert to his wishes and to her own demeanour, to be a better wife and to 'improve'. But when evening fell, she began to dread the moment when Tommy would return from work. The sound of his latch-key in the door became (as it would for the rest of her married life) a signal that made her pound inwardly like a conditioned animal with shapeless fear and cause the palms of her hands to run with anxiety. Like many helpless people when faced with extreme hostility, she soon decided that the only way to avert the violence was to be very submissive and to smile, faintly but readily, with extreme deference, whenever Tommy entered the room. It was the kind of animal submissiveness which does indeed throw an aggressor off balance for a short period. Hilda Thompson found that it both repelled and excited advance, making Tommy waver momentarily between solid delight in the authority he had already accumulated and the possibility of exerting it in even harsher form to one who would so readily bend to it.

"How – how's it been, love?" Hilda Thompson would quietly ask at the end of Tommy's working day, with a faint deferential smile and physical distance well reserved.

"*How d'ye think it's b-bloody been*?" was Tommy's usual reply.

Ellen Hartley, meanwhile, was deeply anxious about her pregnant daughter and realized with painful resignation that difficult husbands seemed to be the fate of both her daughters. Her somewhat estranged older child, X, had married an Irishman she had fully known to be a heavy drinker during their courtship days, and now had several children of her own. X's home was scarcely a model of domestic serenity, but at least X seemed able to defend herself. Like most daughters who are the first-born in a family, X had a kind of combative toughness about her and usefully deep reserves of bloody-mindedness with which she gave as good as she got. It was little Hilda, the vulnerable 'baby' of the family, who caused Ellen such anguish, because clearly she was so unable to deal with the kind of treatment that Tommy meted out to her. Daily, like fragile little Hilda herself, Ellen lamented the fact that Ernest Hartley was long dead. There was no external authority – policeman, magistrate or priest – who, she felt, could successfully bring Tommy to book. At that time, a violent husband could only be dealt with by the family itself and, as the big brass bed she continued to sleep in alone nightly reaffirmed, with no just man in the house to "back her up", she had begun to fear Tommy herself.

As the first year passed at Bowland Avenue, Tommy Thompson gained additional emotional ascendancy over his mother-in-law by subjecting her to simple domestic inconvenience. Because of Chorley's loose-knit, semi-rural character, men who lived in the area tried to have their own means of transport to get to whatever jobs were available. With contempt for an old-fashioned bicycle – supposed symbol of cloth-cap weaklings like his spiritualist stepfather – Tommy rode a big, blustering motorbike to the Commonbank Bleach Works each day and, eventually, he insisted on parking it where it would hurt most: in woman's traditional domain. Ellen Hartley's tiny kitchen was more of a galley, only eight feet or so across, and when she returned from the Hygienic Laundry at night, she found that Tommy's motorbike was now propped there – an evil-looking, black, outdoor thing, coated with coarse dust and oozing oil among the aluminium pans and spartan primrose surfaces of her austerity kitchen.

"You – you don't think, Tommy, you could park it outside, love?" Ellen had once gently asked him.

Towering over her, he had replied with absolute contempt, "It's stopping where it is."

On 15 June 1952, after an agonizing first labour, gapped by panicking and screaming gasps into the dark rubber shoe of a gas-and-air machine, Hilda Thompson gave birth to her first daughter. Then the high eau-de-Nil ceiling of the delivery room seemed to open in an electrical storm of high summer, as the sky had once crumpled with lightning overhead in Duxbury Woods. She was later told that she had experienced a series of 'maternity fits' (eclampsia – an attack of convulsions in pregnant women, or in those who have just delivered, caused by blood poisoning). By the time Tommy Thompson arrived at the hospital, Hilda Thompson was still in isolation in the labour room and pinned to the door was a handwritten notice saying, "Lady Very Ill. Quiet Please."

"Would you like to see the baby, Mr Thompson?" a passing midwife said, steering him away from the door.

"I don't care about baby. I want to see me wife," and, hearing this inside the room, Hilda believed that despite the previous beatings at Bowland Avenue, in his heart he must still love her. Then, in the deep peace which follows the passing of extreme pain, Hilda Thompson gradually rediscovered in the slow-motion day-to-day activity of the maternity ward a life she had almost forgotten. Although, like all the other babies in hospital regimes of 1950s, her new child was kept away from her – brought abruptly to her arms only by the ward sister's infant-feeding timetable when the massed voices of the nearby nursery had been long yelling blue murder ("You must establish a feeding *routine*, Mrs Thompson") – the new mother from Bowland Avenue felt nothing but relief. It seemed extraordinary that here, in this National Health hospital, midwives and doctors spoke authoritatively but quite civilly to her; that people performed small kindnesses for each other and, strangest of all, assumed she was a 'real' person – a 'real' person rather than the worthless thing she sometimes felt she had become. When the day arrived for her to be discharged with little June from Chorley District Hospital, she did not want to go.

> *I found out that being in Hospital were going to be the only Happy Days I would ever spend again. I know this must sound very unusual to everyone but, in spite of how he was with me, he said he loved me.*

From the beginning, Tommy Thompson seems to have had very firm and confident ideas about how to bring up children. Even as new-born infants, there must be no pandering to them – they must be kept firmly in their place. This was a commonly held view of infant care in the 1950s (the complete opposite of modern ideas about 'demand feeding') but, in a way that later became typical of many of his notions about family life, Tommy very readily tipped over into a kind of sadistic excess.

Cruelty, rather than brutality, is a form of human endeavour which is capable of almost infinite refinement. After a few days at home, when Tommy had got the hang of baby life – that a child wanted to be fed when it cried and that its grandmother gently revered the child of her own child – he almost joyfully began to see new ways in which to increase the emotional pain he could inflict on his feeble wife and mother-in-law. He hated crying. As if he had been whipped by a stinging nettle as a toddler, it made him spring alive with compulsive rage. But Tommy now discovered that a woman's love and fear for her child provided a delightful new playground for emotional control and experiment. When he was at home, Hilda Thompson was forbidden to hold or cuddle her new baby – the child was to be fed quickly and then set down. Much as she longed to hold and comfort the infant who, as she grew, cast up a small hand and desperately nuzzled the air for solid contact, Hilda Thompson was forced to ignore her, even as the flood of milk which is stimulated in nursing mothers by an infant's cry set her breasts ludicrously square with engorgement. With his new daughter lying in a makeshift cot on one side of the room and his wife hovering agonized, both physically and mentally, on the other,

Tommy Thompson would recline at his ease on the bed and watch them longing to make contact. Then, he would suddenly give permission for feeding. Suddenly, one day, to Hilda's grief, he decided that breastfeeding should cease altogether.

From the start, although he resented the noise and emotional turmoil of a new baby in the house, Tommy was curiously possessive of his new daughter. Little June seemed to be a useful means for him to turn the screw on Ellen Hartley, who was eventually forbidden to hold or touch her new grandchild or even to speak to her own daughter out of his earshot. In any case, Hilda Thompson was now temporarily beyond the reach of any attempts at communication, shut off from the background emotional struggle in the household behind a grey glass wall of post-natal depression. The young mother's days and weeks flowed into one. Like attempting to walk under water, she was conscious of nothing but extreme effort and the deep silence of submersion, pierced only by a baby's cry.

Meanwhile, around her, Tommy seemed to spring alive in a burst of new activity. He had never been an idle man but his fondness for doing practical jobs seemed to have a kind of malice in it. One Saturday morning he finally brought into his thrall all the women in the household from six months to fifty-five by suddenly dismantling the big second-hand pram to whose familiar rubber hand-grip Hilda Thompson clung, as if to a lifebelt, on the occasions she ventured out. With the clean bedding carelessly pitched out of it, this safe, heavy, reliable pram – the only solid thing in her swimming world of first maternity – had been reduced to chrome rubble and was spread out over Ellen's living-room table on the crazy whim that he would paint the bits maroon. Shattered as if by a giant blow into a score of component parts, the precious familiar pram just lay there for some days. It was then that Ellen Hartley finally decided that this state of affairs at Bowland Avenue would have to change. (Do-nothing politicians who try to mask a national housing shortage by blandly asserting that growing families should 'live together' should try it themselves one day.) Even gentle, pious Ellen could no longer tolerate having her little house turned upside down by a man who clearly loathed the idea of living with his mother-in-law, and one evening she quietly suggested to Tommy and Hilda that they might be happier if they found some kind of home of their own. As if he had been waiting for his *congé* all along, Tommy quickly agreed.

Immediately after the Second World War and the joyous shock of peace, there was a great and universal longing for 'home' – for a home of one's own to retire into and 'improve'; for perhaps a bit of garden which, however small and soot-laden, suggested the unending pull of 'the country'; and for the quiet pottering ideal of British life which amounts to doing nothing very much behind closed doors. It was from the semi-detached houses of the 1920s and 1930s, straggling out along the bypasses near big towns, that the bluebird of suburban happiness (set into the stained-glass panels of front doors) became a shimmering ideal for all. "It is Sunday morning, it is summer, and peace has come again," wrote an ad-man immediately after the war, the purple ribbon in his high-rise typewriter jerking onwards:

> How pleasant it is to lie awhile and listen to the sounds of slowly waking day: the churchbells for early service; the clink of the milkman's bottles on the step; scampering feet across the gravel path. Breakfast, thank goodness, is later today and, with the room to himself, the sun flirts gaily with all that he can find. See the copper gleaming with pride at the warmth of his kisses all laughing and gay . . . because of Brasso and Zebo's winning way with gloomy grates.

But instead of the suburban inglenooks of national longing, most young people like Tommy and Hilda Thompson found themselves in the grim terrain of the post-war housing shortage. There were rented rooms, occupied on tiptoe and grudgingly let out to young couples by landlords who had first extracted the promise "no children"; prefab settlements for the geographically lucky; while the very poor were sometimes obliged to abandon conventional housing altogether. About forty years before, some poor people in England had begun to house themselves on marginalized land, creating rural and coastal slums (the so-called 'plot-lands') where, in wooden shacks, beach huts, sold-off Victorian railway carriages and old gypsy caravans, they had begun an existence which may as well have been a world away. Tommy's mind was now beginning to run along these lines. In the Thompsons' case one thing was certain – that once a married couple had left the home of their parents or in-laws, they were no longer permitted to remain on the council's housing waiting-lists, which now stretched hopelessly into infinity.

One day shortly after Ellen Hartley had asked them to leave Bowland Avenue, Tommy Thompson announced that he had just agreed to buy an old Romany caravan he had found at a builder's yard in the nearby village of Bamber Bridge. They would have to pay it off in weekly instalments, pay to have it towed somewhere and then (wherever that 'somewhere' might be) probably pay rent for the use of the land. That 'somewhere' turned out to be a piece of rough grazing which lay within the lower boundaries of Cuerden Park, the devolved estate of a great house called Cuerden Hall.

Hilda Thompson was now expecting her second child (June had been an 'accident' but Tommy then insisted rapidly on two). Almost as if he already foresaw, or was in the process of willing, the eventual social isolation of the family, he explained to Hilda that one child on its own would be lonely but two would keep each other company for ever.

"They will *always* have each other," he said with some ambiguity.

The prospect of living with him and two children in a caravan on Cuerden Park filled Hilda Thompson with dread:

When we bought the Caravan I had no say in the Matter. Tommy said we would have It. I didn't like It and couldn't

Imagine how we would manage to live in the Bad Conditions But I Daren't say anything . . . I just had to make the best of things. We couldn't get anywhere to live with young babies. I couldn't tell the council why we left my Mother's which was through his violent temper.

Although she had already experienced almost daily fear when living with Tommy at Bowland Avenue, Hilda Thompson suspected that the presence of her mother and the neighbours still acted as some kind of restraining influence on his behaviour. She now dully recognized that as soon as she was discharged from Chorley District Hospital with the new baby, there was much worse to come in the wilderness of Cuerden Park.

Bamber Bridge is the sprawling village which lies at the foot of Cuerden Park, sliced off from it by the broad curve of a fast-moving road. About a year before I had registered Mrs Thompson's sudden chill when passing the lodge gates of Cuerden Hall on the bus, I had been driven through Bamber Bridge once before, this time by Detective Chief Inspector Biscombe. To lighten our mood a bit after having seen the grim colour photographs of Tommy Thompson's post-mortem, we had been glad to talk about almost anything and he had politely taken up my doubtless rather vague remarks with the suavity of a good policeman passing rapidly through a neighbourhood he knew very well. That day, I had been taken with the appearance of Bamber Bridge, which had a long, low, thatched building called Ye Old Hob Inn dangling with baskets of summery planting and, opposite to it, a village green dotted with wooden benches and big horse-chestnut trees which could have been quite idyllically photographed for a central Lancashire tourist brochure.

"What a nice little place," I had remarked, noting a big grey and white cat, dozy with midsummer heat, plodding patiently past the inn in search of deeper shade beneath the trees.

"A nice *violent* little place," Mr Biscombe had rejoined, seeing the village quite differently through the hinterland of past police cases stacked neatly in one of his grey metal filing-cabinets. "The police have a lot of trouble here – particularly on Saturday nights. Everyone is related to everyone else. You know what they say round here about Bamber Bridge? – Kick one and they all limp."

Then, as I had fallen about laughing, in so far as it is possible to fall about when firmly restrained by the very latest seat-belts in a policeman's car, he had added, laughing himself: "Have you never heard that one before, Alexandra?"

In Cuerden Park, the tiny River Lostock trickles eastwards from the old weaving village of Brindle to join the Yarrow. After a long climb upwards through rising woodland, a traveller reaches Cuerden Hall, a large, broad Regency house on which, to contradict classicism in a Picturesque way, half a dozen oblong turrets and a hint of simple embattlement create the suggestion of a pseudo-Elizabethan mansion in the manner of Vanbrugh, particularly against an evening sky. Toy battlements in the hands of a playful architect had led on to a real military history for the house which, to me, now seemed to provide a link with the hitherto unnoticed lives of Tommy and Hilda Thompson.

During the First World War, the Tatton family (into whose hands Cuerden Hall had passed) had opened it in the usual way as a hospital for wounded soldiers and then, as the vast activity of the new Royal Ordnance Factory at nearby Euxton had gained longer reach during the late 1930s, Cuerden Hall had been requisitioned by the army, first as the headquarters of No. 4 Anti-Aircraft Command and then, through outright purchase, as headquarters of the entire North-West Army.

Among derelict terraced gardens commanding the view of a landscape where dying textile mills, sucked down like defeated ships beyond the trees, were being overlaid by the ramifications of the new defence industry, the old house eventually became a perfect official residence for the Major-General. For Tommy, who had first glimpsed masculine freedom and a new order in the roaring military garages temporarily created in the abandoned mills of his boyhood streets, Cuerden Park promised the freedom of action he craved. And, just in case he was left too free among the actual terrors of Nature, the strangely comforting presence of the army was embattled above in stone.

It was an old wooden caravan of the type that nice young people with a Festival of Britain enthusiasm for British 'popular art' longed to restore at weekends with peony swirls of Romany colour. If that proved to be too much of a dream, there was still the magnificent presence of The People in barge art, rug weaving or in trawling country junk shops for the pink coppery licks of Sunderland pottery which could be bought for pence. But to the young woman, now cut off from her mother's house with two babies and a man she feared, it was like climbing up that day into a dark, musty tunnel.

Even in the rounded sunlight of a July afternoon, the interior of the wooden caravan was very dark indeed, lit only by one small window at the bottom end. Beneath this postcard of daylight were two bunks. The long walls of the caravan were lined with solid wooden drawers and, set among them at floor-level, a black solid-fuel stove squatted down in the shadows like a cast-iron toad. For personal washing, Hilda Thompson noted a dusty earthenware jug and a wash-stand bowl. By the time the battered car that had towed the caravan up from Bamber Bridge had bumped away across the park, leaving beside the steps of the van a few cardboard boxes stacked with clothes, hastily assembled crockery, a few pots and pans and a bit of bacon, margarine and lard wrapped in greaseproof paper, the young Mrs Thompson had discovered that the only means of lighting was a paraffin lamp.

Tommy Thompson had hated the close supervision of the Commonbank Bleach Works and, preferring to work outdoors, he took a labouring job with Chorley Rural District Council.

Far from retiring into the warm, clean, serene home she had dreamt of as a child, Hilda Thompson was left to herself to tend the babies and fearfully await his return in the lower wilds of Cuerden Park.

Day by day, the demands of the children brought her body automatically into action, but overlying all this was new anxiety about the fetching and carrying which went with domestic survival in such a primitive place. After Tommy had mercifully departed to work in the morning, every hour of Hilda Thompson's day was now accounted for in hard physical labour, as she toiled to carry water and fuel to the caravan before any kind of washing or cooking could begin. A pram or pushchair is still the car of the urban poor, and at that time in Cuerden Park the faithful second-hand pram – now reassembled from the bits on Ellen Hartley's table – became her literal means of survival. Setting the babies at one end of it and galvanized buckets at the other, Hilda Thompson soon learned that the best way to move the pram over rough tussocks dotted with sheep droppings was to pull it behind her. Like little rajahs swaying in a howdah, the babies rode at her back as she covered the quarter-mile journey three or four times a day to the banks of the River Lostock. Then, putting the brake firmly on the pram, she cooed, gurgled and talked sing-song nonsense to June and Hilda to assure them of her continuing presence as their anxious eyes followed her scramble down to the water's edge. This water was for laundry and general washing – what Tommy in his military way called "cleaning duties" – but for drinking and cooking she would then set off again on a shorter trip to a stand-pipe at the entrance lodge of the park. Drinking water was kept in a deep can on the small platform immediately outside the front door of the caravan and Tommy preferred never to find it empty. Later in the morning, when one of the babies took a reliably deep sleep, Hilda Thompson would seize the other child and, running to the edge of the woods, quickly gather twigs to kindle the coke in her tiny cast-iron stove. Soon Tommy ripped this out – replacing it with a Valor paraffin stove. Then Hilda made the dragging journey down out of the park to Bamber Bridge, to bring back their weekly supplies of paraffin and food in the pram:

It used to take a lot of time, just fetching paraffin and carrying water, she wrote.

In the way that highly motivated British families much further up the social scale also seem to organize themselves on pseudo-military lines in order to manoeuvre social advancement – children in school uniform, strict rules of conduct, mother as sergeant-major and father as Top Brass – Hilda Thompson, with all the drudgery of a military underling, now seemed to be relegated from wife to private out in Tommy's little army camp in Cuerden Park.

As that first summer in the wooden caravan passed by, Hilda Thompson found that she now lived almost permanently in a coat and headscarf. The daily laundry which inevitably accompanies baby life did not cease with the tightening grip of harsher weather. As autumn brought gusting days of cold rain, the urine-soaked nappies which slid from her little daughters' legs in thick yellow twists were carried outside in a bucket. Then, in a parody of Mary Ann Thompson's violent exertions at the dolly-tub in her Chorley back yard, Hilda too now stood at a galvanized zinc bath set out on the grass, thumping at laundry with a set of wooden dolly-legs. She measured time now only by the changing light in the park. On bitter winter afternoons, when she had done her best all day to dry laundry outside to keep it out of Tommy's way, she sometimes found that his shirts, chaotically dancing like thin boards on the clothes-line beside the van, began to give sharp reports as they cracked about in the freezing air – the rigid garments of a frozen man. Like a recurrent nightmare, he only fully returned with the dark. For as long as Tommy stayed away at work, there were still moments, when all this labour was done, that Hilda Thompson could still claim with thin, anxious pleasure as her own.

Her children survived, grew and learned to talk and walk. With no toys at their disposal, they began to make their own small games with stones and bits of grass. As the year turned again, there were things that her own father had long ago pointed out to her on the banks of another river and which she, in turn, pointed out to them – an arc of birds in flight, the simple plants which quietly renew themselves as if in deference to human sorrow and, sometimes, the pleasure of an unexpected pet. From among the sea of greasy sheep which grazed round the van, shaking their dagged skirts, a little, white-faced bletherer trembled up to the steps of the caravan, delighting the children by her wish to be fed by hand:

My only happiness was June and Hilda.

But however much she may love them, young children, with their ceaseless activity and dependency, only intensify the loneliness of a solitary and fearful woman. Used to the greenish glimmer of Chorley's municipal gas-lamps, which, even at this moment, were being replaced by electricity in a fit of post-war modernization, Hilda Thompson was quite unused to the deep blackness of rural night. When the babies slept at last, she became painfully alert, mending or reading by the steady yellow light of the paraffin lamp. At night, her apprehension roved around the warm wooden walls, trying to distinguish the occasional bump and brushing of sheep against the van from the quietly stumbling purposefulness of an intruder. The snap of a twig could mean a hoof or a foot and, for lack of any human voice, she began to discern new subtleties in the night air – the eerie holding back of breath on still nights; the sudden sucking in and release of sound on evenings when sharp gusting alternated with calm and then, in the continuous programme of a storm, the thin rise and fall of spiritual distress among the trees.

One night, Tommy Thompson had been out drinking as usual in the Hob Inn at Bamber Bridge when his dark bulk, both fearful and strangely comforting, suddenly occupied the tiny corridor space of the caravan. He was smiling for once, as if a little joke had occurred to him. As usual when the evening was far gone, his bodily movements were thickened by drink, but as he flung off his coat, she was not sure if it was quite deliberately that a photograph suddenly dropped to the floor with perfect clarity like a leaf to the ground. As usual, when he dropped anything, he signalled to his wife to pick it up. It was a small, square, black-and-white photograph of Tommy and a smiling young woman, their heads close together in a blur of happiness. It was some young woman she did not know.

"Had your photograph taken, love?" she delicately ventured, hoping that this evening might be one on which, since he seemed so good-humoured, he might just drink a mug of tea and fall into the waiting bunk.

"That's a friend of mine," he said, holding the photograph squarely up to the lamp so that she could not fail to see the woman.

"A f-friend of mine *I see a lot of.*"

The photograph was put quite firmly into her hand again and, as usual, having spent five or six hours alone in the darkness of the park, she foolishly still longed for comfort from him rather than some tricky invitation to quarrel. Her nightly confusion about how best to respond to him was nowadays overlaid with sheer physical exhaustion and in this case, surprisingly, a quiet smart of anger that while she daily struggled, heaving even water to the caravan, he now had a woman friend on whom he spent charm and money down there in the proper well-lit streets of civilization. With the effortlessness of depression, tears rose up quite automatically and began to roll down her wind-chafed face.

The trigger that causes a violent man to begin beating his wife can be anything from her preparation of a meal he does not like to sexual refusal, children's 'misbehaviour', a word or movement in which he detects challenge, or just a bad day on the horses. A woman quickly learns the gamut of triggers in her husband, trying to avoid them and to be alert to the possibility of new ones. That evening, Hilda Thompson discovered that crying was a trigger that Tommy Thompson seemed almost to long for because the moment that a tear flowed, he would staunch it with his fist. The confined space of the caravan made the tension between them almost unbearable. As if the temptation to beat or kick a small animal is heightened by confining it in a small space from which it cannot escape, she felt inside like some poor thin thing, racing round and round, low, bruised and desperate, until, finally staying quite still to conserve strength, there is nothing left but the last trick of survival – to take what is coming in mere hope of enduring it. Tommy gave her an exploratory punch on the side of the head and then, as she fell against the wall of the built-in drawers, another and another.

"*Stand still when am hitting ye, ye thick bitch.*"

It was the worst beating that Hilda Thompson had received so far. Above her, the oil in the paraffin lamp lurched dangerously and the small improvised clothes-line jangled painfully to and fro with airing nappies. It was best not to cry out, but as she fell against the bunk where the children were sleeping, June woke and, sliding down backwards to greet her mother, the little girl stood wide-eyed with the pleasure any child takes in joining adult company at night.

"June, love – stand out o't way," Hilda Thompson begged, as Tommy pulled her to her feet once more.

This time, he put both hands round her throat and she began vaguely to sense an arousal in him that perhaps was something to do with the woman he had spent the evening with at Bamber Bridge. With immense care, his two broad thumbs now began to press on each side of her throat and she felt the deep, painful throb of round blots of darkness which his pressure seemed to produce. Just when she felt that something inside her was about to snap horribly and that she was going to vomit as she died, the pressure suddenly ceased and Tommy took his hands away from her. Standing back in the few feet of space that the caravan permitted, he waited a moment for his wife to revive and then, taking her quietly by the shoulders, he looked deeply into her with those very dark eyes and said, quite clearly and simply, "If you're in tomorrow night, ah'll kill ye." Then, shoving June aside, he fell into bed.

The gypsy caravan in Cuerden Park was the place where

Hilda Thompson first understood that Tommy was capable of murder and, supposing from the photograph that, in any case, he wanted the caravan for the entertainment of his mistress, she decided that as soon as he had gone to work next morning, she must – for the sake of the children – get away from him.

> *I'd had a hard life but I wanted to live – if I died what would happen to June and Hilda?*

Even today, to leave a violent man, when one has no money, no clear destination, the underlying threat of revenge, and two babies under the age of three, is an act of utter desperation. The fact that some women choose to sleep with their children on the floor of an over-crowded and often rather squalid battered-women's refuge is an indication of the sheer terror that has made them abandon their only home and personal possessions in exchange for the almost certain poverty and loneliness of the single mother. The first battered-women's refuge in the world, Haven House in Pasadena, California, was opened only in 1964 (initially for the victims of alcohol-related violence), because so many beaten women and children were found to be sleeping overnight in parked cars. In 1954, when Hilda Thompson made her one attempt to escape with the children from Tommy, she was running completely against the culture of the time.

In Britain in the 1950s, wife-beating was not a new social problem – like all forms of human cruelty and disorder, it had been recognized long before but just given different names. In 1878, for example, the Victorian feminist researcher Frances Power Cobbe had published *Wife Torture in England*, documenting no fewer than 6,000 brutal domestic assaults on women during a three-year period – women who had been maimed, blinded, burned and murdered, and in one case, of a woman who had actually been trampled in the face with hob-nailed boots as she lay in bed. But, like the initial public response to child sexual abuse today, wife-beating was felt to be little more than an unpleasant fact of life among the 'lower orders' in which the state could only perilously intervene. Although often sympathetic at a local level, the police were frequently confused about their proper role – domestic violence could not be handled like 'real violence' on the street. In conservative English domestic life there is always a sense of the floating brush of the crinoline and, in the very year (1954) that Hilda Thompson planned her escape, a Commander Hatherill of Scotland Yard, when assessing the annual crime figures in London, remarked, "There are only about twenty murders a year in London and not all are serious – some are just husbands killing their wives."

The next morning, with two maroon thumbmarks on her throat disguised by a wispy nylon scarf, Hilda Thompson prepared for the second adventure of her life. Among her few personal possessions, she still treasured the photograph taken on her one-day honeymoon in Blackpool at what had seemed to be the start of a wonderful new life of love, children and domestic happiness. Now, only three years later, another photograph was propelling her out of the orbit of a man she could only regard with terror. Although she felt she had but a few hours to save her own life and those of her daughters, she felt in too much physical pain to move. Jarred and bruised from the previous night's beating, Hilda Thompson waited until she was sure that Tommy was well clear of the confines of the park and then she sat down on one of the bunks to cry – freely, openly and richly – as June and Hilda, too young to empathize with their mother's distress, blankly stood at her knee and watched. Later, as daylight through the postcard window of the caravan indicated that the morning was creeping towards noon, she dried her eyes, applied lipstick and set about the business of escape. Literally hobbled at every step by two young children, she decided that the chip shop in Bamber Bridge would have to be the first staging-post in getting away.

The people running the chip shop in Bamber Bridge were a nice couple who, in their very flesh, hair and personalities, seemed to have been plumped out with the warm and emollient scent of hot beef dripping. After the drudgery of early hours in the shop was over – skinning thin-blooded fish and mechanically bashing spuds in cold water – the showmanship of deep-frying in public would begin in front of a chrome altar of frying cabinets decorated with laughing fish, turquoise waves and the flick of a mermaid's tail. That lunch-time, over a counter beautifully modernized with a smart piece of Fablon, the fish-fryer's wife (whose name Mrs Thompson could not remember) looked down past the shaker of coarse salt and big bottle of unbrewed condiment at a thin, nervous young woman, carrying a baby and with an older child in tow. Coming up in the queue, she had the yellowish, prematurely worn face of the type that all too often asked for two-pennorth of chips to share.

"Love –" said the young woman, a bit embarrassed by the presence of others in the shop, "Ah'm staying with me mother for a few days and I need these boxes looking after . . ."

Outside the misting window was a pram in which two cardboard boxes brimmed with soft stuff like clothes. Sensing something that was needful but none of her business, the fish-fryer's wife caught the importance of the half-uttered request above the crackle of frying fat and agreed, no further questions asked. Once the precious boxes had been carried in and taken behind the greasy scenes to a back room stacked with sacks of potatoes and impressive icebergs of lard, Hilda Thompson felt the daring emptiness of a plan that had so far succeeded but was destined to fail.

> *I went to my Mother's home. There was nowhere else to go. She was at work but always left a key in case any of us went down to Chorley and could let ourselves in for a cup of tea.*

As if sensing the fragile thread by which their lives hung, June and Hilda had always been unnaturally quiet, "good" babies, and on the bus their mother had an indistinct vision of home in the old days – a fire on, parents waiting and the idea that somehow they could all live together again in the old way with baking, music in the background and kind company. But the house in Bowland Avenue was just the same as it always had been in the dreary years after her father's death. The house was empty, the grate was dead and her mother was at work as usual. She was alone and, even at this crucial moment, when her daughter's very existence was threatened, Ellen Hartley was away as usual, floating in a separate world of her own.

Little June would drink a bit of tea now, with plenty of sugar in it, and eventually as the afternoon passed and it was time to draw the curtains, Hilda Thompson began to pray for the sound of her mother's latch-key in the door.

Tommy Thompson did not bother to sit down in Ellen Hartley's living room when the front door did finally open. He just asked his wife – *told me more like – that I had to go back to the caravan with him*. But at least he seemed genuinely calm for once, even conciliatory, as he gathered up June and, looking down with something approaching a gruff smile, said, "Come on back home. Don't be so daft."

That evening, as the lighted bus, drifting with cigarette smoke, rumbled out of Chorley and off on to the twisting green road back to Bamber Bridge, Hilda Thompson's artificial ease soon dissolved as the distance widened once more between the only place of refuge she knew and the dark, cold park where this man seemed able to do anything he wished to her and the children. She felt his mood alter on the seat beside her, shifting from relief to confidence and then to rising anger. The whisper came to her, *save yourself – save the children*, but how ludicrous it would be to stand up here like a madwoman with crazy hair caught under a headscarf and scream at these other quite normal people whose heads swung like bullocks as they rounded curves in the road: *Help me! When I get off this bus he's going to kill me!* She could imagine Tommy dealing suavely with all this, keeping up appearances as, she noticed, he had begun to do in a quite charming way when outsiders were present. If she stood up and cried out, he would put an arm comfortingly around the bruised, tired shoulder on which baby Hilda now slept and say with such tolerance and understanding, "Take no notice – she's not well. She's touched. Ah'll get doctor to her."

It was not quite dark when the Thompson family once more walked past the lodge of Cuerden Park and climbed the rough track back to their caravan, where the pram, curiously empty of bedding and children, stood outside like a robbed bird's nest.

> *So we all left my mother's before she came home from the Laundry. I never ever told her so not to worry her & I never dared tell Anyone Anything. We went back to the Caravan by bus and on Arriving at the Van He said he would get his own back on me and would never forgive me . . . I knew I would never be able to leave him again. He said he would always find me & Kill me & the young children and I knew he meant it . . . He said he was not frightened of anybody, not even the police . . . Life was Hell really.*

That evening, the usual stray soldier on his way up through the park to a mess dinner at Cuerden Hall would have noticed a touching sight – a young man of good bearing carrying a pretty little dark-haired girl and, walking more slowly behind him towards the old wooden caravan, a tiny young woman with a sleeping baby in her arms. Now that the war was over, it was a national imperative that such people must be properly housed but it was a picturesque caravan all the same.

> Grant me indulgent Heaven! a rural seat
> Rather contemptible than great . . .

A few minutes later, the glass panes at the front and back of the caravan gave out the only man-made light in Cuerden Park. Then, what seemed to be a paraffin lamp – suspended by a hook, no less – swung in a crazy arc before suddenly going out.

1. 193 Skeffington Road, Preston; the perfectly painted exterior of the Thompson family's last home. (Reproduced by permission of the *Lancashire Evening Post*.)

2. Ellen Hartley, Mrs Thompson's mother. She was a pious, gentle, rather withdrawn woman who never recovered from the sudden death of her husband, Ernest, in the winter of 1937.

3. Women workers packing soap *circa* 1947 in the factory far-sightedly begun by Mr A.P. Danischewsky in the redundant spaces of Progress Mill, Progress Street, Chorley during the Second World War. Mrs Thompson, then Hilda Hartley, began work here in 1944 at the age of seventeen. She left school at fourteen and it was her third job.

4. The teenaged Hilda Hartley (third from left on the second row) snapped with work-mates at the back of the mill. She was invited to meet her future husband, Tommy Thompson, on a 'blind date' while working here.

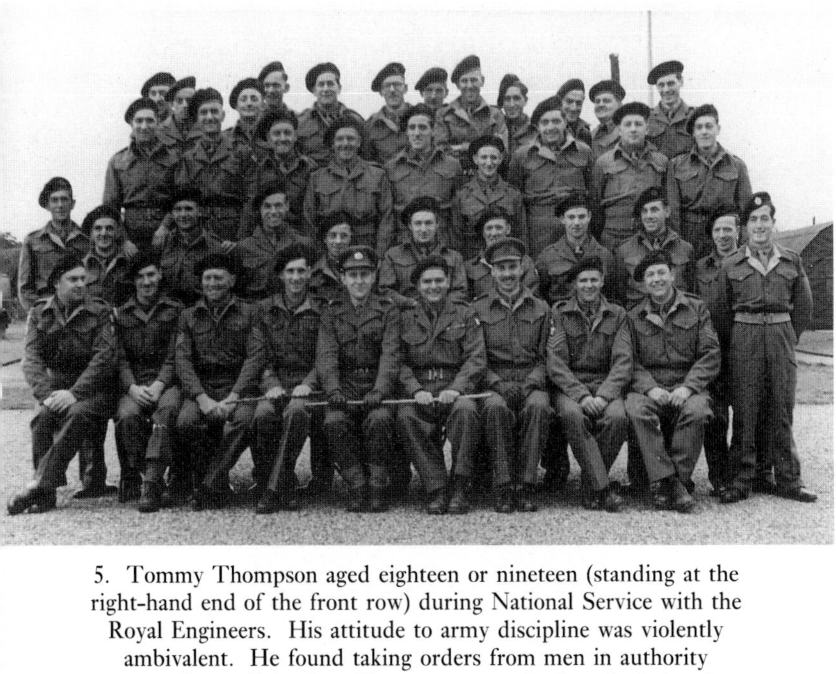

5. Tommy Thompson aged eighteen or nineteen (standing at the right-hand end of the front row) during National Service with the Royal Engineers. His attitude to army discipline was violently ambivalent. He found taking orders from men in authority unusually terrifying but, like many men who have had chaotic childhoods, he was drawn to the formal orderliness of army life.

6. The new Mr and Mrs Thompson, photographed on their blissful one-day honeymoon in Blackpool on 22 September 1951.

7. June and Hilda Thompson aged five and four respectively, photographed in a studio in Blackpool on a rare day-trip to the seaside.

8. Photographed as Tommy Thompson always liked them to be seen: the apparently close, happy Thompson family standing in the garden of his mother and stepfather's house in the old weaving village of Coppull, central Lancashire, sometime in the late 1950s.

9. The only woman for whom Tommy Thompson seems to have had a grudging respect was his mother, Mary Ann Thompson, later Topping, who struggled valiantly to bring up four sons during the Depression and with whom he had a very turbulent relationship from early childhood. Tommy photographed her here with her daughter-in-law Hilda and granddaughters in the garden at Coppull.

10,11. Mrs Thompson with their first family dog, Beauty; young Hilda and June also posing with Beauty, their best-loved family pet. Tommy Thompson's attitude to family pets increasingly became sadistic, but he merely disposed of Beauty very abruptly to a pet shop after she had failed one night to keep to his 'training' programme of crossing a busy road when ordered.

12. June and Hilda with their rabbits in the back-yard of a house in Chorley.

13. June photographed by Tommy on the afternoon she accidentally cut her dress with the garden shears and had to wait for the rest of the day for his promised beating.

14. June and Hilda Thompson entering teenagehood, around the time when Tommy Thompson first began to sexually abuse June. Photography was an element in his sadism. Whatever unpleasant event had just preceded the taking of a photograph, he always insisted that the subjects should smile very enthusiastically.

15. Thompson's 'Red Coats'. The Thompson women are all photographed here by Tommy while wearing identical red jackets he bought for them as a type of pseudo-military uniform. Butlin's 'Red Coats' (there to cheerfully service the day-to-day needs of 1950s' and 1960s' working-class holiday campers) may also have inspired this bizarre idea.

16, 17. As Tommy Thompson's violence to his wife and daughters worsened, he liked snapshots of his wife and himself to appear to be even more romantically dynamic.

18,19. Mrs Thompson and young Hilda photographed by Tommy in apparently casual summery moments as part of Tommy's false portrayal of family life. As the Thompson sisters grew older (note the second picture, also with young Hilda), their body language in such snapshots became less convincing.

20. June and Hilda Thompson, both wearing identical light-blue jackets, pictured by their father in a pub sometime after he had 'married' them with gold wedding-rings in a strange and naïve attempt to avert the attentions of younger men. As part of the pseudo-military regime they now lived under (imposed by a shotgun), both women have placed their drinks exactly five inches from the edge of the pub table.

21. June Thompson snapped by Tommy in her late twenties when she was still working at Courtaulds Red Scar rayon works, Preston. After shift hours and at weekends, she continued to be Tommy Thompson's principal DIY assistant on their random, innumerable and stressful house moves, here captured by him in one of his fanatically ordered tool-sheds. It was when June assisted him in a tool-shed as a child that he first indicated he intended to rape her.

22. Mrs Thompson, after the cancer operation to her face and mouth, flanked by her two daughters. Young Hilda, still very seriously depressed, says she always tried to smile for such photographs and for pub appearances in the outside world, but here only her mother and June are actually able to manage it.

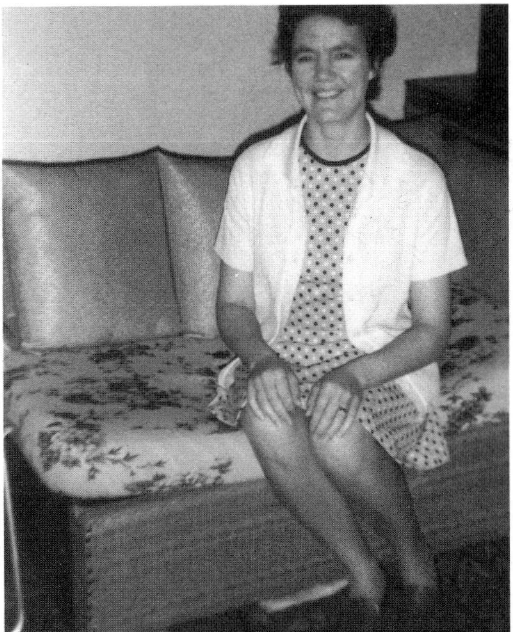

23. Desperation. Stoical June Thompson in her mid-thirties, sitting on a sofa-bed in the downstairs room at 193 Skeffington Road, Preston, still attempting to smile happily for Tommy's insistent camera lens.

24. The police Blue Book shot of part of the downstairs room at 193 Skeffington Road, Preston, where Tommy Thompson was finally murdered by the Thompson sisters in the course of an epileptic fit. The police were surprised at the time by the almost clinical neatness of the room – it more closely resembled an amateur hospital ward and there were no signs of a struggle. Detective Chief Inspector Donald Biscombe, then of the Preston Division of the CID, remarked that it was 'more of an execution, really'.

5

Women of Property

On that day when I had sensed Mrs Thompson's downward plunge of mood on the bus as we rode together past the lodge at Cuerden Park, my relationship with the three women seemed to change a bit. Gradually, I felt able to interpret some of the apparently quite ordinary lines in their notebooks more confidently and, when it seemed appropriate, to ask questions about their past lives in a way that sometimes brought details they had all forgotten back up to the surface. As confidence in each other became a more settled and accepted thing, my visits to Preston increased. I would usually reach the town from Glasgow by 10 a.m. and take a taxi out to the Thompsons' maisonette, inwardly marvelling that no taxi driver ever seemed to be quite sure where it was. Because their home was part of a council estate in a very conservative town, it seemed not to figure very clearly either cartographically or on any 'interior map' in a cabbie's brain – being sunk like some odd artificiality not worth establishing in common memory. As always, I would set my face at the window of the speeding cab as we whizzed past the end of Skeffington Road, trying to catch a glimpse of the neat, old-fashioned street where the murder had taken place and where, in all its violence, the lives of the three women had eventually seized outward significance.

As the year turned to November my vision of the family changed a little when June Thompson, who had already begun to strike me as quietly brimming with things that could be said, suddenly contacted me with the idea of visiting her father's grave – that she and I would visit the place where he was buried by ourselves.

That morning, Mrs Thompson looked particularly frail and wan – grey in the face and trembling slightly when she moved uncertainly about the little sitting room. June explained that her mother had just had another of her "bad nights", while Young Hilda hovered sympathetically in the background, at rather a fluffy-slippered loss as usual. Involuntarily, I glanced up the comfortable rosy carpeted stairs where, only a few hours before, the elderly woman had started awake in the throes of a nightmare which recurrently threw her back in time to married life with Tommy. Then, with both hearing-aids disconnected, a pillow dampened by a dribbling eye (the socket having collapsed from surgery) and with no teeth in, she would stare pucker-mouthed in terror at the darkness and the overwhelming presence of a dead husband who stole to her, again and again, in the sombre illumination of a dream to rage at the apparent impotence of his body on earth ("You – let them – *kill me*!"). Continuing to share a bed with her mother, June would then produce the new reality of kindly bedside light and, bending over her, reassure her mother that Tommy was truly dead and that in life as they now knew it he could never again enter any room they were in to advance with the swift and smiling decisiveness of malice.

Inwardly rather nervous at the proposed expedition to Tommy's grave, I stood about that morning with my coat on. The pressing question of the moment seemed to be whether we should, or should not, take umbrellas.

"I dreamt he was against me . . ." said Mrs Thompson, speaking wide-eyed with the dazed directness of a child who has wandered barefoot into its parents' room at night. "I dreamt he was against me and he was trying to turn everyone against me. I have no enemies though – none to speak of."

"But no one is against you," I tried to tell her gently, as June busied herself with the putting on of a warm navy-blue coat and black gloves, and anxiously looked about for her handbag and umbrella. "No one has any reason *at all* to be against you. June and I will be back very soon."

Slightly reassured, Mrs Thompson then shakily followed us to the front door of the maisonette and, as June and I set off for the cemetery, she waved in the sad, mechanical way that a nanny cheerfully teaches a young child to wave at a departing mother.

It was a bitterly cold day. Only a short bus-ride away, the cemetery rose on higher ground, already whipping with a profusion of leafless trees. In contrast to the little industrial streets of Accrington brick close by, we found ourselves deposited by the bus in a neighbourhood very consciously Gothicized at some time during the preceding century for the decent reception of the dead. The cemetery itself was bounded by huge cast-iron railings and immediately to one side of them was set a handsome stone pub called the Hesketh Arms. Its façade bore an imitation hatchment hanging like a stone lozenge and, just inside a square Gothic porch, the sweet medievalizing heads of a man and woman had been corbelled out of the walls like angels' faces worn to smoothness by centuries of weather on some ancient country church. Continuing the Victorian Gothic into modern times, a bizarre waft of vinegar and frying fat was carried across the road on the turbulent air from a small black-and-white shop lettered in big Chaucerian script with the comfortable words YE HESKETH CHIPPY.

I had never been out in June's company before and, as we passed between the pointed stone piers of the massive cemetery gates, I suddenly became conscious of the very quiet and elastic determination of her gait as she padded swiftly on, head down against the icy gale, like an absentee cat unwaveringly set on the course for home. I had fully expected to see Tommy's grave set amid the aching neatness of some dismal municipal cemetery, verged in the aquarium manner with bright-green marble chips. Instead, beneath a steely-grey sky already burdened with ice, June led me on into a deepening forest of rugged stone crosses, draped urns crazily set at the point of toppling and the pointed arches, pinnacles and knobbly crockets of small family mausoleums on which some doors, solid with Greek studs, remained closed, while others, standing open, were now rifled by the wind. It was too breathtakingly cold to talk much. Deeper into the cemetery lay a banked undulation of simpler headstones, gracefully rounded like the tops of early Victorian drawing-room mirrors ("In charity pray for the soul of Lizzie, daughter of Thomas and Eliza ... who departed this life aged 14 years ..."); greenish table-top tombs with sides pierced by big ace-of-club trefoils and everywhere, around and beyond us, stone angels seemed to light on the scene with one foot. The whole place looked like an angels' party at which, rising and falling with heralding pinions – now opening to land and then folded in contemplation – the air swam with the winged paraphernalia of High Victorian funerary art.

I was rather apprehensive as to how June would cope with this visit to her father's grave and, as we plunged on, I tried to trample down the prurient thought that I was now accompanying a woman I scarcely knew and who, only a few years before, had been more than usually instrumental in putting her father into the earth. June was deeply wrapped in her own thoughts too but, simultaneously, we halted before a rather strange tomb set a few yards in from the broad cemetery path. Close to some holly bushes, a life-sized white marble girl of perhaps twelve or thirteen appeared to have accidentally fallen asleep in the open, her head and arms resting on a very low stone bed, while the rest of her body remained slumped on the bare earth. By its very nature, figurative sculpture must idealize the human body to some degree, but here, as in recently rediscovered Pre-Raphaelite sculpture, the tension between idealization and realism had been left unresolved, producing a very startling effect in which a 'real' frozen girl appeared to be sleeping in paltry clothes among the wet, roaring trees of November. Suddenly, the thick mats of dry orange beech leaves which had been periodically lifted by gusts of icy wind to bowl and rattle on end down the cemetery path, were now joined by the light bounce of hail and, unable to bear the stationary cold any longer, we blew along once more in search of Tommy Thompson's grave.

Tommy Thompson appeared to have been buried in a far distant part of the cemetery, bordered by a thin line of leafless, whipping larches which bent this way and that against the sky like upturned twig brooms. As we drew near to this place, June seemed both angrier and more able to talk.

"When – when your Dad was buried here," I ventured, "I suppose you, your Mum and Hilda were the only people to attend the funeral?"

To my surprise, it seemed they actually *had* attended it.

"Oh, aye," said June shortly. "We'd never been to a funeral before. We'd never done *anything* before except eat, drink and go shopping for things to exist on."

Longing for a glass of white wine and safety, I suddenly thought of my own warm little room back home in Glasgow and of June's often quite perfunctory notebooks which, in setting down the past, had given no clue to the rounded power of this desolate place (*Friday was one of the days he also had sex with me because he would send them out to go to a Jumble Sale. I used to hate Fridays . . .*).

Unlike the rich grey tumble of Victorian funerary monuments that we had just left behind, the spot where Tommy Thompson was buried appeared to be a roughly kept field clotted with tussocks of coarse grass, as flat and open as some rough piece of grazing. The headstones on it were few and far between and it was noticeably empty of the trashy sog of mourners' Cellophaned tributes. Here and there, on graves which were no more than simple oblong holes in the ground, sods of earth were still yellow and wet from recent turning and bore the slicing champs of a spade. Suddenly stopping at a patch of rough ground on which the grass had chaotically risen up again, June jerked her head sideways in dry contempt: "That's it" – and, quite by accident, I found myself standing on top of Tommy Thompson's grave. The only thing that defined the ground on which I stood as the place where a human being was buried was a tiny piece of white stone, no bigger than two cigarette packets, which slanted among the grass like a hard white fist.

The last time June had seen her father, he had been still technically warm and flexible, lying on his downstairs bed in Skeffington Road with the rich soak of two massive shotgun wounds in his chest temporarily disguised by the bright-red folds of a cheap sports shirt. Unfortunately, I had seen the photographs of his subsequent post-mortem (which June had not) and, instantly leaping off the grave, I could not help but recall with a rush of nausea the professionally probed, sawn and reassembled wreckage of the man's body which now lay, with the same shocked, dark eyes, only a few feet beneath us. Keeping my feet well clear of the grave, I carefully walked round it to see the name on the tiny piece of marking stone, suddenly overwhelmed by a childhood fear that something under the bed was waiting with a long grey arm to catch my ankle as I climbed in at night. Then, to avoid the withered hand that might fly out, I had propelled myself through the air. But Tommy Thompson's tiny headstone had no name on it – just the strange inscription: SS20.

"But it doesn't have his name on it!" I shouted, as June continued to stand sardonically by, looking into the distance with her back to the hailing wind.

"They don't have names on't graves in this part of cemetery," she said.

Sure enough, the other tiny headstones I now investigated ran on in bald sequence: SS21, SS22 . . .

"Is – is it because the people buried here have done bad things?" I asked, horrified at the anonymity of it all and, for some reason, thinking of medieval burial strictures, not on those who had fearfully died 'unshriven', with the great weight of sins on them, but people who had committed the ultimate sin of despair and taken their own lives.

"Oh, *no*," said June, mildly amused, as I continued to run over the wild clumps of grass, desperately searching for any name that might lighten the anonymity of those buried here. "They're for social services people – people who aren't bothered about names."

I then realized that this graveyard was an innovation of the 1980s in Britain and that we were standing in the new equivalent of a paupers' burial ground.

In the winter of 1988, shortly before their trial for murder, the Thompson women had been asked whether they wished to attend Tommy Thompson's funeral. Despite all that he had done to them, they had wanted to go and were driven from their separate places of remand to carry out the in-born conservative duty of seeing the last of those who have been, in one way or another, family or friends.

"We'd sooner have had him living and being OK with us like other fathers and husbands," said June bitterly.

Dazed with fear at the prospect of the forthcoming trial, but already enjoying the first emotional freedom of being released from daily oppression and terror, the three women had stood weeping in confusion at the graveside and a cemetery official, whose dismal duty it was to see the unmourned into the ground, had quietly asked them, "Do you want to say any words?"

"No."

"And then," said June, "we looked at each other and went home."

As we turned to go, June Thompson threw one more glance back at Tommy Thompson's grave, and I knew she would never visit the place again.

"There's one thing we're making sure of," she said, referring now to her younger sister. "We're not having Mum buried in the same plot as '*im*."

One evening, as abruptly as he had once announced his intention of buying the wooden caravan, Tommy Thompson said that the family would be shortly moving back to Chorley. Tommy usually brought an evening paper home with him from work and he had made it Hilda's job to scan the ads for cheap, derelict-sounding houses that they might be able to afford. She was never invited to accompany him to see what such houses might actually look like, but now he had his eye on an old terraced house in Hindley Street.

Despite the fact that Tommy had continued to go drinking

most nights at the Hob Inn in Bamber Bridge, the primitive way of life that Hilda and the children endured in Cuerden Park for three years had enabled them to save a little. Those small savings, plus the price that Tommy was certain he could get for the caravan now that he had internally 'modernized' it, meant they could put down some kind of deposit on the house and pay the rest off in weekly instalments. To Hilda Thompson it was a signal to depart to the promised land. On a summer morning in 1956, she packed most of their belongings in a galvanized zinc bath, which served as wash-tub, bath and packing-case, and then, as someone in a van bounced them out of Cuerden Park, scattering sheep across the rough grazing, she felt a grateful sense of at last returning to civilization. They were going to a real house in a real street with paving-stones underfoot, street lighting, running water and neighbours next door. On that glorious morning, dazed and slightly slower in reaction from having lived for so long in the open air, she felt that to enter what turned out to be the grey, derelict rooms of a two-up, two-down in Hindley Street was like being pulled into a lifeboat from a sea of darkness and isolation.

From the moment he had begun quite arbitrarily to take the second-hand pram to pieces on Ellen Hartley's living-room table, Tommy Thompson had realized that any material progress he would make in life, particularly with a wife and children round his neck, would be literally by his own hands and, after listening day by day to the Saturday afternoon intentions of men who worked alongside him on building sites, he reluctantly became a classic DIY man of the 1950s. This was the first period of mass modernization in Britain, when ordinary people felt impelled to do something, anything, that would give their homes the appearance, if not the actuality, of newness in a frantic national effort to expunge the outward signs of a failed Victorian working-class past. Unlike his wife, Tommy felt he was out alone in the world and, as with all handymen at that time, floating above him was a dimly perceived Scandinavian dream of simple solid teak surfaces, vast windows of glass which created the illusion of living in the open air and of new, simple furniture stripped clean of daft, parochial fiddly bits. As soon as he set eyes on the derelict house in Hindley Street and realized that it could be his own, Tommy Thompson visualized the gruelling task in which he as a man must not fail – that of modernizing it 'throughout'.

On the first day back in Chorley, when they had luxuriously eaten a take-away lunch of fish and chips, Hilda Thompson saw things rather differently. The house in Hindley Street was a type over which a national veil was rapidly being drawn, but despite its cold, filth and terrible dereliction, she felt there were good things in it. The house had a small garden at the front, which she instantly earmarked for the pleasure of June and Hilda. As in her old childhood home in Leigh Row, the ground floor was entirely flagged with venerable stones, there was an old cast-iron range in the living room and, after passing up steep, dark stairs, she could look out from the windows of two small, fusty bedrooms over the familiar grey slate roofs of her home town, to which she had now returned, older and saddened, as an established married woman.

Like most women, Hilda Thompson instantly sought out the emotional possibilities in objects which arbitrarily surrounded her. Even in the terrible caravan in Cuerden Park, she had soon grown to respect the old, solid, built-in drawers which lined the two long walls. When pulled out, they had glided easily through long years of use on well-seasoned wooden runners. Smoothly lining them with sheets of newspaper before setting in a few hard-won layers of clean clothing, she had recognized them as things true, tested and burnished by the use of previous generations. One Saturday afternoon, when Tommy had arrived back at the van with wood, nails and anything he could scavenge from the building site he was then working on, she had not been able to say otherwise when he had coldly hacked them out with an axe, replacing the old rich drawers with simple, open wooden shelves to create 'kitchenette-style' fittings around the new Valor paraffin stove. But Tommy had been right about one thing – by modernizing the caravan, they had just about made money on it.

After the Thompsons had bought a few beds, a table and a sideboard from a second-hand furniture place in a disused mill round the corner in Pall Mall, the modernization of the house in Hindley Street began straight away. One thing that Hilda Thompson immediately discovered was that Tommy would rarely attempt any practical job on his own. Driving onwards in a cacophony of sawing, hammering, raking out walls, slapping on plaster, hacking up floors and laying screeds, he demanded close and dextrous assistance from her as if he were a huge toddler, truculently setting about a challenging nursery-school project. The work seemed to make him depressed and more violently angry than usual and, if she failed to read his mind at the precise moment he required the passing of a tool or the steadying of some component part, he would instantly correct her fault – without speech – by butting her on the side of the head, where he had learned that bruises would not show, or in cursing or slapping her face or with the terrible pain she feared most – the crack of his hard working boots against her shins. Day by day, as the Thompsons gradually expunged the familiar traces of a domestic past – ripping out the old black range and replacing it with a new tiled hearth in buff and maroon, concreting over the flagstones so that Tommy could smoothly lay lino on the newly levelled floor, setting a new kitchen sink and a second-hand gas stove into the scullery and replastering the crumbling walls – Hilda Thompson thanked God that her two children sat about in corners or discreetly played outside in the garden, quietly fingering the odd dandelion or pebble that were still their only toys. By staying out of Tommy's way and remaining silent in the grey malaise of building work in progress, they seemed to have instinctively understood the art of their own survival. As the young woman fearfully laboured outside with a spade, striving to mix enough concrete to keep up with Tommy's demand (he was a fast worker), she consoled herself with the thought that once this terrible episode had passed, the family would at least have a proper settled home in which things might possibly get better.

> *I soon got the hang of being his Labourer although It seemed hard at first. He was used to the type of work . . . Tommy never had any patience when doing Jobs so you will be able to understand what It was always like for me. It was a good job June & Hilda were always good while we were doing jobs. Although only babies and were too young for school, they used to play quietly together. They were good children.*

At odd times, Hilda Thompson had inwardly permitted herself to look forward to wallpapering the four rooms of the old house in Hindley Street, as a clear sign that the end of this grim DIY journey was in sight. But when the decorative stage of the work was reached, Tommy's temper only seemed to worsen as they attempted to handle more delicate materials. In a horrible parody of the old song 'When Father Papered the Parlour', a sharp slap across the face or a punch in the stomach meant that she had failed to paste a length of wallpaper properly, so that its extreme margins would not stick closely to the wall, or that she had not been quick enough in passing a newly pasted length up to him at the precise moment he was ready to hang it. She was a DIY novice and it was a terrifying thought that her two thumbs might accidentally tear through a soft, warm length.

"You're bloody dozy," Tommy would say from the top of the step-ladder, looking down on her as she struggled at a drop-leaf table to slap on the warm flour paste so perfectly that he could have no possible complaint. Then, as she rushed forward to pass him the soft, warm bundle of wallpaper, looped up back and forth in the professional way and smelling of porridge, milk-puddings or of old-fashioned bread poultices, he would strike away her confidence with words when even she could not provoke reaction from his fist.

"You know what you are?" he would say by way of comradely thanks. "*You're a bloody waste of time!*"

But when all this cold, tedious and frightening work had been done and the little house in Hindley Street, although a bit spartan, at last had the appearance of a clean, gleaming 'modern' home, through whose windows the light of a new life could begin to shine, Hilda Thompson found that, just as the terrible days in the caravan in Cuerden Park had intimated, her life with Tommy was going to be nomadic. Almost as soon as they had finished refurbishing their first proper home, Tommy came up with the idea of immediately selling it. Within months of arriving in Hindley Street, they were going to move house again.

Although her dreams of a permanent home were eroding, Hilda Thompson felt that one good thing about the return to Chorley was the fact that she and her mother could resume contact again. During the three years in Cuerden Park, Ellen Hartley had stayed away, thinking that Tommy resented her and hoping that by being flung together in such an uncompromising way, the couple might find space to settle maritally. Now they had returned to Chorley, Ellen began cautiously to visit them, usually on the pretext of bringing new clothes for the children, but always letting several weeks elapse between brief visits. As in the days of her courtship, Hilda Thompson still did not get on with Tommy's jealous mother, Mary Ann, but she was very glad of the odd afternoons when he cleared off to visit her and his stepfather, Jack, usually rowing violently with Mary Ann while trying to do some small DIY job for her.

Roughly a century before, the sophisticated French traveller Hippolyte Taine had noted one economic vice of the English: their compulsion to make money from property rather than manufacture. Now, drinking in the effects of the recent handiwork at Hindley Street (down at the other end of the social scale), Tommy Thompson also began to discover the idea of the 'rising' and inflationary property market and realized that he could not only pay off the Hindley Street house entirely after selling it but cover the cost of materials used in its repair and then make a small profit. With unemployment benefit and odd bursts of outdoor labouring work to keep up appearances with the authorities, he sensed a future way of life in minor property speculation which would be ideally to his taste. 'Doing up' houses and then instantly moving on might one day mean that he could spend more and more time at home and less in the company of adult men, among whom he felt strangely uneasy.

Like most men of his social background at that time, Tommy Thompson passed his days at a pub when not at work or at home and, eventually, I discovered that when in a pub he always preferred the company of a woman, if that were possible, as if to distance or shield himself from other men in this tough, street-corner domain of his violent natural father.

Arnold Thompson, Tommy's older brother, had told me that Tommy had found his time as an army conscript particularly hellish (well – few National Servicemen seem to have actually *liked* it). But on the other hand, Tommy seemed to obsessively admire army life for its extreme orderliness in which he and others knew their place and, I suppose, relations between men are not 'social' but highly formalized. Nowadays, with his spell in the army well behind him, as a casual labourer Tommy was thrown into ebullient male company for a lot of the time and without much in the way of imposed external boundaries which, as a physically, possibly sexually, abused child, would have been particularly frightening to him – the horse-play, joshing and crude physical competitiveness of a building site. Getting out of that world while putting his only skills to some useful purpose by constant house renovation, seems to me to have been Tommy's way of making a dignified withdrawal from the fiercely masculine world of his father which had terrorized him as a child. In any case, part of the pleasure in controlling Hilda was to do exactly as he liked with their home – to keep her unsettled and pained by the prospect of constantly moving on from houses which she had jointly laboured to repair.

> *I'd love to have stayed at our first house*, Hilda Thompson wrote wistfully. *There was no need for us to move.*

Apart from Tommy's violence and contempt, Hilda

Thompson's sense of powerlessness lay in never being allowed to settle in one place or to have any say in the interior arrangement of her home – a deep frustration for every woman with natural 'nesting' instincts, particularly when she has young children. Hilda longed to surround her small daughters with cleanliness, peace, order and pretty things. Instead, as they next moved on to a decayed house in John Street, Chorley (*which was his Idea*), and Hilda again packed their clothes and bedding in the galvanized zinc bath, she realized that she might never have a settled home of her own, nor any say in the interior softening of a house to make it a feminine ideal of safety. With no option but to make the best of it, and hoping that this time Tommy might settle for at least a year or two, Hilda Thompson resigned herself once more to pulling out the old range, fitting a new fireplace, concreting the floors, fitting a new kitchen sink, replastering soft, damp walls and redecorating throughout.

> *I was quite pleased with the house though it would take us some time to get all the jobs done. I knew I would have to work hard labouring on Tommy as it needed everything doing from top to bottom like we did at Hindley Street. I only hoped that Tommy would settle at John Street for years maybe. It was so convenient for everything & only five minutes to town which was great.*

One early summer morning, when John Street too had been painfully refurbished and, through the passing of a year, Tommy had nightly kept her in suspense that they might soon move on again, Hilda Thompson had just begun her weekly washing at the new kitchen sink when a neighbour of her mother's from Bowland Avenue arrived with the news that Ellen Hartley had been suddenly taken ill in the night. Luckily, Tommy was still obliged to work and June had started primary school which gave Hilda a little time to manoeuvre. Immediately, Hilda Thompson dropped everything and, half walking, half running with little Hilda off and on in her arms, the young woman hurried round to Bowland Avenue, counting the minutes – thirty – in alarm.

Ellen Hartley had been unwell in a vague way for some time and, fully aware of the domestic difficulties of both her daughters, she preferred to depend, as ever, on her elder sister Mary Ann. But something about this illness could not be shaken off and, eventually, Mary Ann had arranged for the big bed Ellen had continued to sleep in alone since Ernest Hartley's death to be moved downstairs so that its occupant did not feel so remotely cold and isolated. Hogging unwarranted space in the living room, the bed now lay within inches of the old Bungalow range and, during the hours when Mary Ann was obliged to go back to her own home in Wordsworth Row, the sick woman watched the red embers beyond the open door of the range gradually shift downwards, settle into a grey torpor of ash and then peacefully fade away.

Arriving that morning with the urgency of fresh air, anxiety and youth, Hilda Thompson was shocked at the change in her mother, who lay strangely small and wizened in the bed she remembered from her childhood days in Leigh Row. It was a big brass bed and once upon a time both parents had seemed big and buoyant in it. Jumping on it in the morning was like boarding a high bright ship in which the entire family might sail away (*My mother & dad slept in a Iron Bedstead with Brass knobs on. That's what they used to be like.*) Ellen had asked her sister to fetch a priest. He had been and gone. Trying not to appear too uneasy, Hilda darted out for a doctor, begging him to come quickly, and then ran on to the shops. With her mother's wan face before her, she decided to risk a beating from Tommy by spending money from her own household budget on soft invalid food that the sick woman might like to eat. Soon, flushed with profligacy and momentary economic freedom in a nearby corner shop, she decided on a yellow custard pie with an amber freckling of burnt nutmeg, a tin of sweet rice pudding and, in a dazzling brainwave, on a large glass siphon of soda water to wet the grey, stale mouth which, most worryingly, now refused even tea.

After the doctor had arrived at Bowland Avenue, pronounced

some kind of minor heart trouble and prescribed pills for it, little Hilda was lifted up on to her grandmother's bed and sat quietly holding her hand, which the old lady seemed to like. Again, Hilda Thompson noted with dismay the transparency of those hands, grubbily pale with light-blue veins flowing so clearly through them as they lay on a faded cotton bedspread with white flowers woven into it. When away from her and locked into her own domestic strife, perhaps she had always carried in her mind a youthful picture of her mother: handsome, serene-eyed and slightly remote, her hair always perfectly waved in the old Buty-wave manner, particularly on Sundays and 'best' days, when she liked to dress up in a special silky blouse with a softly tied floppy bow at the neck. Now, after several weeks of vague malaise and one particularly bad night, that dense hair had lost its wave and looked more like thin wisps attached to an all-too-prominent skull. Ellen Hartley's calm blue eyes had also suddenly lost their colour, like flowers past their best and, with a sense of something fragile taking a slow leave, Hilda Thompson trampled down the thought that one day her mother was going to die. As the hands on Ellen Hartley's tinny alarm clock moved on towards three in the afternoon, when it would be time to pick up June from school, Hilda tried to comfort her mother as best she could.

"You'll be all right, Mum. This medicine doctor's left will soon put you right."

But Ellen Hartley seemed to be troubled by deeper things and, as this was the first time she had been able to speak to her daughter without Tommy's threatening presence for almost five years, she lightly drew Hilda to her by the arm and asked her very quietly, "Love, how is Tommy with you now?"

"Better, Mum," said Hilda, who hadn't the heart additionally to burden the sick woman with the living terror of her married life, so near but emotionally so far away, in John Street.

"You're quite sure he's all right with you now, love?"

"I *promise*," said Hilda warmly.

Shifting uneasily in the big bed, so that its brass bits suddenly clinked a little, Ellen Hartley quietly closed her eyes, as if exhausted, and asked her daughter to come back again that evening.

"You promise you'll come back and see me tonight, love . . .? *Promise you will*," and Hilda, thinking that even Tommy could never object to that, instantly reassured her. "I'll be back tonight, Mum – to see how you are."

But that night, Tommy Thompson was having none of it.

"No way," he said, when Hilda timorously mentioned that her mother was ill and that she would like to pop out quickly after tea to Bowland Avenue. "You're stopping here."

Bent over the new kitchen sink with her back to him – circumstances in which she could sometimes safely permit herself a controlled grimace of anguish – Hilda Thompson was again forced to recognize that Tommy's art of inflicting pain from one day to the next would be always novel and extreme. Like taking a flower bulb or a common onion to pieces, there always seemed to be one more layer of his inner workings to lift off and examine before stripping on to a bitter, tightly wrapped core.

"Tommy, love –"

Suddenly he was standing very close to her in the kitchen and, inwardly knowing what she had already secretly and illicitly spent that day in the corner shop near Bowland Avenue, Hilda braced herself for the onslaught of the almost toddler-like explosion of fury which flared up with a terrible internal logic of its own into twenty minutes of punches to her painful breasts, face-slapping, thumping, head-butting and kicking. But on this occasion something seemed to draw Tommy back. Looking very acutely at her eyes, rabbit-pink with suppressed crying, he had begun to smell the heady mixture of death and money on the air.

"The old bitch has insurance policies, hasn't she?"

"Tommy, love!"

"*You go round there and you'll suffer by it.*"

That evening, as she finally put down the soft, string-headed dish-mop, Hilda Thompson finally weighed up the warning of a severe beating against the promise she had made to her mother, who now swam inside her head in the big brass bed beside the fire, glancing at the clock, dozing, wondering and listening to every footfall beyond the street window in expectation of her younger daughter's approach. By speaking so cruelly of insurance policies Tommy had suddenly put Hilda more fully in mind of the possibility of death, the thought of which she had forced away that afternoon. Now, like a child panicking after a long absence from home, all she wanted to do was to run to Bowland Avenue, cling to her mother and be told that all was well, that she would not die:

I was worried June & Hilda would Suffer also, knowing him. I was too Afraid to disobey him, as I knew his Violent temper If he didn't Always get his own Way in Everything. I asked Tommy if I could go to my mother's in the morning when he had gone to work and he said, yes. Tommy had only one thing in his mind & that was if my Mother was going to die, How much he would get from my Mother's Insurance Policies.

Like most respectable working-class people, Ellen Hartley had paid weekly into a burial insurance fund which would ensure that whatever comforts she had done without in life, she would at least leave the world with dignity and without being a financial burden on her precariously married daughters. Closely watching his wife that evening, as she stifled misery and apprehension in his presence and mechanically got on with the business of putting June and Hilda to bed, Tommy Thompson was teased by the prospect of unlooked-for money lying about somewhere, a wad of something warm, crisp and useful that needed only a purposeful hand put out to secure it. The thought of how he could put that extra bit of cash towards buying and refitting another house pricked him like a thorn and, as he tried to sit still and calmly mull over the day's events, it was like the shifting stab of a fever which makes the body involuntarily move in sudden irritation. Like his mother, Tommy had a respect for spiritualism when it suited him and, on that evening in 1958, the possibility of a death in the family put him in mind of his old fool of a spiritualist stepfather, who still cast his eyes up to the ceiling when Sunday hymn-singing burst out of the radio, to garner what the spooks could foretell. Eventually, when Hilda came downstairs again, having got the girls to bed, the whole subject brought Tommy strongly to his feet. Hilda Thompson would indeed go out that night, he had decided – not to Bowland Avenue but to One who could predict the future.

"Bugger off round to Cat Woman," he instructed, "and get cards read – I'll let ye go."

Miss Sharples was a tiny old woman in her eighties who was known in Chorley as the Cat Woman because of the vast numbers of these creatures who slipped in and out of her strange little house for chaotic food and shelter. With the back-street degeneration of inter-war spiritualism into fortune-telling, she was one of half a dozen elderly 'wise women' in the town who were alternately scoffed at and feared. For some older people in a country weighed down by the grief of two world wars, spiritualism, both pure and decayed, was a way of keeping in touch with the recently killed, whose youthful photographs, usually taken in smart military uniform, were quietly enshrined on mantelpieces and china cabinets up and down the land. For those whom even the wonderful new National Health Service could not help, the predictions of a female seer like Miss Sharples were an old way of discovering the likely outcome of illness or sudden physical decline.

Miss Sharples's house, as dark and narrow as a crack in the wall, was set back at an angle off East Lane, a gloomy cobbled passage well away from Chorley's municipal lighting improvements. Like a child's home-made doll's house (perhaps an upended shoe-box with one thin cardboard floor set into it), her house had just two rooms, one set above the other, no back door and only two windows, both of which closely overlooked the gate lodge of a dusty old mansion still called 'Brown's House'. The Brown family (Chorley's early Victorian cotton-masters) belonged to the time when a manufacturer often built himself a big house and half a dozen trifling terraces for his work-people, close up to the gates of the mill. Nowadays, all that was left of Brown's clamorous empire was this silent house whose windows, thick with rich brown dust, bore signs of being partly occupied as offices. Then came a towel factory, set a few doors down from Miss Sharples's house, and the remnants of another mill, refitted shortly after the war for the manufacture of hosiery. It was part and parcel of Chorley's famous 'cotton patriotism' that the looms in some abandoned mills were never cleared out, as if loyalty to them might one day draw back the trade, and cobwebs as big as wedding veils slowly gathered on the machinery of the past. Like the ancient servant of an extinct family, ekeing out the rest of her days at the gates of their mausoleum, Miss Sharples continued to dwell in 1858, literally within six feet of the defunct cotton-master's mansion.

A little later that summer evening, when Miss Sharples's cats seemed to glint and flick in the twilight of East Lane, like fish in a nocturnal stream, Hilda Thompson arrived, tear-streaked and anguished, to have her fortune told. Miss Sharples was four feet eight or so in height, so small that even Hilda Thompson felt tall and gangling in comparison as she looked down on a once-blonde head, now pure white with hair pulled up into a tight little bun that was painfully restabbed each morning with an arthritic handful of old steel hair-pins. Few people attempted conversation with Miss Sharples ("she was a very serious woman – a bit stern, really") and, once she had passed through the old woman's door, the reluctant inquirer into the future regarded her with courteous awe, mainly because "she were very abrupt".

Reserving her walking stick for outdoor trips to empty her sanitary bucket in the communal lavatory three or four doors down, Miss Sharples moved shakily about her little house on tiny boots beneath a fusty ankle-length skirt. The stone-flagged room was lit by the low, damp hiss of a gas mantle but a brighter, happier light came from the tiny black range on whose hob, even in summer, Miss Sharples permanently brewed a pot of tea. Warmed by this domestic glow was a peg rug of Hilda's childhood, two rocking chairs and a plain deal table on which the young woman was now invited to shuffle a pack of cards and to cut it in three. The dark warning of spades came up and an inconsequential heart.

"You're going to lose someone very dear to you," said Miss Sharples immediately, beginning the reading in her own uniquely abrupt way. Then, as the old stern voice elaborated and busked the variations on this theme, Hilda Thompson could not help but disengage from those sharp blue eyes on the other side of the table to think of other eyes, now closing in resignation, only a matter of streets away.

Like most women of her generation, Ellen Hartley put long-term faith in a school of man-management by which a difficult husband could be 'brought round' by a good meat meal and (although it was never spoken of openly) by sexual enthusiasm. The old saying, when poverty comes in at the door, love flies out of the window, seemed to be true, and after the Thompsons moved back again to Chorley, Ellen had begun to drop in on her daughter and son-in-law, casually bringing them a bit of good steak and an onion to contribute from her earnings at the Hygienic Laundry towards a sound evening meal – the bringer of harmony. As a perfect mother-in-law, Ellen had tried not to impose herself on the young married couple but to confine her visits to fortnightly intervals, offering to babysit while Tommy and Hilda went out for a drink together. Hilda knew that her mother had never come empty-handed into Tommy's house but, in the most tactful way, had tried to spoil him like a cherished son. She would bring little treats to let him know that he was respected by the women in the family and that his economic efforts on their behalf were recognized and appreciated.

My mother used to bring him lean steak or Pie Meat for stewing & a big onion. He liked eating that. She also Bought him Prawns or Shrimps. She would get the Meat from the Butchers & the shrimps from a Fish stall on the Market usually. My

Mother liked to bring him his Favourite cakes also, like Tennis buns they called them in those days or Vanillas. My Mother made more fuss over him than me & never came between us or spoke out of turn.

On days when Tommy had enjoyed a bit of good steak or had devoured the thickly iced buns that her mother had proffered from a fancily printed paper bag, he might later refer to his mother-in-law as "the old lady". But once the immediate pleasure of eating Ellen's gifts had worn off, he verbally used her behind her back as he used most women. Always suspecting that she gave greater gifts to her first-born daughter (whose family size was now creeping up to five or six), Tommy Thompson continued to burst out against Ellen in a refraction of spite against women in general. "*The old cow – she's no fucking good to us*".

That evening, from her first abrupt declaration, Miss Sharples had said all that Hilda Thompson needed to know. In the usual meshing of expectations between fortune-teller and client, the old woman's words merely confirmed Hilda's anguish and now, still calculating the short distance between East Lane and Bowland Avenue, particularly when taken at a run through the short cuts of back alleys, Hilda Thompson agonized over the possibility that if she took even minutes longer to return home, Tommy might start some new cruelty with little June and Hilda. Sensing that she had long since lost the attention of her young client, Miss Sharples looked penetratingly into Hilda's eyes and brought the reading to a close with words she used so often to Chorley women who sat with her in the shadows of her tiny, filthy house: "*Somebody's not being as he should be.*"

Then, after Hilda had passed a shilling across the table, she called upon her to do the thing that brought even giggling parties of young girls intent on knowing the outcome of a love affair to their senses – to go upstairs in the pitch dark to prepare the way for her to later crawl painfully up on her hands and knees to bed:

"Go upstairs, love," said Miss Sharples, "and light gas mantle before ye go."

Next day, with June kept back from school and hobbled by the small steps of both her daughters, Hilda Thompson immediately set off for Bowland Avenue. Even at 9.30 in the promising light of a fine summer's morning, she found the curtains drawn at all the windows of her mother's house and that overnight, with her sister Mary Ann at her side, Ellen Hartley had gone for ever.

Tommy Thompson could not stand crying of any kind, either in children or adults. It seemed to trigger something far too painful in him – perhaps his own useless infant tears of the past – and in his presence Hilda Thompson was obliged to suppress all visible signs of an intense grief made all the worse by her failure to have appeared the evening before at her dying mother's bedside. In contrast, Tommy was cock-a-hoop that Miss Sharples's shapeless predictions had been right and he immediately set about securing the better part of Ellen Hartley's burial insurance money. It was up to Hilda, he decided, to ensure that as little as possible was spent on the actual funeral and, to this end, she was dispatched late that afternoon to Mr Moss, the local undertaker, as a front for Tommy's designs.

Mr Moss lived in quite a nice house just off Eaves Lane and, apart from running up coffins for that particular neighbourhood of Chorley, he ran a wood and decorating business from a nearby shop specializing in paint, wallpaper and DIY materials. Mr Moss looked after the undertaking side of the business from home and, like all good undertakers, particularly those in poorer areas, he had learned both tact and pity. At that lovely point in the late afternoon when the shop was closed and his own skilfully modernized home wafted with the scent of a savoury tea and the prospect of Hughie Green (Double your mon-eee) on the thick green screen of his new television set, he instantly understood from the trembling and pain-racked young blonde in his living room that her mother was to have the plainest coffin he could supply.

"Yes, love. A nice plain pine one. Something dignified but not too fancy."

"N-no satin inside, or anything . . ."

"Yes, love. It's all one to them that's gone on to happier things before us."

"And – and – no shroud."

Her last request meant that, when he had placed Ellen Hartley in her coffin, the lid should be immediately screwed down. It was unusual for a family to ask for that but, of course, Mr Moss would comply.

At that time, in the poorer parts of Lancashire and the North, it was the custom for neighbours to lay out a body at home and for an undertaker merely to supply and fit the coffin and to arrange its transport – in this case, to Chorley Cemetery. Earlier that day, while Ellen Hartley's family gathered at Bowland Avenue to pay their last respects, Hilda Thompson ran about on errands as she always did, like a leaf blown along the road, to set in motion the banal clearing up which usually takes place immediately after a death. Her mother had a few outstanding bills which needed paying with money kept in a kitchen tin. Then, after being sent for, her tougher half-sister, X also came to Bowland Avenue. Sitting trance-like beside the coffin now set up by Mr Moss on three wooden trestles beneath the living-room window, through whose drawn curtains the summer sun continued to filter warmly, X smoked twenty cigarettes, solidly and ruminatively, for the rest of the day.

Ellen Hartley's elder sisters, Mary Ann and Lizzie, blamed no one in particular for the striking simplicity of the coffin but they were rather surprised, and then affronted, to discover that the lid had been screwed down so quickly. Knowing what she had been forced to order from Mr Moss, Hilda felt it keenly when Mary Ann eventually ordered that the coffin should be opened, so that the assembled female family could take a last glimpse of the departed woman. Even here in Lancashire, apart from a clean nightdress, there was not a shred of cloth in it.

I had to say My Mother had no Money or Insurance to Cover the Funeral. Tommy made me say she had not to have a shroud on even & the cheapest Coffin & that the Lid of the Coffin had to be screwed on as soon as her body was put In so no one could look at her. I was terribly shocked with having to do this. I will never forget how I felt by Tommy's Orders. I know Mary Ann could not Understand. I just had to take the blame And when My Mum's Eldest Sister came round to see her in the Coffin she got the Undertaker to take the Lid off & put a shroud on. My Mother and the Coffin was made to look much better Inside with Satin and the Lid was left off till the funeral.

Quietly taking matters into her own hands, Ellen Hartley's oldest sister, Lizzie, recalled Mr Moss who discreetly returned to the house with a length of white satin and, in fifteen minutes or so, he again set the dead woman back to her rest, properly presented like a grey wax rose. Never another word was said about money and Tommy's rather small windfall for investment in new property was secured. Although her mother had often failed to be there at Bowland Avenue when she was a child, had failed to be there on that terrible day when she had made her one bid to escape from Tommy and Cuerden Park, and even in the intervening years since then had seemed only the vaguest source of support – an elderly woman with a few paper-bag bits of shopping set against the suffering that Tommy was increasingly inflicting on her and the children – Hilda Thompson, like most adults who have newly recognized the loss of both parents, suddenly felt strangely alone in the world. In future, both to herself and her own children, she would have to be what is meant by 'mother', 'father' and 'family' now. Carefully reserving her grief for the hours when Tommy was away from John Street, Hilda Thompson looked at her own daughters, too young to understand the complexity of her pain, and felt that, apart from them, she *didn't know what there was to live for.*

With his own inimitable timing, Tommy provided the answer when he announced one evening that soon they would all be moving on once more to another old terraced house in Trafalgar Street. In the laconic way that many people of my generation describe some wreck that with the eye of faith will be eventually repaired and 'restored' after a great deal of domestic upheaval and physical effort, Mrs Thompson merely described the third decayed house in her short married life as a place that "needed quite a bit doing to it".

6

Learning to be Miss Thompson

As she paused inside the open classroom door for the first time that autumn, the little girl saw and sensed a new kind world specially made for children. Unlike some other children, who were frantic at being suddenly separated from home for half a day, she did not need to be disentangled from her mother's hand on this first day at school because, quite unlike anything at home, five-year-old June Thompson was magically drawn in by an enveloping physical warmth, a strange air of relaxation and the utterly unexpected dazzle of small things coloured red, yellow and bright blue which were too tempting to hang back from in shyness. There was a strange lady in a soft jumper and grey hair whose big face looked down with a welcoming smile; very small chairs and tables – lots of them – quite unlike the high, sparse furniture at home, and in a far distant place edged with red wood on the other side of the room, mounds of something yellow which reminded her of earth in the garden but was called 'sand' in a 'sandpit'. Until this inviting time, June Thompson had only had a few battered things from jumble sales to hold in her small, interested hand and call a toy. Like all children who have spent their early years in what is dubbed 'sensory deprivation' (plus a grey burden of tension which she felt squashed under but could not resist), June ran without hesitation from the cold fearful place to a bright kind one.

I always loved going to school, wrote June Thompson. *Not because I was clever but it was so much nicer than being at home.*

I could no longer put off looking more closely into the developing lives of June Thompson and her sister, Hilda, but already knowing something of these particular children's lives –

decades of physical, emotional and sexual abuse, ending in Liverpool Crown Court during their early middle age on a charge of murder – I too wanted to run, not forwards with June into her growing life but backwards to the ordinary, kind safety of Mrs Thompson's early childhood of flower festivals and serenity in Chorley and, indeed, back to memories of my own childhood, many miles away and a long time ago.

It was the family photographs, particularly those taken during June and Hilda Thompson's primary-school days, that became some of the most painful things to examine in the history of this family. For many months after first meeting the Thompson women, I actually avoided the place in my room in Glasgow where, after returning as usual one night from Preston, I had set down in a carrier bag the cache of family snaps meticulously labelled, filed in white envelopes and then double-wrapped in clear plastic by June Thompson herself with her strange, silent efficiency. For a long time, I did not want to go near those photographs and the reason was this – the children in them not only looked perfectly normal, they could have been me or my friends at that age.

Perhaps it is just a trick of memory but in England in the 1950s and 1960s all young children seem to have looked the same, particularly in summer, when little girls were snapped outdoors in classic English cotton frocks, sandals and hand-knitted cardigans, with the inevitable squint against the sun. Perhaps when children are left to themselves there is always at all times a superficial similarity and expectation among them. In age, June and Hilda Thompson are my contemporaries – the one reason why I had been tempted into the painful job of examining their lives in the first place – and I too came from the North of England (though from the other side of the Pennines). Around us too, beyond the fields, the distant heavy industry of the Victorian age was dissolving into rust (literally hastened in this case by airborne salt from the sea). I suppose I was appalled that from this very old-fashioned northern start in life, the lives of the Thompson sisters had turned out to be so horribly different from mine.

One day in July, when June was nine, she had been photographed at St George's Primary School, Chorley – the individually taken official school portrait which parents are then invited to buy in a variety of sizes and decorative mounts. Like most girls of that age, June's dark hair had been rather haphazardly cut at home; she wore a simple cotton dress with a white piqué Peter Pan collar slightly crumpled under a hand-knitted cardigan and her willing smile revealed the settling of new teeth. It is only a trivial thing, but I was somehow deeply shocked that even the cardboard mount of June's primary-school photograph was the same as mine had been at that time. Beneath her black-and-white portrait, in fancy blue printing (specially looped and joined up to imitate the neat, flowing handwriting we were all struggling to achieve in wide-lined exercise books) were the words SCHOOL DAYS 1961. Then, around the frame of the photograph were little drawings of the things that symbolized school days for millions of ordinary children in that year and on which parents looked so approvingly: a little drawing of a globe ready to spin on a stand, piles of hardback books with markers sticking out of them, a tennis racquet and balls, and a mixture of other objects suggesting literature, science, sport and art – all meant to ram home the ancient ideal of a sound mind in a healthy body. To the top right of June's head was depicted the concrete gear of elementary mathematics: a couple of protractors and the sharp steel points of a pair of small brass compasses, which demon boys liked to straighten out entirely, to throw into an old wooden desk like a dart and then pull out again, in a fantasy world of extracting the sword from a stone. Above all this, immediately over June's head, was a little drawing of the sun, which in normal memory always seems to shine down, especially on children.

That afternoon in Glasgow, as I turned on through the first packet of Thompson family snaps, I next came across an almost identical school photograph of June's younger sister, Hilda – the perhaps more hesitantly smiling portrait of a child whose father had already held her right hand close to the flames of an open coal fire until the scorch of her screams had taught her never again to go near the fireside and, indeed, still prevents her from daring to light the gas ring of an ordinary kitchen stove. But with artless people's compulsive willingness to smile in everyday snapshots, there was still no clue in this photograph to the domestic reality of the Thompson children's lives. To me, always dubious about visual appearances as a way of ever knowing the truth, these conventional family photographs merely confirmed that one may smile and smile and be a victim.

At some time during the late 1950s, Tommy Thompson's mother, Mary Ann, had moved out of Chorley to the nearby weaving village of Coppull. The photograph suggested some kind of light-coloured terraced house with a long, overgrown garden at the back. Already imprinted with a sense of vast greenness and open-air space from her infant days playing round the caravan in Cuerden Park, June had been momentarily captured in her grandmother's garden as if in her own element. The photograph spoke of sun-lit freedom, away from the angry, grey squashing of everyday life when she was not at school but at home. In his own way, I reflected, Tommy Thompson must have thought of this as a good day too. Just as he often seemed to be a perfectly ordinary father, Tommy had taken a few black-and-white snaps out in the garden with a heavy, oblong camera which smelled faintly of leather and into which a coil of bright-yellow film had been inserted with a great deal of fussing and fuming about the need to fix the thing up in darkness. Despite what I had already divined – I think accurately – about Mary Ann Thompson's emotional life during Tommy's childhood, I was amazed now, even abashed, by how sunnily ordinary and normal she also appeared to be when fixing her eyes on the lens of her beloved son's camera. Mary Ann wore an old-fashioned cotton pinny and round, wire National Health specs. Her hands were proudly placed on the shoulders of little June, as if to say, "I did my best all those years ago, back in Buchanan Street – and, as you see, I succeeded."

On another afternoon, when pretending to manipulate a big

pair of garden shears, June had been snapped by Tommy again, this time smiling and crouching low among unkempt grass in a cotton dress bleached out by the sun. But the emotional reality behind this little monochrome window on the past was already known to me. That day, June had manipulated the shears all too well. She had not only trimmed one tussock in some field of a garden, but had made a small, clean cut in her dress as well. As if always looking for some reason to rain down disproportionate hatred on those beneath him, Tommy had rapidly closed up on her, a familiar shadow with her mother's voice at the edge of it, attempting to placate him. There had been loud words and his raised fist, quickly followed by artificial calm, because Tommy did not want his mother to see him hitting his little daughter. For June, the sun had gone out for the rest of the day. She was now old enough to know that, as far as Tommy was concerned, a beating halted was only a beating postponed. Putting a finger surreptitiously through the hole in her dress on and off for the rest of the afternoon, she knew that once the coolness of evening had driven them all home on the bus, big hard smacks from a man's hand would send her upstairs to the bed she shared with her less adventurous sister. In the manner of all younger sisters, Hilda seemed to have some agile quality which often kept her one step ahead of trouble.

The Thompson women's sitting-room had changed. It seemed brighter and more cluttered than usual. This time Mrs Thompson sat on a cheerful cherry-red velvet sofa – the old brown suite had been expunged.

"A pretty colour," I said, thinking that in some way she was beginning to bring to life her dream of what a 'proper home' should be. But a hand fluttering up and down to the side of her head indicated that she was having trouble with her hearing-aid.

"Sorry, love. I can't hear too well today . . ."

Then I remembered that cherry-red was the colour of the stiff Edwardian *chaise-longue* on which she had lain as a child when staring up at the hissing gas-mantle of the old stone cottage in Chorley.

Out in the kitchen, June and Hilda were preparing tea with their usual eerie silence. Averting my eyes from Mrs Thompson, who was still fiddling about in the agitated inner world of the deaf, I realized that week by week, when I was 250 miles away and often sunk into the gloom of trying adequately to reconstruct their past, the Thompsons' home in Preston was taking on a new life of its own. It was slowly filling up with newly bought things. On the light-oak veneer of the mantelpiece Mrs Thompson had recently placed little glass domes full of yellow cloth flowers and bright-blue butterflies. There were images of animals, flowers and 'The Country' everywhere – swans and trees; a big photographic mural of two white Yorkshire terriers wearing blue satin bows; and, above the fireplace, the old picture had appeared, narrowly framed in gilt, of three white kittens peeping out of a half-opened drawer. Other pictures seemed to be made from silver paper and showed improbably thatched cottages arched over by a rainbow and almost dwarfed by tumbling Victorian gardens standing high with hollyhocks and delphiniums. Even the vast new TV set bore little china baskets full of equally china flowers. Through the kitchen door, I glimpsed a new wall-plate which said, in sweetly curving script, "You're the Greatest Mum in the World".

"IT'S ALL CHANGED," I said very distinctly to Mrs Thompson, who still smiled remotely on the other side of the room. "YOU'RE MAKING THINGS THE WAY YOU WANT THEM NOW."

As if stepping forward to explain this new life, June silently appeared at the kitchen door with a small plate of fancy biscuits and said quite simply, "We like anything that's bright and cheerful."

One thing I had learned from skilled oral historians who encourage ordinary people to make tape-recordings describing their supposedly 'insignificant' lives is the usefulness of old photographs in stimulating the memory. Mrs Thompson had the naturally patchy memory of an elderly woman for whom bright childhood days shoot up to overgrow the sagging recall of middle life. 'Young' Hilda Thompson felt that her memory had been artificially wiped by the ECT (electro-convulsive therapy) she had had for severe depression some time during the early 1980s. Although June had somehow retained the management of her own brain (despite having borne the brunt of sexual abuse in the family for almost thirty years), it was largely by suppressing her emotions altogether. I always felt ambivalent about trying to stir memories in the Thompson women too much. The family photographs might well draw up incidents 'useful' to me in the telling of their story, but, on the other hand, I was often afraid of making them recall things too painful to remember. Perhaps naïvely, I was truly afraid of sending them all mad. Nevertheless, we began, as usual, to 'talk through' this new batch of family snaps.

It was the frequent presence of animals in these childhood photographs (mainly dogs and rabbits) that gave me a clue to the next stage in the Thompson children's emotional history. At a time when most ordinary people still relied on natural daylight to take family photographs, June and Hilda Thompson always seemed to have been snapped outdoors in summer. "July 1958" or "July 1962" was frequently scrawled on the backs of the photographs in big, coarse, incompetent stabs. With a curious sting of fear I then realized that this was Tommy Thompson's own handwriting. Days when the children were caught happily crouching down in the warm grass were, in fact, a rarity. Year by year, in one terraced house after another, the backdrop of their summer lives was always a backyard, deeply shadowed on one side, stone-flagged, with the broad sill of a living-room window somewhere behind them, a cast-iron down-pipe to one side and the afternoon sun slanting in over a high brick wall through the terracotta haze of industrial summer. Here, in one snap, the young sisters stood, dark hair blunt-cut, in cotton frocks, simple sandals and slightly shrunken Fair Isle cardigans. This time, June's right arm was spread protectively around the shoulders of little Hilda, who turned to her as naturally as a plant turns towards the light. Another July and Tommy had snapped them quite charmingly with Beauty, a big Alsatian dog whose tongue lolled out as if smiling in the heat. June had her arms round Beauty's neck with the proprietorial control of the elder child, while Hilda, also enjoying the company of the dog, sat quite daintily to one side on a small wooden stool. In the prunes and prisms manner of some quite naturally genteel little girls, her hands lay clasped on the lap of her cotton frock and her knees and feet were set perfectly together.

"In a way," I said, as we all thought a bit about this picture, "I'm surprised that Tommy let you have a dog. I thought he didn't like you to have anything to play with."

"Oh, we always had lots of animals, Alex," Mrs Thompson quickly interjected.

Young Hilda remained silent as usual, just fondling Candy, the white Yorkshire terrier that seemed to live almost permanently on her lap.

June, though, was faintly sardonic. "Oh, aye, we allus had lots of animals."

And then, for some reason, all the Thompson women seemed to twitch away from the photographs with animals in them.

Beauty had been their first dog. She was a big, soft-natured, easy-going creature, patient with children and of the type that is known as 'soppy'. June and Hilda were forbidden by Tommy to play with any local children ("You've got each other"), but sometimes they were let out with Beauty at weekends into the backyard, over whose high brick walls they could hear the buzz and yells of neighbouring children's activity. Beauty represented half an hour's freedom before the sound of their happiness rose above the living-room windowsill, the back door opened and Tommy hauled them into the house. These children's mother had never been permitted to cuddle them in Tommy's presence but they could hug Beauty. When things inside the house felt bad but were not in any way understood, out in the yard there was still a broad living neck, muskily scented beneath the leather collar, and those sharply pointed ears, responsive, quickly and naturally, to the slightest sounds they made. Beauty obeyed Tommy too but, unlike them, they recognized that she still had an unquenchable freedom of her own.

Beauty may have been the Thompson children's only playmate during daylight hours, but after they had gone to bed she had another life. She was Tommy Thompson's ticket to local acceptance among men he knew were different – somehow bigger and better than him. In the evenings he now liked to swagger out with her – a big dog and he in charge of her – for an evening walk. He had decided to buy her in the first place only to prove how well he could train her. Even when dozing obediently with one ear still vaguely cocked to and fro against the beery din of the pub floor, Beauty would instantly sit up on command when he ordered it ("*Sah!*") and then – wait for it, wait for it – present a paw to shake hands.

"Aye, ye've got a good dog there, Tommy" was music to his ears when Tommy Thompson stood, curiously tense in other men's company, at the bar.

But then Tommy Thompson pressed Beauty on to the next trick, or 'training', which to his timid wife seemed quite irrational.

"I tried to tell him it were dangerous, but I couldn't say too much . . ."

As if he had been somehow arrested around the age of seven or eight himself, Tommy began to place Beauty on one side of a pedestrian crossing and then go over the road by himself. There Beauty would sit, alert and obedient, beyond the river of traffic, until Tommy gave the lordly signal: "Come, Beauty!"

Then, and only then, to the wonderment of all who had recently and uncertainly turned out of the pub, would Beauty cross the road all by herself – just like Lassie on television.

One terrible morning, when the children sat on the bed as usual (there was no table) to eat half a slice of margarined toast each before school, they learned from Tommy's glowering silences that Beauty had very badly misbehaved while they had been in bed. Quite oblivious to her crime, Beauty lay head down, perfectly affable, near the fireplace, but after school that afternoon she was going to be sold.

"He didn't want her after that," said Mrs Thompson, abruptly setting down the forgotten black-and-white snap of Beauty, Hilda and June: Hilda so quaintly pleased, and June with her thin arms clasped so desperately around the big dog's neck.

"I once tried to mention the danger. It could cause an accident mebbee . . ."

After more than thirty years, quiet still came down like a pall on the pink brassy room.

That previous evening, Beauty had been distracted by something when sitting quite alone in the darkness on the other side of the pedestrian crossing. Long before Tommy had given the command, she had dashed violently across the road. In the convivial shadows of pub-closing time, there had been a horrible screech of brakes as a car had swerved. Then a car window had been rapidly cranked down – "*You stupid bugger*!" – as anger, fear and death momentarily hung on the air.

The dog was so big and her children so small, but, as June and Hilda knelt in anguish on the floor of the pet shop in Market Street to bury their faces in the neck of Beauty for the last time, Mrs Thompson completed the transaction with the adult art of making all seem smooth and socially acceptable – "A lovely dog . . . beautiful nature with children. But too big for us in a small house . . ." Then June had finally offered up the familiar worn loop of Beauty's leather lead into the hand of a stranger.

"We were crying our eyes out going down Market Street," said Hilda, glancing slowly at June, and I was surprised that this time she spoke up of her own accord. "But, in a way, we were glad he wouldn't kill it."

"Aye. I were glad when he got interested in parrots," Mrs Thompson more lightly remarked. "You could sell them like dogs – instead of killing them."

To me, the startling words "kill it", "killing them" hung

among us briefly before the Thompson women began to look at each other with an air of recognition.

It was Mrs Thompson who had first discovered Tommy's sadistic interest in animals. One day, she caught him standing absolutely entranced by some faint presence in the kitchen sink. He had merely tipped out the children's goldfish bowl when they were at school, to watch with those intense, dark eyes as the pathetic creatures leaped and thrashed with the comic desperation of truly small things. Then he wetted the fish with a spurt from the tap to see their momentary joy in salvation. Tommy had no sense of the dignity of minor worlds. When, still inwardly rapt, he had drifted off to the corner shop, Mrs Thompson quickly refilled the glass bowl with water and returned the fish, nearly dead, to their own element.

A few months later, when another thump in the breast and a kick on the shins were healing, Hilda Thompson became less casual about Tommy and animals when she returned home one day and, as if sensing a bad spirit about the place, knew that he was upstairs. At that time, in whatever house it was, there was an old gas geyser which leaked and sputtered a few scalding drops at the end of each service to an upstairs wash-basin. Taking a slow glance round the bathroom door, Hilda again found Tommy in a twilight world of his own. They had recently fitted a new bathroom window. It was a pane of ripple glass and yellow beads of linseed oil occasionally oozed from the still malleable putty round the frame. The window was wide open all right, but the room reeked of gas. Holding a canary upside down, its thin legs tightly pressed together between his finger and thumb, Tommy was carefully gassing the bird at the unlit geyser. When the fluttering stopped and its pale eyelids closed, he hung it out of the window, wafting it backwards and forwards to revive it in the air. Tommy still loved to partly strangle Hilda – to take her, in the front of the children, to those vomiting gates of unconsciousness and then, to suddenly release his pressure on her throat. This time, Hilda Thompson did not intervene but glided away downstairs, and when the canary had revived, Tommy began to gas it again.

Like most violently abusing parents, Tommy Thompson was hypersensitive to what he took to be the slightest challenge to his authority at home. Gradually, he began to notice that after the age of eight or so, his children seemed to be changing inside in a subtle way to which he felt he must respond. June and Hilda were beginning to read rather haltingly, even though he would not let them have any books at home. In speaking (when they dared to) sentences sometimes came out of their mouths in a new way which suggested a different, almost adult, means of thinking. Now Tommy was uncannily aware not of soft, dismissable baby stares following him round in a room but of four very dark, observant eyes behind which he occasionally sensed a maturing judgement. From time to time, Tommy Thompson wondered if June and Hilda ever, as he put it, "talked outside", or gave hints at school of what "went on" at home.

At this age, through animals, children usually begin to understand the idea of 'otherness' – that all living things have an independent value of their own. They also learn about the importance of nurturing weaker beings, and move on from the very young child's view of death as a 'sleep' from which a parent or pet can suddenly pop back next day, to a better idea of the physical finality of death. Crudely sensing the emotional importance of the relationship which exists between children of this age and family pets, Tommy knew that a few open demonstrations of his power over animals would serve as a clear reminder to June and Hilda (should they now need one) of his unshakeable hold on the family. It was only within the strict confines of the enclosed family that he felt himself to be a powerful man.

The opportunity came soon enough. After Beauty had gone, the Thompsons acquired a family cat, one of dozens. It was a grey, partly Persian cat, bony beneath the long-haired fluff. Mrs Thompson, I gathered, was never allowed to house-train kittens and, like all cats, this one was chaotic and nervous in a house which lacked underlying peace. This time, before Tommy could push its flat, pretty face into what it had done, the cat fled upstairs like a low, broken thing at his sudden advance across the room. Frantic for a bolthole, it had then shot into an empty bedroom grate, breaking its claws when attempting to scramble up the chimney. Tommy had clutched up their cat so roughly by the scruff of the neck that it could not close its mouth to mew in pain – white needle teeth in a pink ribbed mouth.

For Tommy, small animals were always an irresistible invitation to creative cruelty. Like some deviser of a medieval ordeal either by fire or by water, this time he decided on water.

"*Get that big bread-mug ready!*"

Mrs Thompson had a creeping idea of what he was intending to do when she obediently went out to the kitchen and lifted down the big earthenware bread-crock. It was resounding, deep and narrow, and wrapped in pearly wax-paper, down at the bottom there were still a few slices of white Sunblest loaf. Quickly she rinsed out a few remaining crumbs.

That Saturday afternoon, June and Hilda Thompson sat taut as two bowstrings, hands folded, knees together on the edge of their parents' big bed, which hogged most of the space in the living-room. It was as if Tommy were about to begin a simple scientific demonstration and they were the classroom audience. Nowadays, June no longer asked the question that most normal children ask of a parent hell-bent on some intriguing piece of business – "What are you going to do, Dad?" Instead, she knew that whatever Tommy was going to do, it would not be good and, on behalf of the agonized cat, she ached with a feeling she called "crying inside".

"*And fill it wi' water – not right up t' top!*" commanded Tommy.

Out in the kitchen, the hollow sound of a cascading tap meant their mother had obeyed.

They were white cotton bags, very loose-meshed and soft, in which flour was still sold at that time. After the very last sprinkling of flour had been shaken out of a bag, Mrs Thompson would wash, fold and store it with the others, because they were always useful as dusters. The mewing started when the cat could open and close its mouth again and was suddenly rammed into one of the bags. As if teaching a toddler to enjoy its first dip in the sea, Tommy dunked the lumpy, moving bag up and down in the cold water of the bread-crock, pushing it under, drawing it up and explaining – almost gently, for once: "That's it. Just till the fur's nice and soaked and it gets used to the water."

Little Hilda was conscious only of her mother's shins, bruised behind a ladder in her nylon stockings, and of June's feet, standing quite ordinarily in white socks and sandals, as she knelt on the kitchen floor beside the brimming bread-crock.

"See?" said Tommy, opening the bag to reveal, close to her face, a curiously shrunken soaked thing, the furry aura of its beauty gone.

"Now, Hilda, put yerr ands on top o' that lid."

Tommy Thompson loved a drowning. Calmly he contemplated the moment when a submerged thing, head down in darkness, must leak out its last thin breath, and then draw in that first solid lungful of pain and panic. For once, his wife had done her job well and not a drop of water had spilled over on to the floor.

Kneeling beside the crock, little Hilda felt the lid move a bit beneath her hands with the faint bobbing of the drowning animal.

"Smile," said Tommy Thompson to her, suddenly crouching down low to meet her face to face. They were very dark eyes in a big tanned face, with possibly a trace of friendliness or amusement in them. She wanted to cry out but the child continued to press down on the lid and to keep her face utterly impassive as seconds moved on and the animal continued to die.

"Smile!" said Tommy Thompson more sharply, as the cat's hind feet ceased to churn against the lid.

"Smile!"

Then the big brown face came very close to Hilda's and, while crying inside, she still managed to make her lips crimp up a bit at the corners. She had the sense of an invisible photograph being taken.

"*Smile!*"

On the front wall of the suburban house which I eventually reached alone, a small brass plaque was soft, dented and rosy after a century and a half of fiercely house-proud Lancastrian polishing. In curling, faintly archaizing script it said ROMOLA HOUSE, and I was truly amused by the name.

Romola House is a modest welcoming 'private hotel' set in a row of rosy brick villas (some Gothic in fancy and others Italianate) blurred by mature trees on an airy ridge at the very edge of Preston. Fresh off the early Glasgow train that morning, I also discovered, under fluttering pink cherry trees half a mile from the house, a small concealed tunnel – the lovely presence of a railway which always seemed to say I could go home soon. At that moment, a local train slowed and then quietly hummed on over the remaining mile to Preston station. Romola House is partly bounded by a high brick wall – a good, venerable wall for growing things against, and which indicated that many years before, this neighbourhood had been a place of minor English consequence. Inside it, the garden had the sweetly curving remains of mid-Victorian flowerbeds, now as genteel as paper-lace doilies and still defined here and there by the brown pointed teeth of old glazed edging tiles. Up close to the front door (where a brass-set bell had been abandoned), one of the beds, in a long-forgotten way, had recently been pressed with big white sea shells beneath the forget-me-nots.

Mrs Rowe turned out to be a slender, active woman in her early fifties, with fluffy faded hair elegantly shaped and flicked up by a hairdresser. She smiled as she opened the door and then, rather alarmingly, bent forwards deeply from the waist. Behind pink fluffy mules and tan nylon ankles, she was trying to restrain the rummaging scuffle of a big Alsatian dog.

Since that bitter mauling day in Preston cemetery when June Thompson and I had ventured out alone and she seemed to my conventional eyes and ears to have expressed for the first time something akin to real emotion – a kind of sardonic contempt – I had wanted to speak to her alone in warmth and peace, away from what I supposed to be the restraining influence of her own home. When I was with Mrs Thompson I liked her and, of course, sympathized with her always, but as the point in their story was reached at which Tommy Thompson added sexual abuse of the children to the existing torment of his family, quite frankly I wanted to see how June's version of events tallied with that of her mother. Mrs Thompson, with all her physical frailties, was one of life's great survivors, and I was beginning to resent the way she always seemed to be the principal fount of memory and moral interpretation in the family.

Young Hilda Thompson would never agree to see me alone. She was still rather depressed and, although keen to tell her story, usually felt inadequate to cope with questions because of her damaged memory. That left June, who had somehow clung on to her sanity but only by some aptitude for driving down memories of the very worst that had happened to her.

Some time possibly in 1964, when she would have been twelve, she had been raped by her father and then used by him two or three times a week (particularly in the summer) until the age of thirty-six. This was not, I felt, the kind of background that could be examined when squared up in the usual way – interviewer to subject – in a pleasing restaurant or bar. Nor could I anticipate how long such an interview might take – a few days or a week possibly – and at £90 a night, the swagged polyester grandeur of Preston's only business hotel was out of the question. In any case, it was a terrible system-built monolith of a place overlooking a stretch of motorway. Then, for light relief on the other side, lay the huge bush-hammered concrete cushions of Preston's 1960s, award-winning bus station. The nightly sum quoted at Romola House sounded all right, but in a bed-and-breakfast hotel, where guests are usually expected to clear out by 10 a.m. each day at the latest, I realized that to interview June there for a few hours each day was going to require some kind of landlady's dispensation.

Over the line from Glasgow, Mrs Rowe's voice had been pliably understanding but not untinged with the sharpness of the professional landlady. Preston has no major theatre and, unlike many other bigger provincial towns, I supposed there was no hidden web of cheap lodgings in which landladies expected true peace and quiet only between the professional stage hours of 6 p.m. and midnight.

"I know you probably like guests to depart no later than 10 in the morning of each day . . ."

"As a *business lady*, you'll be wanting to be gone by then."

"I – I'm not exactly a business lady *as such*."

Then, without mentioning the shut-down, turn-off word 'journalist', I tried to explain the remaining and perfectly true things about needing to stay in Preston to speak to a lady – a very-nice, long-suffering lady – "Who's had a lot of trouble in her life and she wants to speak to me about it privately."

I could hear from the weighed-up silence at the other end of the line that Mrs Rowe was more intrigued than repelled.

"Is she a *local lady*?"

"She's lived with her mother and sister in Preston for more than twenty years! If my room could have two armchairs in it – just for a few hours each morning. I'd be happy to pay you more for the inconvenience . . ."

In the end Mrs Rowe was sharp and fair, and I liked her.

"No. That's all right. As long as I can have the room by 12.30."

And then, whether June Thompson had anything to say that might turn out to be emotionally revealing or not, at least a quiet place in a strange town had been secured for as long as it might take.

That morning, I left the Dillon's carrier bag which had my papers, toilet bag, the stupid black tape-recorder and a long nightdress in it, and went off in a taxi to collect June from her home. As spaghetti junction flies, the Thompsons' maisonette was over on the far side of town and I felt it would be wrong to ask her to hunt out my obscure hotel on the bus. But now the other practical complication of the day occurred to me.

Only a few years before, the most unflattering photographs of the Thompson sisters had been plastered all over the national tabloids and the *Lancashire Evening Post*, and I knew that in Preston sympathies were still occasionally divided about these two self-confessed murderers who, because of the harshness of their lives, had been rather stunningly 'let off' with only a couple of years' probation.

"Aye. They had hard lives," a young solicitor's clerk had said to me one day when I was hovering round the Georgian legal offices, mainly concentrated in Preston's elegant Winckley Square. "They had hard lives all right, but it was still cold-blooded murder."

In offices, shops or when I was just asking directions in the street, the people in Preston had an alert, bright friendliness, but I am far from being the first stranger in that town to have noticed that, beneath it all, Preston can be a curiously harsh place. Perhaps foolishly, I was now rather apprehensive that Mrs Rowe, landlady of Romola House, might instantly recognize June Thompson and possibly dispatch us both from her house. For some reason, the confidential voice of nice, dancing Phyllis Entwistle played on and off in my head – "We didn't want *undesirables*." Apart from the annoyance of losing a useful place in which to interview a tragically elusive person alone, I myself would not care if Mrs Rowe kicked us out. But I was worried that June, still living a life of abnormal seclusion, might be offered one more jot of unpleasantness.

There is nothing very novel about the entrance hall of Romola House. Like all English 'private hotels', the walls had been given their annual bleak coat of pastel emulsion for the approaching summer season and, against one, a narrow polished table bore a scattering of radio-taxi cards, a small bowl of pink cloth flowers and some colourful Lancashire tourist brochures. But that morning, to my surprise, neatly dressed in navy blue and with her hair specially trimmed for the occasion, June Thompson lingered around in the hall, looking about in wonder while, sure enough, Mrs Rowe advanced swiftly and curiously from a kitchen at the back. Smiling brightly – "Hello, Mrs Rowe! Here we are . . ." – I blushed with embarrassment in a totally trashy way, while inwardly willing June to move on, quickly, up the stairs.

Mrs Rowe was a kind enough woman, with the true conservative's respect for private suffering, particularly in women, but as if winding in the lead of an invisible Hoover, she stayed vaguely occupying herself at the foot of the stairs, and behind her eyes I could see a mind trying to riffle back in time as slowly and overtly as the thumb on a card index.

"We'll just have our little chat now, Mrs Rowe, and leave you in peace by 12.30."

But pausing on the stairs of Romola House, Preston (room with television, shower and bath on request, £15–£30 per night), June Thompson turned full-face in perfect innocence and said very happily, as if a new and glamorous world had been suddenly opened up to her, "Alex . . . Is this a hotel?"

The biggest piece of furniture in my room was a formidable light-wood dressing table, dotted about with beige tatted mats. Its huge swing-mirror was neither heart-shaped nor kidney-shaped, but had some amoeba-like form of its own. In the usual way of suburban 'master' bedrooms, all this had been carefully placed in front of the window to block the maximum light. Mrs Rowe had been as good as her word and close by she had set out two easy chairs, one in brown Rexine with a beige embroidered cushion on it. Almost reverently taking this seat, June continued to look round the room with immense pleasure – at walls emulsioned white over swirls of textured wallpaper, at the huge TV set at the foot of the bed and at the carpet of soppy 'old rose' pink (which, I knew from experience, was going to feel faintly sticky underfoot when I walked on it barefoot that night). Then, over on the far wall, stood a small wicker table sprayed green and gold, where I was now making instant coffee from sachets on a tray.

"Alex, are all hotels like this one?" June asked, apparently lost in happiness on the other side of the room.

"Thousands of small hotels in England are like this," I said, keeping an eye on the smart, new plastic jug-kettle, which was spilling up to a boil. "But more expensive hotels have different things in them. You know – posher furniture or a bigger bath, and more space."

Then, as I answered questions about price, location and what hotels were like abroad, my own thoughts moved at random over things that June, although my age, had never seen – marble floors, hidden courtyards with the secret splash of fountains in them, long heavy shutters that suddenly opened back the roar of foreign traffic in places like Naples, Munich or Seville, and then, back in the days of Uncle Erich Honecker and the GDR, came that system-built 1960s hotel in Dresden where I had first happily discovered I was pregnant.

June was enjoying herself so much that when I eventually gave her the genteel cup and saucer of instant coffee, I scarcely had the heart to try to draw matters round to the question of her lost childhood. Just like a child, severely dressed in a navy-blue school uniform and with a plain scrubbed face, she was still utterly enchanted by her new surroundings and the things it now seemed, in a strange reversal of roles, that I could tell her. I gathered that apart from a few months on remand with her sister Hilda in 1988, immediately after the murder, she had never spent a night away from home – no package holiday, no bed-and-breakfast by the seaside, not even *one night* away from Tommy Thompson's grim domain.

"June," I said eventually. "If you would rather not talk about your childhood, we don't have to, you know."

But then she sat up all alert, hands clasped neatly on her lap, knees and feet very properly together, as if I had suddenly drawn her back to school, or to a court of law.

"That's all right," she said in her small, dry, remote voice, and I felt sorry to see that her pleasure in the day had gone.

"June –" I began, "when you were little, can you remember any of the times when you first began to feel really frightened of your father?"

And, somewhat reluctantly, we moved on from there.

During the Thompson sisters' early school days, Tommy Thompson seems to have been fairly measured in the way he hit his young daughters. Perhaps he was conscious of his own physical strength and was afraid of damaging small children so severely that he would be up on a charge of murder. In the late 1950s in Lancashire, murder was taken rather seriously and I could just see Tommy relishing the gossip in pubs on those special days when murderers were hanged. I asked June how and where her father had hit her at that time. Having experienced violence on a terrifying scale for almost forty years, she merely said – almost airily – in that small remote voice, "Oh, nothing too bad at that time – just big hard slaps round the face."

Tommy terrorized the children by beating their mother in front of them, almost daily. Every two or three days, Hilda Thompson would be knocked to the ground by a punch on the side of the head and kicked in the stomach. Then came the thing they all feared most – the moment when Tommy would pause and deliberately sit down to put on a pair of hard outdoor shoes, specially kept for the purpose of kicking Hilda Thompson on the shins until she wanted to die with pain.

"Have you seen Mum's leg?" June asked.

I recalled that one day Mrs Thompson had indeed modestly raised a few inches of skirt to show me her right shin, permanently clotted with big brown blisters.

"The marks are still there," said June, "all this time after."

Cowering in one corner of the cold, grey living room while their mother curled up on the floor, crying for mercy only a few feet away, the children soon learned that any 'bad behaviour' on their part would cause this to happen to their mother. She was their only source of love and protection and the two little girls tried to deflect attention from themselves by never moving as much as a facial muscle. During these attacks, they learned to bide their time in 'frozen watchfulness'.

Tommy Thompson was confident that his wife would never

attempt to involve the outside world again. She had tried to escape from him once and had failed. Even if she had tried once more, I could see now, that in the early 1960s there was little that the outside world seemed able or willing to do.

Although June and Hilda were glad every morning to escape to school, both children were stultified by thoughts of what Tommy might do to their mother while they were away. Stretched out on wires of high anxiety, they moved very little about the classroom, found it hard to concentrate and, as the chalky light in the room moved round to the time when the first morning break seemed like yesterday, the children were torn by ambivalence as home-time approached. They wanted to see if their mother was all right – but they did not want to go home. Of the three Thompson women, 'young Hilda' was always the one who seemed least able to speak or write about her experiences. But at some point even she had committed this memory of early school-days to paper:

I think I was a poor learner because of dad's temper at home. When we were at school we were always thinking about Mum.

June wrote more fully:

I couldn't concentrate on lessons at school because my mind kept going back, thinking how bad Dad was with us & strict & how Mum would manage to cope with him during the day.

Immediately after school, when the painful ringing of the brass handbell sent them scattering out across the yard, the Thompson sisters scanned the school wall in panic for a glimpse of that one face, embedded somewhere in the row of other mothers' faces. But when their mother appeared, smiling as usual, lightly passing the time of day with other grown-ups at the school gate, she always made it look as if they – the Thompsons – were the most normal and happy family in Chorley. As they grew a little, the children began to look carefully over their mother for any marks which might indicate what Tommy had done to her during the course of the day.

Sometimes, as they all three walked reluctantly homewards, June and Hilda noted with silent anxiety new bruises on her shins, or even a glossily rising mound of a black eye which had not been there in the morning. With a child's keen but simple sense of justice, all that little June and Hilda could say about this anxious afternoon scanning of their mother for injuries was: "*It wasn't fair*."

As with most young children who are secretly and severely abused at home, the young Thompson sisters gradually developed two lives. Like their mother, they were obliged to learn the art of lightly retaining 'normal' relations with the outside world while also keeping a clear distance from it. At school, this eventually took the form of always finding neat explanations for not playing with friendly classmates after school hours in the way that most ordinary children love to do. To me, this fobbing off schoolfriends with light, vague excuses marks the beginning of the Thompson sisters' own personal dissembling with the outside world, until their 'outer' and 'inner' lives eventually imploded in early middle age in 1988 with the murder of their father.

In June's case, the names of her schoolfriends remain indelibly printed on her memory. They are the sunny, simple, upright names of first friends – Ann Warne, Patricia Robinson and Margery Moore – and, over them, June exuded a remote kind of regret.

"I don't think I will ever forget those names," she said (and I certainly hung back from the old adage that we choose our friends but not our family).

June felt bitter and, I think, still amazed by those schoolfriends – that with all her hidden difficulties and sense of personal worthlessness, they had seen something in her that her own family could not see. Other children had valued her and wanted her company. There was love and regret for the long-ago path of simple friendship, which in gregarious small-town Lancashire life she had not been able to take.

"A lot of times they would say, 'Why don't you come over to our house tonight?'"

"And I suppose Tommy wouldn't let you go – was that it?"

"I think they just thought at first that I wouldn't go anywhere without Hilda."

Then these same friends – nice Ann Warne, Patricia Robinson and Margery Moore – had plied her again. Younger children in a family often find it harder to make friends and tend to rely more on elder siblings for company. Little Hilda was now also included in the endless invitations.

"They always said, 'Bring Hilda with you as well', but I always had to tell them the same story . . . That we don't like going anywhere at night and that we have each other to be with at home."

As usual in speech, June always referred to her father as 'He', drawn out to *ee* with a mildly contemptuous emphasis.

"The truth was that *ee* wouldn't let us go anywhere out of the house – only if *ee* wanted anything from the shop nearby home for himself."

Then she added, neither miserable nor happy but high up on some objective plane, as if her past life had been that of a stranger, "They must have thought I was a funny sort of friend at times."

What seemed centuries ago – the beautiful day when I had climbed the steeply winding path up to Clitheroe Castle and then sat with the sound archivist, Andrew Schofield, among the yellow lozenges of light in his medieval office – I had glanced through some pages of a great *English Dialect Dictionary*, an old eight-volume work of no small fascination. For some reason, my eye had fallen on the word "tup". There had been no fewer than fifteen principal definitions of "tup" ("a push, a butt with the head"). Now that word came up again, as June Thompson described the ways that Tommy felt able to hit her more confidently as she grew in height and strength, and was dragooned into helping him with endless DIY work.

"When we were doing jobs about the house, if we didn't pass something – a screw or a bit of wood – just when he needed it, he would tup us."

"Tup you?" I said rather vaguely.

"Of rams," the dictionary ran on, "to cover the ewe."

"Yes, you know – he would tup me on the head."

Then came "tuppin" ("to butt as a ram") and, more romantically, "to tup and lamb" ("to live together in conjugal amity").

Then I thought of the times when little June, standing taller now in a skimpy tweed skirt and jumble-sale jumper and trying nimbly to assist Tommy Thompson in his DIY endeavours, would, without word or warning, suddenly receive a vulgar blow on the side of the head from his hard nut. June had become his preferred DIY assistant, eventually supplanting her mother. It was in these tedious intricacies of house improvement that I suddenly began to sense how June had emerged as Tommy Thompson's new 'wife'.

One thing I had gleaned from the stack of brand-new American child-abuse books which were stacked gloomily round the walls of my little room back in Glasgow is that extreme force – rape – in which a female child is totally unprepared for the first sexual assault seems only to occur in a comparatively small proportion of child-abuse cases. It is claimed by some American experts that most acts of incest perpetrated by fathers initially involve psychological coercion without physical force. It seems that most abusing fathers lead slowly up to the first sexual act with a daughter in the way that a new suitor pays court to an adult woman. This slow preparation of the daughter takes two forms. There is 'evolved incest', in which a father pays special attention (usually to his elder daughter) over a long period of time, singling her out as his apparent 'favourite' and making increasingly intimate sexual advances as time passes. Other fathers embark on incest another way – by 'devious behaviour', which usually involves the father molesting his daughter while she is asleep. She wakes from time to time to find the big face and touching hand of some adult presence, quietly breathing beside her in the dark.

June believed that some time in 1964 she had simply been taken upstairs and raped without warning. Tommy Thompson was an extremely disordered and sadistic man, and I felt that it would have been perfectly in character for him to have brutally raped June one day – that she fell within that supposed minority of children who, within the family, are sexually seized out of the blue by no means other than physical force. But, on the other hand, I felt that Tommy Thompson himself may have *believed* that he had prepared June in some way for this terrible event (not that psychological 'preparation' makes incest any easier for its victims to bear).

That morning, as we edged forward in time over cups of instant coffee at Romola House, I wondered if June and I might discover any long-forgotten but quietly inevitable steps by which Tommy Thompson, to use the child-abuse jargon, had 'groomed' her for the first sexual act.

June never willingly referred to her father as 'Dad', because she had a perfectly clear idea of the kind of man who deserves that name. He was always "*ee*", or sometimes simply "Tommy", as if he were a shady grown-up brother or some kind of big disordered child. From first to last, her memories of him always seemed to be meshed with DIY work or home improvement, as he drove them all on in oppressive isolation towards some leisured property-owning ideal.

"He seems to have spent a lot of his life doing DIY jobs, doesn't he, June?" I said, and, with her usual remoteness, she agreed.

"It was always as if he was wanting to change something – like, say, a couch. One day he might suddenly want to saw the arms off it . . . It was always like he was spoiling the look of things. Nothing ever seemed to suit him really."

Although Tommy had always obsessively built wooden shelving in upstairs 'military' storerooms wherever they went, I had not realized that he had compulsively altered furniture as well.

"When he was altering furniture, can you remember what else he liked to do?"

June almost sighed at the boredom of it all. "Well, for instance – like he suddenly decided to put two sets of drawers together. They were supposed to be separate but he would take the legs off one and screw them together to make one complete tall chest."

"And I suppose it didn't look very nice?"

"That's right. They weren't the same – they didn't match, you know – but it didn't matter to *im. Ee* never asked us, 'Well, what do you think about that?'"

And then I had a picture of a home not only completely shut off from the outside world but where, in a surreal way, like the crazy magnifications of fairground mirrors, even the furniture was stacked about, crudely nailed together in the random distortions of a dream.

"June," I finally ventured, sensing that her interest was stretched rather thin on the subject of Tommy's practical obsessions, "do you know whether Tommy ever trained with a builder as a carpenter or something? He used to make a lot of shelves, didn't he?"

"We always had to have a room upstairs to keep 'spare items' in. But *ee* was never the main man in any job. With *im* it always seemed to be like there was a lot to every job – that he found it difficult."

By the time she was ten or eleven, all that June was conscious of at home, apart from Tommy's almost 'normal' violence to them and to their animals, was the need to assist him perfectly. She steadied ladders when he was mending the guttering and stood about for hours on end, holding this or that.

"I could have passed water many a time, but I never dared to ask him if I could go."

Like a surgeon's assistant, trained to foresee the progress of any procedure, June tried to hand him a tool in the nick of time to avoid (when his hands were full) being instantly "tupped" on the side of the head. Beneath her dark hair, the bruises would not show next day at school.

Looking in on the family from the outside, I began to notice the slow swapping of roles between mother and elder daughter which classically takes place in an incestuous family in which the father rather than the mother or a cohabitee is the abuser. As in the inevitable winding, facing, passing and handing on in the progress of an invisible reel, June was becoming (at the age of ten or eleven or so) the principal woman in the family. With just one look, she could now signal to her sister when she was on the verge of putting a domestic foot wrong and she helped to clean up her mother after a beating when Tommy had finally cleared off to the pub. As in Mrs Thompson's early days of marriage, June too was now painfully alert to any tiny domestic detail that might 'trigger' her father's violence. Quite automatically, when all else had failed, the Thompson sisters now glided to each side of their mother when Tommy began to punch her. The idea was to stop Mrs Thompson from injuring herself further by falling backwards or sideways under Tommy's blows. Tommy Thompson no longer needed to yell (as he had done during the caravan days in Cuerden Park when his daughters were mere infants), "Stand still when I'm hitting ye, ye thick bitch!"

Around the same age – ten or eleven – June became more conscious (in whatever house they occupied) of being increasingly secluded with her father in the woody, creosoted twilight of Tommy's garden shed. As he glowered over some piece of work in a vice and she stood silently beside him, she was conscious of his DIY tools, so perfectly arranged, cleaned, greased and hung above him in the shadows he retired to, taking her with him. It was her job to clean up the tools when he had finished for the day and she ached with fear at their appropriateness to a job.

As if he always needed to emulate his mother, Tommy Thompson also increasingly preferred to keep control of the cooking for the household. In the manner of some elderly, genteel English bachelors who attempt to cook for themselves and their rare guests using austere methods remembered from woman's domain in the past – involving ancient aluminium saucepans and chipped enamel dishes – Tommy too, in a rather bizarre way, liked to retire to the shed to chop bones for broth. Vegetables were always sliced in the kitchen but bones went out to the shed.

Tommy Thompson had a big steel knife of spiteful sharpness and it was with this that all vegetables had to be cut – just so. As if performing some heroic act of surgery, his concentration on this 'cutting up' was intense. The blade was always drawn across carrots, onions and potatoes at exactly the same angle, the pieces falling like coins always to the same thickness. Once, when June had ventured into the kitchen and passed a little too close to him, even with her accustomed cat-like silence, Tommy had sensed the very suspension of her breath, spun round with a hiss of rage and then she felt the imposing line of the blade held very gently across her throat.

"*Stay away!*" he said through clenched teeth. "*Knives are dangerous.*"

Then came the part of soup-making which Tommy seemed to delight in most – the chopping up of big knuckle bones to enrich the pan with succulently churning blood and marrow.

That day, when she was ten or eleven or so, Tommy had taken June out to the shed with a parcel of marrow bones as if he were about to initiate her in some art so pleasurable that he preferred an almost erotic seclusion. In the shadows of the shed he laid out on his work-bench a handsome, creamy bone with red remnants of tattered flesh still hanging from it. The chopping block, set on his work-bench, was a pleasingly dense block of wood with a faint dip in the centre from half a century of blows. Always conscious of the severe greased saws, chisels, screwdrivers, metal cramps and trowels which hung above them in such an orderly way, the little girl now understood that this time her job was to steady the big knobbly end of the bone while her father steadied the other. Then, as if to demonstrate his prowess and exactitude, the small, heavy axe which Tommy seemed to take especial delight in using crashed down neatly and heavily along the shaft of the bone, and she sensed his pleasure in the work. When the bone-chopping was done, Tommy gathered up the pieces for soup. June's job was simply to collect on to a piece of newspaper the small chips and splinters of bone which had flown off the dark perimeters of the block. They were in her hair, stuck to the wool of her cardigan and sometimes spattered the sparkling clean window of the shed. With a child's sharp eyes, June did not miss any, and she wiped up neatly, because Tommy's discovery of just one fragment could wreak terrible vengeance on them all.

When the bones were smaller, June did not have to hold them but concentrated instead on steadying the wooden chopping block itself.

"I had to hold it down – you know, to stop the board flirting."

"Flirting" struck me as an extraordinary but good word to choose when describing the quick, random movement of a chopping board moving under what must have been the truly savage blows of a cook's axe.

"Flirting," June explained again in perfect innocence. "Sometimes, the board was *moving*."

June had reached the age when she was able to stand slightly apart from her parents. She was becoming old enough to pass judgement on them. On that Saturday morning when Tommy had made such a to-do about making a bit of soup, she had permitted herself to glance up at him as he chopped the bones. Despite all that he had already done with his fists, head and feet to her mother, her sister and herself, June had been able to look at him for the first time from the strangely detached viewpoint of an emergent woman – he was a pathetic lump of a crazy who, despite all his swagger and violence, felt compelled to cook like an old woman.

As June haltingly described all this as we sat in my hotel room, I suddenly felt her mood lighten. From sheer nervousness and anxiety, I burst out laughing.

"I'm not laughing at *you*, June," I said quickly, appalled that my laughter was quite inappropriate. But I knew that her own mood had provoked it.

"Knuckle bones were the most dangerous – *ee* would have to have four goes of an axe at those. That knife he used to cut the vegetables was called a 'devil knife'. It were a devil 'n' all if he were holding it."

Then, to my relief, June laughed too – quite openly and genuinely. She had small white teeth like those in a cat's mouth and it was the first time I had ever seen her laugh in almost two years of pretty assiduous visits. I then supposed that at this point in her relationship with Tommy, his emotional hold over her had been loosening. She had begun to see him merely as a pathetic grotesque in control of nothing, including himself. But harking back, she also captured perfectly the child's gift of still desperately trying to love the better parts of a bad parent when she added, "Sometimes I used to think he was a funny old thing – not that bad really, in his own way. If he hadn't have been that bad with us – always hitting and thumping us, a lot of this would be laughable."

Retiring to her normal sardonic state, June then went on to make a joke.

"*Ee* was always supposed to have a bad back, but it never seemed to bother him when he were throwing us at wall."

Chopping bones in the tarry twilight of the shed became just another regular job that June always did with Tommy. One day (she could not remember in which year) she was out in the bone-chopping shed with her father and, always wary of that sudden crash down from his head, she held the end of the knuckle bone so carefully. Then Tommy began to explain something to her in a voice which seemed kinder and even calmly reasonable, in the way that teachers talked to her at school.

"Ye know I have sex with your Mam, June?"

She said nothing and just held on tightly to the bone, because she both knew and did not know exactly what "sex" was.

"Well, now I want it with you as well."

Tommy did not seem so intent on smashing up the bones that time and, in the shadows of the shed, June began to feel, in some new form, the grey pressing down which happened inside her when she was waiting for punishment.

I was so deeply shocked by what he said. I wanted to say (no never) but I was too afraid of him to say it.

So in a bright, ameliorating way, as she continued to steady the marrow bone, June just said, "Do I have to, Dad? I don't want to do it and it's wrong."

Then the axe flew down from the air, the shell-like bits of bone flew up and in a rising bout of anger he put his face very close to hers and said, "Whatever I tell you to do, *you do it*, whether you like it or not. And if anybody gets to know anything at all about what goes on in this house, it doesn't matter who or what position they're in, I'll shoot the lot of ye."

On a day when he had taken June and Hilda out shopping in Chorley, Tommy had bought a shotgun, speaking very nicely and calmly in the way he kept for 'outside' people.

"Aye, it's just for a bit of clay-pigeon shooting."

Beyond the counter in a dark, funny kind of shop full of glass cases and linked with chains, there had been the blur of men's agreeing voices. Then, as he had produced the money, a big smile of approval came from the other side of the counter.

"Two nice little lasses ye've got there, Tommy."

After that, a brown cardboard box of cartridges and the big shotgun which broke into two were kept upstairs in the store-room for "spare items".

After that time in the shed when Tommy first verbally broached the subject of sexual intercourse with June, perhaps weeks or months had passed. June continued to help her father as usual and, although his words were no longer so vivid, they had sunk down into her and she stored them against some other time. When she was enjoying something at school and there was a kind of happy lightness in the air, she would be suddenly thrown down again to her desk with the knowledge, like a blow on the back of the head, that some time – perhaps tonight when she got home from school, or during the two terrible days called "the weekend", which lasted for what seemed the slow passing of years – something very bad was going to happen to her and there was nobody at all to stop it.

I couldn't understand why he would put me through such a terrible thing as to have sex with me when, if any boy gave me a second look or would speak to me, he would get angry . . . From the day he told me he was going to have sex with me, I felt so Frightened and worried. I knew I couldn't turn to anyone for help. I didn't know how I was going to cope with it when it happens.

Slowly, June was tuned up to a pitch of excruciating anxiety. She began to watch closely the movements of the family in the house – who was in what room and when – knowing that for as long as her mother and Hilda were still about the place, perhaps 'It' (whatever 'It' was going to be) could not happen.

The only thing that Tommy Thompson read was the *Lancashire Evening Post*. No women's magazines were allowed in the house and certainly no books. In the manner of an unenlightened Victorian paterfamilias censoring the reading matter of his 'angels in the house', Tommy Thompson would sometimes shake out the evening paper and say, "I'll tell you anything ye need to know."

One thing he scanned the local paper for was news of church jumble sales. Although he often bought new clothes for himself and was smartly turned out, jumble sales were the only source of clothing for his wife and daughters. New school uniforms were the exception, because he did not want any unwelcome attention drawn to the girls at school. Naturally slim and delicate, and with a good eye for the cut, texture and hang of a garment, Hilda Thompson managed on pence to remain curiously chic, always keeping up appearances by bleaching and setting her own hair with Amami lotion on small plastic rollers. Outside the house, lipstick restored a dash of carnal authority to her face. On a Friday or Saturday, Tommy would usually let all three of them go to a jumble sale. To appease him, Mrs Thompson would first rummage round to buy some pleasing trifle for him and then they had an hour and a pound or so at their own disposal. Back home, the Thompson women would try on their new purchases for Tommy as he lay pasha-like on the downstairs bed to pronounce whether, to his eye, their new clothes became them or not. If Tommy did not like a particular second-hand blouse, skirt or jacket, they all knew well enough never to wear it in his presence again.

June could not remember what day it was but it was summer and she was aged twelve, thirteen or thereabouts, when, rather unusually, Tommy sent the two Hildas off to a jumble sale on their own. Leaving his presence, getting out of the house without him, was always an overwhelming relief, but almost as soon as the front door had closed, June knew that this time her moment had come. In his usual curt way, Tommy told his daughter quite literally, "I want you upstairs."

The stairs were narrow, steep and dark, almost a vertical tunnel. At the top of them, on the small, square landing, June paused uncertainly. Immediately before her was a lavatory, stifling with a near-poisonous block of artificial pine. To her right was the room with the three-quarters bed that she still shared with her sister, Hilda. Its only other furnishing was a crude 'wardrobe' knocked together by Tommy himself, with a dragging jumble-sale curtain hung at the front. This room was always cold and dank. On winter nights, when the young sisters held each other for warmth, their clothes in the wardrobe slowly turned green with mildew. To June's left was Tommy's strange storeroom, scented more pleasingly with untreated timber shelving – yards and yards of it – which she had again helped Tommy to construct. Silhouetted against the banal daylight of the street was all the stuff of siege – tins of food with fading labels, tools, ropes, axes, plastic vats of paraffin and, of course, the gun.

"He was always worried about the weight of it all," June explained. "That it might crash down to the room below."

This time, Tommy was not aiming for the military stores. Advancing up the stairs behind her, slowly as if he carried a quiet weight, he did not abruptly signal her into the storeroom as usual, but right – to her own bed.

"Take your bottom clothes off," he said, in the manner of a PT teacher at school, "and then lie down on the bed."

When he sat down on the edge of the bed to untie his shoe-laces – the route and impediment to a man removing his trousers – June felt the bed strangely restive around her with his weight.

"Now, keep your eyes closed. Don't open them till I say so."

"No, Dad. No! It's wrong!"

"*The more you struggle, the worse it'll be.*"

And then, after a kind of dry butting, the child screamed as she felt a deep, hollow pain.

When June Thompson knew that she was still alone in the house with Tommy but all was quiet, she slowly got up from the bed and walked, dazed, to the landing with a funny feeling of being open and hurt ("*I was crying my eyes out*").

"The first times, it seemed to last a long time, but after that, it seemed to be over quite quickly."

With a bit of hard, shiny paper which would not absorb water and which had a little bright green word printed across each corner, she tried to clean up some kind of running, sticky mess. Eventually, when the child descended the steep, narrow stairs on shaky legs, her father was just lying on the big downstairs bed as usual, watching television. Football was on and, as she crept into the room, Tommy barely gave her a glance. On the thick, blue-green screen, men scurried in clouds after the random bob of a ball, with mad roars coming up in the background. When Tommy eventually gave her a longer look, it was as if nothing out of the ordinary had happened at all. "Crying inside", where the tears would not show, June now knew what 'It' was, and that 'It' was going to happen again and again far into the tunnel of the future, and all she could do was watch and wait. Silently sitting down at the perimeter of the room, robbed and stolen from, all she wanted was for her mother to come home. But for the sake of her mother and little Hilda, she hoped she would not cry out when she saw them.

"And I suppose," I said, "that after that . . ."

"Like, before it happened, when he used to get bad-tempered chopping bones in the shed, at least I thought – well, in other ways, he's probably OK at heart, you know. But then, with that happening – that just . . ."

Another long silence fell.

"That just . . .?"

"That wiped it out. There was no way anybody can say he is good to you and do that to you, you know . . ."

It had taken us about three hours, broken by endless cups of instant coffee, to get round to this point and the atmosphere in my hotel room was pretty lowered. In the English way, there seemed really nothing else to do but to make yet another cup and, downstairs, I could feel Mrs Rowe's agitation that the bed-and-breakfast room was not being "vacated". But as I made the coffee, or perhaps it was tea this time, June began to glance again with interest through the open door at the side of my room which merely contained the shower, loo and wash-basin. It was the kind of wash-basin which always seemed to contain one curving hair of a colour and length that was probably not one's own.

"It's just a little bathroom, June," I said. "I don't like showers myself. I'm going to ask the landlady if I can have a bath tonight instead."

It was almost 1 p.m. and I knew that we must very soon get out of the room.

"Look," I said. "After all this – we've both worked so hard this morning – I think we'll go and have a really good lunch."

I didn't know much about restaurants in Preston, but there was a passable place I had been in once near June's former solicitors in Winckley Square. It was a lunch-time haunt of young solicitors and accountants. One day, chawing through a plateful of vegetarian stuff behind a shielding copy of the *Lancashire Evening Post*, I had realized that these people were the young northern professionals who had probably processed June and Hilda Thompson's 'paperwork' leading up to the trial at Liverpool Crown Court – to them, mere names in crude local circumstances. Tanned, swigging and guffawing, the young men's bodies had seemed quite artificially pushed back into the sober pinstriped suits of the Law, and the clever young women with whom they flirted had topped their slightly passé 'power suits' with sleek hair tied back in black-velvet Mozartian queues. Usually, I do not care for restaurants with pink neon handwriting on the outside saying 'The Inn On The Something', but it had taken credit cards. Not knowing June's taste in food, I also knew that it did safe things like big grilled steaks which looked OK or, failing that, chicken-and-mushroom pie.

Down in the hall of Romola House (which I was hoping quickly and discreetly to leave) Mrs Rowe suddenly darted out once more, as fast as her faded fluffy mules could carry her.

"We're just going out now, Mrs Rowe," I said brightly. "The armchairs were perfect. Thank you *so much*."

And if eyes could have photographed June Thompson's face in a Polaroid shoot of – fancy that! – hers did so.

Out we went, across the faltering Victorian garden, then right past the cherry-trees to the main road, on which I hoped a taxi might be hailed. Outdoors, June walked very quickly, precisely and firmly, and above the hum of traffic and dispersed impressions, I could barely take in what she was saying.

"Everything's new to us," she said. "You see, after 'It' happened –" and I was not quite sure whether she meant the rape or the murder – "It's like our life has only been going on for a few years."

Then she, aged thirty-nine and having earned good money as a skilled textile worker for almost twenty years, voiced a fear that drifted away like vapour on the air.

"Hilda and me, we've never been in a restaurant, Alex . . ."

The solitary librarian on late duty in Preston's Harris Museum was quietly plodding about, wearily returning large-scale maps and piles of books to their cases. That evening, on the big oak table where I had killed an hour or two tidying up my notes of the day while the squiggles were still fresh, someone had left out a stuffy-looking Victorian book with heavy marbled boards and yellowing pages which smelled faintly of vinegar. It had been written in the 1880s by some rambling antiquarian bore who, in the usual way, tells all and nothing in extreme detail. I was not looking forward much to spending a solitary evening at Romola House and, lingering on, my eye eventually fell on the words "Bannister Doll . . . Preston's most celebrated apparition". In the distance, the librarian was keeping his eye on the clock and me. I kept an eye on him and the book and, while making some show of gathering up my papers, I rapidly turned on.

In 1700 a man named Bannister had been governor of Preston's "House of Correction", a place of "harsh work, spare dyet and whipping in a building now a cotton mill". One day, Bannister's daughter had "confessed to him that she was with child" and, enraged at the shame he thought this would bring on the family name, he had beaten her to death. Only afterwards (and it was not clear whether he had been "taken up for it" or not) did the wretched man learn "that his daughter had been violated". The raped and murdered girl was still said to follow evening travellers, "apparently trying to convey some communication to them . . ." A polite pair of male hands then closed the book, tidying it into a pile and, looking down on me with a gentle bookworm face and tired grey eyes, the young librarian said at my elbow, "The library is closing now."

No "Bannister Doll" bobbing lightly beneath a white linen cap followed me back to the hotel that evening but I was suddenly taken aback by the presence of the deserted streets. The steely undertow of Preston always seems to rise up with the approach of darkness and, for some reason, I had always avoided staying overnight there before.

It was about three in the morning when, drawn up layer by layer from deep sleep, I became aware of a thin, grey wailing. At the foot of the bed, an occasional high-pitched tone came from the blank television screen because the comforting presence of Jeremy Paxman on *Newsnight* had long gone and, as I turned over, a copy of the *Tatler* and the books I always sleep with when alone slid with a thump to the floor. Quite unable to rise, I was conscious of the outer walls of the house becoming strangely defined as if a long, grey arm, bent at the elbow, was encompassing the corner of the building. Light through the open door of the bathroom still burned and then I realized that outside there was a terrible gale fiercely wrapping round the house as, some years before, there had been in the passing of the London hurricane. Sleep-sodden then, finding all lights fused and the children terrified, we had only discovered next morning in Gray's Inn Road that reliable municipal trees lay uprooted from forgotten beds of clay at the unusually silent roadside. The storm in Lancashire that night was so severe that next morning I learned that half the roof of a local girls' school had been completely lifted off in the night. Thoroughly rattled, I began to think of the Thompsons, now only a mile or two away on the other side of the town.

I have always admired eighteenth-century satirical prints and the foul accuracy of their cruelty. In one, quite wickedly, I could visualize Mrs Thompson – her thin hair possibly secured in pins to reinforce its bulk during sleep; first one and then the other hearing-aid disconnected but still containing within her fragile head the drizzle of tinnitus against the storm. Then would come the taking out of her teeth so that her mouth shrank back to a greyish hole. In her recurring nightmare, this was the hour when Tommy advanced on her in sleep and she had once prosaically called it "Mum's Dream", as if she were some other person entirely. As usual, June and Hilda had just shot Tommy and he was lying there on the downstairs bed, truly soaked in death. They all knew he was dead, but at night he seemed able to disengage himself from physical events and look down on his own leaking red body to scream to her, "*You – let them – kill me!*" Her punishment for not guarding his life would then begin again, shifting the scenes, just as her father's death had caused the floor and walls of her old stone childhood home in Chorley to fly away. *He tore down the curtains in the room and he pulled down the furniture on top of us*. As he had so often promised when things did not go his way, "*You'll all live Rock Bottom again! No electricity and no light!*". Often, in spite, he had chipped the handles off china mugs and said they would have to drink from rusty tin cans.

Sleep had departed from me in the middle of the night with that bright assurance which means it will not return. In the way that a photographer sometimes gets the best picture when a sitter thinks the formal session is over, I was still shocked by what June had casually revealed at lunch the previous day. Mrs Thompson too had *known*, long before it happened, what lay in store for her young daughter – she too had anticipated the rape.

"I didn't know how I was going to cope with it when it happened," June said, referring to Tommy's words in the bone-chopping shed. "As soon as I had the chance, I told Mum what he had said to me."

June had never tasted mushrooms before and the waitress was explaining to me that even though they were on the menu, for some reason the restaurant could not produce any that day.

"She felt so sorry for me," continued June. "She said, 'His temper and hitting us is bad enough but to demand *sex* from you as well!' She said, 'I've never once refused to have sex with him, even when I've got a bad headache or I've not been well.'"

"So, for quite a long time – probably in 1964 – your Mum knew that Tommy was going to rape you?"

As usual, June's point of view seemed to coincide totally with that of her mother.

"Mum *said* she wished she could do something to stop him, but she was just so frightened."

In an empty house on some terrible summer day in the 1960s, Tommy Thompson had calmly led his young daughter upstairs to rape her on her own bed. Later, when the child had been too profoundly shocked to resume crying and she had seized the moment to tell her mother, Hilda Thompson's reply had been, to my conventionally spirited ears, a shade too accepting: "I never thought he'd sink as low as this."

Then, after a bit of physical mopping up, life had simply gone on as before – one margarined slice of toast each before school and then Tommy had continued to rape June once or twice a week and almost always on Fridays. June had eventually become his new 'wife', with the two Hildas (one still sexually unassailed) held in reserve.

Like most women who have never experienced domestic violence of any kind, I was now full of resentment against Mrs Thompson herself. That night in the hotel room, as the storm continued to rage outside, I wanted to whizz back in time like one of the Furies in a slipstream of avenging Greek draperies to make these children's enemies my footstool. Next time when, over a desultory tea-table, Mrs Thompson was shushing, lisping and twinkling on about her previous life in old Lancashire with no small degree of charm, I wondered if I would be able to avoid rising above the chocolate-coated biscuits to shake her fragile shoulders and yell, "You stupid little woman! Even in Lancashire in 1964 incest was a *crime*!"

Why didn't you take June straight away to the police station and get a police surgeon to note the evidence while it was still fresh?" She was a monster of pathos.

Eventually, the clear light rattle of the first train of the day indicated that the storm outside had abated and, like most insomniacs, I briefly fell asleep at dawn.

There was pleasing normality in my room next day when June arrived and settled herself once more into the brown Rexine easy-chair. Again, she looked around the room with pleasure and seemed to be full of the experience of having been taken out to lunch the previous day. I was surprised that she still retained the old habit of keeping a diary – simple but assiduous diaries that Tommy had instructed her to begin writing sometime in 1970.

"I've written it all down," she said happily. "It was a very special day – something to remember."

Then, as I fiddled about with the plastic jug-kettle once more, filling it from the bathroom tap to make coffee, June drew a small white envelope from her bag.

Mrs Thompson genuinely loved writing and I had come to admire the apparently effortless way that she seemed able, in her own style, to pour out thoughts and memories, never giving the act of writing a second thought. As I had not seen her to speak to on this trip to Preston, I supposed it was just one of her usual friendly notes that I sometimes received at home – notes of the see-you-next-time variety. But this was turning out to be more than a note. In fact, it was a five-page letter.

Dear Alex, it began, *I have something I would like to tell you about the time we lived down Blackburn Row. June and Hilda must have been about eight and six at the time . . .*

Like a child exploring a Wendy House, June had wandered into the bathroom and, as I kept an eye on the distant corner of the room where the kettle was rumbling up to a boil, other words emerged.

. . . having an abortion in those days was out of the question . . . Tommy said that if I had the baby I would have to kill It (smother it). He decided he would give me an abortion . . .

For the first time in the researching of even this story, my head swam. I sat down and said to June, "Do you know what's in this letter?"

Remotely smiling and pleasant as usual, she emerged from the bathroom and merely said, "Mum told us a bit about it last night . . . She's never told anyone for thirty years."

In the throes of the previous night, when I had raged in judgement and contempt against Mrs Thompson for failing to protect her young daughter, never, in a thousand years, could I have suspected the utmost depths of her physical slavery to Tommy. Mrs Thompson had truly believed that Tommy would kill them all with the gun if she broke the silence of the household, because he had, by that time, already personally murdered her last child.

June watched as I finished reading the letter and then I folded it and rather shakily put it away in my handbag. Continuing to smile, her face now seemed to have a mild kind of triumph in it, as if to say – If you didn't know what we were up against all those years ago, try that.

Late one summer night in 1960 when June and Hilda were both apparently well settled into primary school, Tommy had come home rather more drunk than usual and, too fuddled to be bothered with the usual contraceptives, had forced himself on his wife. Three months later at a local clinic she had discovered she was pregnant.

> *I felt in a state of shock knowing Tommy's Temper – how he would react when I went home and told him. I knew he wouldn't want another baby & as my health was not bad at that time, having an abortion in those days was out of the question.*

In the way that an ordinary, quite reasonable man or woman often initially resents the insidious power of Nature to connect one casual and long-forgotten sexual act with a long-term result, Tommy Thompson was at first caught up in fury. Then he became surprisingly calm but adamant: "There's no way you're having *that* to keep."

Day by day, while his little eight-stone wife hovered about, sheltering something inside her like an animal or bird, Tommy considered what could be done. Smothering a new-born baby was easy and it was also a thing that could be readily explained: "Well, if you have it, you'll have to kill it."

But Hilda Thompson then thought of the agony of labour – "Going through all that" – and then being forced to put a pillow over the child's face while he stood by and watched to see that it was truly dead. She was terrified of labour, *having had such bad times before.*

Tommy bought a medical book – being a classic DIY man, he wanted to see "what was what". And now I realized why Mrs Thompson, who was not naturally given to reading, had also frequently, said that she "liked to read medical books".

"You've heard of what they call 'the cervix', Alex?" Mrs Thompson said. "Well, he had to find that."

Plastic was coming in in those days and one night Tommy brought home a bright-green plastic clothes-line, cut a bit off it and sharpened one end to a point.

"I knew I had to live and protect my children, June and Hilda."

I insisted on everything being clean with Dettol on his hands and everything. If I hadn't, I would not be alive today.

Over a stretch of three weeks, when little June and Hilda were safely out of the way at primary school, Mrs Thompson lay down on the Fablon'd kitchen table ("it was a lovely yellow Fablon that the children always called 'cheese'") and, seated between her drawn-up legs, Tommy Thompson stared into the biggest DIY job of his life.

I am a small-made woman . . .

and with no anaesthetic, the fear of haemorrhage, of the police and of visibly living children waiting, panic-stricken, to be picked up from school, she fixed her eyes merely on the kitchen tap.

Tommy Thompson knew how dreadfully wrong this operation could go, but if anything did go wrong, his wife would have to say that she had done it herself. In the eighteenth-century way of knowing how a woman can always plead her belly in court, he supposed that as long as she could continue to stand up afterwards, Hilda would be OK by the law. After the fifth attempt in three weeks, Tommy succeeded. There was surprisingly little bleeding and, after climbing the stairs bent double with fierce, griping pains, Mrs Thompson eventually found a tiny foetus floating in the lavatory pan.

It was a male baby, very very Tiny at that stage but Formed. Even the little fingers. It was DISTRESSING for me.

A GP on a house visit was shown the foetus, now captured

like a minnow in a clean jam-jar, and he prescribed tablets which made her head clang with loud bells, "like a fire engine". She took to her bed, but she got better and could continue to love June and Hilda.

Shortly afterwards it was Christmas, a time which Tommy loathed and never recognized at home. But this particular Christmas, when Chorley's two ancient markets twinkled with temptations beneath the lamps and the dark outside world was festive, Tommy bought the girls a present each on a whim. They were two stiff white bride dolls that the children briefly looked at but never cuddled.

"I tried to tell him they would be better off with a soft toy they could cuddle."

As in many families, the ghost of a lost child now floated between June Thompson and myself as we continued to sit rather quietly in the big front bedroom of Romola House.

"June," I said. "If you and Hilda had been boys, do you think life would have been any easier for you as children?"

June actually laughed at the idea.

"'If you were a son,' he used to say, 'I'd take me shirt off and get into that room with ye and beat the living daylights out of ye.'"

She thought for a moment about the brother whose existence she had only discovered the day before.

"He'd have had a hard life if he'd lived."

Then, thinking of Young Hilda, who sat at home in the daily shifts of continuing depression and the unrecoverable blanks of a shocked brain, she added rather strangely, "We're privileged, really, that we weren't sons."

That afternoon, I actually ran to Preston station, bag and all, simply to get away on the first train to Glasgow. The way trains run now, the one I should have missed was so late that I still caught it and, willing the familiar journey into speedy reverse: Preston–Lancaster–Carlisle–Oxenholme-in-the-Lake-District–Penrith–Motherwell, ending up in the muzak bagpipe welcome of big, open Glasgow Central, I eventually arrived home early. Back in the house, there was a blur of two-day-old stew, homework, tomato ketchup, dirty school socks, a word-processor chattering all by itself in a darkened room like mad teeth and spouse rather glad to see me.

Around 9 p.m., when the telephone rang, it was Mrs Thompson speaking from Preston with the perfect tact of a mother who knew my children would be nearing sleep.

"You got my letter, love?"

"Mrs Thompson," I said, "I don't know what to say to you – apart from the fact that I'm very, very sorry for all the terrible things that have happened to you."

"I've told no one for thirty years . . ." and when it came to the abortion, I knew that this time even her own daughters could not quite appreciate the horror of what had been done to her.

"You'll know, Alex – you'll look at it differently because you've already had children . . ."

Then, for the first time in my two-year knowledge of her, Mrs Thompson's voice dropped in a strange way that I had never heard before and she seemed to put her mouth very close to the receiver, speaking words like "look" and "book" with long *oos*, as in "daring to say *boo* to a *goose*". It was an odd phrase and one that seemed to cast me as some kind of unwilling exorcist.

"*When the book's finished – I'll be free of him!*"

7

Golden Rings

Although she had only seen them on big holiday posters in shop windows in Preston and sometimes on television, Young Hilda was concentrating with closed eyes on the outline of very dark palm trees. It was approaching dawn somewhere on a tropical island and the sky was just dark enough for her to see the last few stars. Raggy-headed, like upright dish-mops in the dark, the palm trees lined a cool white beach. Casting her mind back to a childhood trip to New Brighton (stuck out at the tip of the Wirral peninsula), she tried hard, as instructed, to re-create the taste in her mouth and nostrils of salt sea air, now aided by the sound of lapping waves which hushed, ran in and withdrew beneath idling seagulls somewhere deep inside her new Sony earphones.

Sometimes, when Hilda had been very young, her father had still attempted to do the things that most ordinary families take for granted, such as going on a simple trip to the seaside, because, despite everything, he had some idea of what ideal family life should be like. That summer morning when the jaunt had been undertaken and the ghost of industrial July was already baking the orange brick in their part of Chorley like a kiln, Mrs Thompson had tried to see to Tommy's forceful needs as usual – particularly coffee, because he would not drink tea out of a vacuum flask. Then she had cut sandwiches of some kind, economically wrapped in the waxed paper saved from a big sliced loaf. But once little June and Hilda had reached their destination – seen the sea in its vastness and freedom – they had gone wild, as most town children do – running, laughing and jumping over the hard, stony beach, which "had no sand really". Then, by a miracle of good fortune, came the vague resounding bounce of a stray ball and, wavering like a mirage in the distance, the slight forms of two other children impassively signalling to play. Tommy Thompson had jumped up to smash his own children down, as if he always carried the confining propriety of a house around with him. Boundaries must be imposed. There would be no noise, no playing and no wild running with strangers; they were just to sit perfectly still on a thin, damp towel beside the grown-ups, like the upright dead.

Beside Hilda's bed was the little pottery 'statue' of a baby rabbit, snuggling down beneath the turquoise covers of a cot while winking with one eye. Nowadays, it was her totem of sleeping alone, like an adult at last.

"All your mental and physical desires are satisfied . . ." continued the golden voice of a man, rooted firmly in California, over the sensual wash of the sea. Obediently, Hilda tried to sense that the sky of his tape-recorded world was indeed becoming lighter and lighter. But beneath her own eyelids, she wondered if inner night as she knew it could ever completely fade away.

"Feel your feet relaxing," instructed the Golden Guide, "and now, feel that moving *awn up* into your legs . . ."

Every night, when the three Thompson women climbed the yacht-like wooden stairs of their new maisonette in Preston, June and her mother retired to one bed in the room opposite to await the almost inevitable approach of Tommy Thompson in his widow's dreams. Opposite their room and with her bedroom door also wide open to admit the landing light, Young Hilda now attempted to sleep alone, lulled by a New Age *Ultimate Relaxation* tape which someone at the psychiatric unit had said might be worth a try.

Life on a desert island had crossed her mind before.

> *I think we were the only ones in the world that wished we didn't win anything on the football coupon because Dad kept saying we would go on a Desert Island away from people and where it will be quiet.*

Young Hilda had no clear memory of how old she was when

her father had attempted to rape her – possibly thirteen. She simply knew that he had tried and then, for some reason, he had given up the attempts and sexually set her aside. She was the youngest child and, in all senses, somehow impenetrable. At first, an idea of what might happen to her was transmitted only by June's stricken face on a Friday evening when, after an hour or so of rummaging among rancid heaps of cast-off clothes at a local jumble sale, Hilda and her mother would reluctantly return to the house. At the end of an evening's television, when both sisters eventually crept upstairs to the three-quarters bed which seemed almost wet with cold and damp, June would cry quietly in the dark and Young Hilda would hold her, in the powerless and futile way that one child tries to comfort another.

Although she had little choice in the matter, June Thompson believed that if she could comply with Tommy's sexual demands without resistance, without even crying, her younger sister might be spared the ordeal.

> *I thought that with having sex with me, he wouldn't have wanted it off Hilda as well. He always took precautions so that we wouldn't get pregnant but he only did that because it would have been inconvenient for him.*

On the Friday evenings when Tommy ordered her upstairs (and sometimes now at other quite unpredictable moments in the week), June kept her eyes tightly shut and tried to send her mind elsewhere – floating up to the ceiling or close to the window – to pretend that his fiercely concentrating face, the small heap of still-warm clothing neatly folded beside her on the bed and the motion of his body might belong somewhere else, with no real connection to her. Some female long-term incest victims report having learned 'disembodiment' or 'disassociation' as a means of survival and I took this to account for June's continuing 'remoteness'. I supposed that June, by eventually separating 'body' and 'spirit', had sometimes looked down from the ceiling of her bedroom and almost persuaded herself that, although bad things happened down there to her body, they did not happen to *her*.

The first few times it seemed to last a long time but after that it was over quite quickly.

Like a perversion of the peace of adult lovers, locked together in whispered intimation, the continuing assaults on June passed into Hilda in the dark, and like all younger children who, under the shadow of great stress, absorb and internalize an elder sibling's experiences as their own, Hilda too now shared and anticipated June's daily tension as the Thompson family sat together watching television. At some time in her middle teens, Tommy Thompson, long confident of his hold on all the members of the family, did not even bother sending Mrs Thompson and Young Hilda out of the house on those days of the week when he fancied abusing his elder daughter. At first, when kindled by something he had seen on television, or once the regular cycle of desire and easy release had been established as a kind of sexual addiction, he would go upstairs by himself to his military store room, as if to itemize or check the 'stores'. Then, his voice would pitch downstairs, "June, come up here and help me a minute."

June knew that even when her mother and younger sister were downstairs, the act from which she was now so detached was inevitable, but at least it would be brief and 'neat', because nowadays Tommy seemed to pass through her almost without physical trace. Then, the crashing flush of the lavatory would announce Tommy Thompson's descent to the lower floor of the house and she followed shortly afterwards. As time went on and still no resistance seemed to be offered by any woman in the house, Tommy dispensed even with the decency of deception in the military stores. Like an addict who instantly needed a shot of his baby, just how and when he needed it, he would merely lock June's eyes into his own across the flicker of the television screen in the darkening room and, almost imperceptibly, jerk his head sideways and up. Like a well-trained dog who takes the briefest signal as an invitation to a walk, the girl would rise and mount the narrow staircase first. Already recognizing the power of visual images to stimulate sexual desire in men, June and Hilda watched television every evening of their lives on a rack of tension.

Coronation Street was utterly sacred, and twice a week the Thompson family, on Tommy's command, had to be assembled in silence with plenty of time beforehand, as if in a public theatre where 'patrons are advised to take their seats five minutes before the performance begins'. Mrs Thompson and her daughters were not permitted to visit the lavatory or to stir after 7.25 p.m. precisely, when, after blazing through the preceding ads, Tommy's eyes would eventually settle on the simple roofs and familiar brick terraces of would-be Salford, while the wistful line of a quiet trumpet expressed the free flow of neighbourly feeling in troubled times. June watched Tommy as he watched the blue-grey screen. She took to praying that no salacious scenes – flirtation, dancing, a pretty girl pertly leading a man on – would put him in mind of what he could so easily do to her upstairs. Should any hint occur that sex had already taken place in some mysterious flow of true and mutually imperative feeling (and that pregnancy might now be the outcome), Tommy, sitting over there in the quivering shadows of the downstairs room, would laugh like a demon at the star-crossed lovers and their lack of scientific foresight.

"Ye didn't take precautions, ye silly buggers!"

He liked wrestling and boxing, with plenty of crowd yells and men slugging it out ("I'd take me chance with a man before a woman any day"), and after all that his great love was Westerns. The women in the family hated this choice of programmes in which they had no say, but at least when the television was on and Tommy was reasonably sober, there was a chance he might not be so violent. In Westerns, where the men seemed to leap into horses rather than on to them, seizing their mouths quickly and painfully as one might rapidly run up the gears in a sprightly car, sometimes an American heroine would pop up, very beautiful in bonnet, bustle and petticoats, but with the quite undisguisable idea that she was home-town 'sassy'. It was 1968 in the north-west of England, but Tommy behaved towards the TV set as if he were back a century before, at a barnstorming play set with lamps at the foot of a moor or in the drunken turbulence of an urban music-hall, no turn unstoned. Should a bright, attractive woman temporarily set her lover back by the heels (the sort of woman locally known as "a bad 'un"), his fury would boil and, crashing his right fist into his left hand in the dark, he would yell, "I'd show her!" or, for variation, as another self-inflicted punch fitted into his other palm, "Just leave 'er with me for a few minutes and I'll sort 'er out!"

Beneath it all, with a smile set and prepared for the outside world instead of homework for school the next day, June would sit, taut as an arrow in the artificial twilight, praying, "Let there be no sex in this film. *Please*, show something different." Otherwise he might want her again.

Solidly sheeting West of Scotland rain was drumming our sodden garden to pulp when, some weeks later, I got up at 5 a.m. to cut the children's school sandwiches, check that the makings of an evening meal were clearly labelled in the fridge and then prepare myself for another trip to Lancashire. My next job was to look into the working lives of the Thompson sisters and, nowadays, because I had become obsessively determined to learn *everything*, this meant visiting an Edwardian laundry in Chorley. Some time in the summer of 1968, when she had left school at the age of sixteen, it seemed that June Thompson had begun her working life there, following almost inevitably in the footsteps of her maternal grandmother, Ellen.

That day, even from the train window, something in Preston was very different. Steaming in waterproofs and squelching trainers, extraordinary crowds thronged back and forth on the platforms and, beyond the dripping glass canopies of the station, came drifts of municipal turbulence and excitement. Deciding on impulse to break my worthy journey to Chorley out of sheer curiosity, I soon found elaborate red bunting sogged and swagged across Preston high street; that huge grandstands had been set up and, even at this time of day, every café, shop and by way in the place was jammed. Standing in a shop doorway to peel back page from page of a special souvenir edition of the *Lancashire Evening Post* which almost dissolved in my hands, I learned that this was Preston Guild Week, a vast festival which (with a bit of a hiccup during the Second World War) had occurred every twenty years in the town since 1179, when Henry II had granted the town the right of free trade.

It seemed that half a million Lancashire people descended on Preston for this week and that the two previous days had been occupied by vast religious processions, with every tiny church in central Lancashire taking part. Today, despite the weather, the same crowds had gathered again to watch the great Preston Guilds Trade March, which would take three hours to pass. Running like a water rat past the massed backs of the procession route, I eventually met with the spine-tingling explosions of a thumping good military band and the slow passing of vast painted sets which could have been towed out of a theatre in a dream of rain and music.

Tottering slightly because of its great height (and with its truck engine idling at a purr), the float was designed like a Roman temple and on it three vaguely Classical maidens, heavily made up, in simple white robes and with loose-flowing hair, pointed lightly and signed like rain-swept Fates at the virtues of floral stretch-covers on sample armchairs. As if to show where textiles had gone in Lancashire – what some skilled people actually made now – it was wonderful Plumb's Stretch Covers, employing 500 people at Brookhouse Mill in Old Lancaster Lane. Overhead, big swags of pastel fabric snaked as if they had freshly fallen from looms around gold and white architectural snatches of Ancient Rome, and the float commanded respect from the crowd.

"I met my wife during last Preston Guild," said the dripping man beside me, ruminating on the slow passing of the stretch-cover Norns. "We're twenty years married now."

Although all this was novel to me, I began to realize that many people in the town must measure the passing of their lives by it.

"I've seen *three* Preston Guilds," rejoined an older man, topping him in the way that some elderly people compulsively sidle up to the subject of death. "You're an old man if you see four."

Noticing them – and then quickly looking again to confirm it – I suddenly saw the Thompson sisters, alarmingly clear but far on the other side of the procession route. For some reason, that day I was shocked to find them there, out in the real world of Preston, rather than sitting at home with me in some cosy journalistic appointment. Now that Tommy was dead and their lives were their own, the sisters were impassively watching the first Preston Guild they had ever seen. Standing closely together, feet neatly pointing forwards and with identical umbrellas primly held aloft, they were watching the goings-on in the town, standing high and remote on the upper steps of the Guildhall. Feeling strangely guilty that day and quieting my futile waves, I passed on about my own business as if I did not know them.

As if to wash away the sins of the town, the Hygienic Laundry is set apart at the very edge of Chorley. It stands at the foot of Harpers Lane, no suburbia intervening, on the shocking razor-sharp divide between a small northern town and open country. Although nowadays given over entirely to commercial laundry (roller-towel supply for offices and work for supermarkets, hotels, restaurants and butchers), the faded white letters of the old name, CHORLEY & DISTRICT HYGIENIC LAUNDRY, are still visible on a band running round the top of a sweetly curving Edwardian building, cut like the shallow slice from a brick-built barrel.

A few feet away, across a quietly flowing road now hissing with wet, Chorley's bit of the Pennine Chain was swimming pure and green beneath bales of raincloud hanging weightless and remote as airships around the barren snout of Chorley Nab.

During the summer of 1968, when she was sixteen, June Thompson had begun to work here, in the year (SAY IT WITH COBBLESTONES) of supposed youthful revolution across Western Europe.

Soon, passing beneath a huge suspended sign saying in bold red and white THINK QUALITY! A COMPLAINT A DAY KEEPS BUSINESS AWAY, I walked with Richard Swift, a kind and rather quiet young process supervisor, into the vast neon-lit sorting room of one of the biggest commercial laundries in central Lancashire under a deafening blare of Red Rose Radio FM.

For just one difficult year, the Thompson sisters were separated while June forged a path into the outside world of work, leaving Hilda behind at St Alban's Secondary Modern School, Chorley. Still tied to her desk, and trying to be 'one of the girls', Young Hilda wished her days away. Without the presence of her adept elder sister to smooth over the gulf between home and school, appearance and emotional reality, she felt her 'outside' relationships were failing. But in the afternoons, when her laundry shift was finished, June brought home the promise of another world where if only Hilda could hang on, they might both enjoy some new degree of freedom together.

June was taught by an elderly woman called Lizzie (whose husband drove a laundry van) how to sort the endless brown-paper parcels which poured into the sorting room like proper Christmas. At first, in the way of all first stabs at a grown-up job, June found the work exciting. Carefully, she classified each stale garment, noting it down in the book before clonking each item with a hot metal arm which mysteriously deposited a customer's laundry number. Taught by Tommy to obey without question and quite fearfully to watch her step in every tiny detail of daily life at home, June excelled at work to which she was intellectually superior. Then, hoping to prepare her younger sister for the great day when she might join her at the laundry, June rushed home to teach Young Hilda, with quiet words and on bits of paper, the various factory processes so that she too might get a job: GET IT WHITE FIRST TIME – EVERY TIME!

"But," I said one day to Hilda, when the idea of work in a laundry – what it might entail – had been still a complete mystery to me, "didn't Tommy *mind* that June came home in the afternoon and then sat down with you after school? You know, perhaps you were huddled together, talking quietly about things he didn't understand?"

"No," said Hilda, looking back on those surprising days when the violent rampages of her father were curiously held in suspension and Tommy stood back for some reason, allowing his daughters to be closeted together in daylight by themselves.

"No," said Hilda, thinking quite clearly of money. "He didn't mind that because he knew that as fast as I learned, the more bonus I'd get."

In the old-fashioned way of working-class economic survival, which was becoming a source of conflict between ordinary parents and children in the 1960s, the young sisters' pay packets were just handed to Tommy on a Friday evening unopened – straight over. Then, to complete the bounty of the week, if he felt like it, June would quietly go upstairs at the slightest inclination of his head.

Tommy Thompson ran a hostage system, allowing two women out of the house at any one time but always keeping back the third. Like all successful male incest perpetrators, he felt himself to be living in a constant state of siege and this was his way of ensuring that "no one talks outside about what goes on in this house". Just as June and Hilda had been 'safely' together, supporting each other at school while excluding the real world, Tommy insisted that at all times in adult life they should work together too. In future, should one sister be laid off during bad economic times in a factory, the other must also resign. In some fierce inner battle, Tommy was still fighting on two fronts – to keep the outside world shut out and the grown-up family (on which he was as dependent as a huge child) firmly under control. In 1968, the year that June began work at the laundry, Tommy traded up his old shotgun for a better model. As Young Hilda wrote:

He told us he bought it to protect us if anybody broke into the house . . . it was like we were sitting on a time-bomb. That when he fell out with us at any time, it could get out of control & he would shoot us all.

I noticed that, unlike June, Young Hilda still continued to sometimes call Tommy "Dad" and, in another notebook, she was more explicit about the breadth of his threats with the gun.

Dad meant what he said . . . If anybody got to know about what was going on in this house we were all Dead. Even if he had to go to prison, if anybody did find out, he would serve his time in prison & he would be all nice as though he had changed to a kind person. Then he would dedicate his life to finding us all (wherever we went) & kill us all.

After a day at the laundry, if she should accidentally break one of the House Rules which Tommy had quite arbitrarily devised – some amazingly trivial thing like failing to shut a drawer properly, so that it stuck out by half an inch, or forgetting to switch off an electric light very, very slowly, because Tommy started up like a madman at the barest hint of a click – the young woman did not question her father's sanity or real power over the family when June was sent upstairs for the gun. Slowly and lovingly loaded and then pressed to her head for quiet minutes at a time, Young Hilda found that the cold metal muzzle gradually warmed against her scalp.

Although it was repetitive daily work which would have made me scream after two or three hours, laundry work was a sweet release for June and Hilda Thompson after evenings and weekends with Tommy at home. Every day, as three vast conveyor belts droned past, the sisters chucked up flannelette sheets (which spewed out clouds of fine fibre dust) onto the top belt; shirts, blouses and underwear on to the middle belt; and greasy cotton sheets, big with stains, on to the belt below.

In the way that even the humblest working person can often think of ways which would improve an industrial system, June remarked. "I suppose it would have been better if they'd told us to throw the flannelette sheets on the *bottom* belt really – less dust!"

But, even when thinking about the worst jobs in a laundry (and I could only suppose that work in a hospital laundry might be worse), the atmosphere in the Thompsons' maisonette lightened almost to one of jollity when it was just June, Hilda and myself recalling their days of work.

"There used to be a restaurant," said Hilda, "and they must have stored the table-cloths in some damp place for weeks, because when we threw them up on the belt, their cloths always had maggots in."

Momentarily, even she seemed to step from the shadows of mental illness, and I could not quite believe it.

"There was some terrible underwear," said June, joining in the fun. "You learned," she said, doubtless mentally throwing thousands of fundament depeinted underpants, neck-ringed blouses and grey slimy vests upwards on to the conveyor belt of memory, "just to angle it carefully and get rid of it."

Eventually, no matter how long it might take, the Thompson sisters sensed a new, free world in which their mother might be able to join them. Then they would no longer have to fear, as they had done as children, what Tommy was doing to her at home when they were out. These days, Tommy had given up work altogether, withdrawing from the world behind the shield of the dole. Trying to find some way to spare their mother daytime beatings seemed to be the modest limit of the Thompson sisters' hopes.

"Did you not think," I said, "that once you were earning a bit of money of your own, you might all be able to get away some time?"

"Oh, no," said June. "We were too frightened really . . ."

Then she added, with her old bitter emphasis, "Mum would have loved a job to get her out of the house and away from *im*. But *ee* would never let her away from *im*."

*

Having gone from one derelict house to another, doing it up and then moving on, something like eleven times in Chorley since the early 1950s, the Thompson family made the major house move of their lives in 1970, when Tommy ordained that they should all move to Preston. Now retired and on invalidity benefit, with vague but convincing back complaints, Tommy heard from a next-door neighbour in Chorley that Courtaulds were not only taking on trainees at their Red Scar rayon works out on Longridge Road, at the edge of town, but paying good wages too. Now totally dependent on his adult daughters for money to improve on what was available from the state, Tommy looked as usual for an old, cheap decayed house in Preston where he could ply his obsessive DIY skills. Consequently, from 18 May 1970 until they collected their redundancy pay packets on Friday, 28 March 1980, the Thompson sisters were employed as creelers and beamers at one of the most impressive textile mills in Central Lancashire.

During the years Tommy was alive, this decade of unbroken work for Courtaulds was the Thompson sisters' happiest. From the beginning, they each earned £50 a week, plus productivity bonuses – good money for teenaged girls in those days. Until I later discovered the bizarre truth behind it, June's diary (which also began in 1970) always seemed to confine itself to exceptionally bald facts and figures about the Thompson family's life. But in one entry, recalling the sisters' eventual parting from Courtaulds, she came closest to expressing emotion:

28 March 1980

We have nothing more to do with Courtauld's Red Scar Works, Longridge Road, Preston. We are not employed there any more. Collected a wage & a cheque for redundancy pay. We put both cheques in Halifax.

Hilda's redundancy pay: £398.88
June's redundancy pay: £471.03
Hilda's severance pay: £531.84
June's severance pay: £538.32

Later, in one of her notebooks (which were more freely written), June remarked that in comparison with living at home with Tommy, *going to Courtaulds was like a holiday camp to us.* The sisters loved working overtime when it was available – not so much for the extra money it would bring in for Tommy, but simply to stay away from home for as long as possible. But Courtaulds Red Scar rayon works had become a haven for the Thompson sisters for another reason: the exceptional welfare policies of the company's management at that time. Like very poor children who once found not just education but personal warmth and good school dinners at primary school, Courtaulds seemed to them not only a workplace but a good place.

Even by the 1950s, when June and Hilda Thompson were still at primary school, textile work in Lancashire had become something of a locally despised occupation reflecting the recurrent British contempt for manual labour. The younger women who worked in it were largely drawn from secondary-modern schools and, as one annoyed correspondent to the *Chorley Guardian* put it at that time, there was a "disparaging dismissal of all who labour by hand and brain in mill and mine and workshop". Far from being the enviable work of an Edwardian industrial princess, weaving and spinning were seen throughout the years of the Thompson sisters' schooldays as being suitable only for what another *Chorley Guardian* correspondent called "the soft ooze of the secondary-modern school".

This post-war attitude in Lancashire towards its ancient female crafts of spinning and weaving meant that employers who were still in the textile industry increasingly had to lure young women into it not only by stressing the new socialist perks – an emphasis on welfare facilities, a first-aid room and subsidized restaurants – but with social activities, gifts of dress fabric and dancing, to emphasize the old femininity of the industry. At his mills, the flamboyant Lancashire textile magnate Cyril Lord even staged mill workers' mannequin parades. After an annual fashion show, the chosen models were allowed to keep one beautiful dress each, and this was followed up by a dinner-dance to which employees were allowed to bring family and friends and at which free cigarettes were distributed. Cyril Lord owned Greenfield Mill in Chorley (to whose gates Mrs Thompson had so wistfully put her ear on the day I went walking with her round the town). Here Cyril Lord's personnel officer had almost pleaded for trainee weavers in 1950 by addressing recruitment ads to the parents of female school-leavers: "Parents interested in our Mills are invited to visit Miss Symons, Personnel Officer, to discuss the Welfare, Amenities, Canteen and Medical Services etc."

By the 1960s, when June and Hilda Thompson were of an age to begin work, the big new boom in man-made fibres such as rayon meant that employers like Courtaulds not only provided exceptional welfare facilities to attract trainees and older skilled labour but were happy to pay the high wages of new technology as well. For the Thompson sisters, secretly semi-starved and beaten by Tommy at home, good subsidized meals and sympathetic company medical staff (as well as cheerful workmates) were the things that kept them going. Finding one or two of those former workmates from the long years at Courtaulds – someone, anyone, who had known the Thompson sisters during working hours and who would agree to speak to me – became the next job in hand.

Rising above a ground mist of subtle colours which suggested a good plantsman's sleight of hand, the pretty semi-detached house which the taxi driver eventually found on the outskirts of Preston was laced up the front with trellis. It was a few days into September – not quite summer, not quite autumn – and in that middle-aged English turn of the seasons, the damp flowers which hung in cascades from pots on every ledge were slightly faded. In the quite magical way that English people turn a recently bought council house into echoes of Devon cottages, Georgian town houses or moorland barns, this house spoke quite simply of patient work in the garden, a domestic haven with a touch of 'the country' and of sheer normality. Holding down a raggy, jumping dog which scattered cats back into the house in all directions, Dennis Preston, a warm man in his fifties with a craggy brown face, important nose and bleached blue eyes, shook my hand and welcomed me into the house to meet his wife because at last I had discovered her whereabouts – the workmate who had known the Thompson sisters best.

That morning, like me, Dennis and Maureen Preston had been up since 5 a.m., driving in their car out to the depths of the country to begin the early shift (6 a.m.–2 p.m.) in Bees Mill at Ribchester, and by this point in the afternoon we were all ready for a sit-down. After the somewhat synthetic glories of the Preston Guilds trade procession that day, I was amazed that these two, married for forty years and with grown-up children long flown away, continued to work together, man and wife, in the old craft of Lancashire – as weavers in a genuine cotton mill.

"You know, bees, as in the buzz of bees," said Dennis, explaining what was nowadays their rather unusual situation. "It's an old mill set down in the middle of the countryside really. If I say there's 100 people living in the village it would be too many. It was a Roman village, you know – try buying a house there these days and you're talking telephone numbers!"

Bees Mill specialized in dress fabrics – some for Laura Ashley and a big order from Viyella for tartan had just come in ("It's good stuff. When it leaves us they charge £8 a metre for it!"). But although the mill was presently running twenty-four hours a day, and Dennis had once enjoyed working in the small hours when the looms clattered on in the pitch dark and stillness of rural night, he feared that short-time working was on the cards again.

"I was laid off for some months once and I had the garden spick and span. It's so demoralizing having time on your hands. When I was out in that garden every day, passers-by would say, 'I wish I had time to do the garden', and I used to say, 'I wish I *didn't* have time to do it!' These people on the social, I don't know what they do all day . . ."

Then, sitting on the sofa beside me and having quietly assessed that I was a genuine inquirer into the hidden lives of the Thompson sisters and meant them no harm, Maureen Preston – very small, pretty and round, dressed casually in pink and with pale-blue eyes the exact match of her husband's, behind clear-rimmed specs – began a flow of her own in the way that well-married people slide in and out of each other's thoughts and conversations. For her, the murder of Tommy Thompson might only have happened yesterday and, fondly supposing that he was in for a long haul, Dennis, sitting on the other side of the mock-stone fireplace, lit a cigarette with the high-minded concentration of a recidivist smoker and turned his gaze up to the ceiling.

"Now, June and Hilda – They were two *lovely* girls. It was just after Dennis's birthday and we heard it on Red Rose Radio. There's been murder in Skeffington Road and I said, 'I think that's June and Hilda.' I don't know *why* I thought it was June and Hilda, but I just did. I said to old Mrs (a name I didn't catch in the flow), 'I think that's June and Hilda!' And *she* said, 'There's a lot live down Skeffington Road.' But I don't know why I *still* thought it was the Thompson girls.

"Just after it happened" (and I took this to be a matter of weeks after the murder, when the Thompson women had been released from the medical wing of Risley Remand Centre and were awaiting trial in sheltered accommodation in Preston) "I saw them in a small coffee bar in town and I didn't know whether to speak to them or not."

"But you'd been working with them in the old Courtaulds' Red Scar mill for about eight years, hadn't you?" I chipped in hopefully, as Maureen barely drew breath to assess the English subtleties of the situation that day in the snack bar.

"Yes, but if I speak, they'll think I'm nosy but if I didn't speak, they'd think I'm cutting them."

But then Young Hilda had come across to the Prestons' café table, stood quite simply beside them and said, "Did you hear about us?"

"Yes, love, and I'm really sorry . . ." And kind Dennis had resolved matters by saying, "Why don't you come up and see us at home some time?"

Eventually, while still on remand, June, Young Hilda and Mrs Thompson had come up to the Prestons' house on the bus to speak for the first time about their true situation to someone who had known them as workmates and vaguely as neighbours for a very long time, but who, of course, did not really know them at all. As a man who likes and understands women, Dennis had known the moment when he wasn't supposed to be listening, because, explained Maureen, "Sometimes a woman can only speak to another woman. June and Hilda came out to the kitchen and told me all about it and how they'd been tret. They were such nice-mannered girls, such good workers and such hard workers. I used to say long ago, 'If ever I had daughters, I'd like daughters like that.' Just imagine going home and handing your wage packet straight over.

"The evening they were here in that kitchen, June told me how her father used to go to front door. Some nights he'd say, 'I think I'll get some air' but then he used to go with a knife stuck in his belt. Just down to front door! He were just like something in't army."

Later that evening, shocked to the core by what they had heard – and in Dennis's case, supposedly not heard – of Tommy Thompson's violence, incest and cruelty to animals – "One of their dogs, he used to drag it behind him on a lead until its paws were bleeding" – Dennis had quietly run them back in his car. Soon after, when called upon by the Thompson sisters' solicitors, Maureen had written a letter, standing for both of them as a character witness.

To Whom It May Concern

I have known June & Hilda for the past eighteen years, working alongside them both from 1970 to 1976.

I have always found them both to be quiet, hard-working & sober young ladies, Showing great consideration to everybody but mostly their Parents. Two young ladies, in Fact, that I would have been proud to call daughters.

Yours, Maureen Preston

And then, in the way that tiny bits of astonishing information sometimes fly off in a torrent of speech like sparks of light which suddenly illuminate a greater whole, Maureen Preston, thinking quite literally of the intense fibre dust which once hung in the shafts of light feeding in to older mills, remarked, "Courtaulds was a very nice atmosphere – not dusty because it was rayon, you see . . . Their mother was only working there for a few hours when she was called to the phone."

"You surely don't mean," I cried, completely bewildered. "that Mrs Thompson actually *did* get away from Tommy to work at Courtaulds too, beside her girls?"

"Oh, yes," said Maureen, mildly amused at my alarm. "But their mother was only working there a few hours when she was called to the phone, and it was her husband. Could she go home because he couldn't manage without her!"

From the beginning, Preston was a town that Tommy Thompson did not like and, for some reason, even feared. Shortly after moving there, he took his shotgun out into the new backyard as if expecting a state of siege, and tested it by firing it once into a thick piece of wood. Then he handed it to June (who was always sent upstairs to fetch the gun), instructing her to fire one test-shot too.

It was frightening the noise it made. He made me fire one shot as well. I knew I couldn't say no because he said If anybody breaks into the house & I hadn't used the gun on them, he would shoot me in the legs and make me suffer.

It was then, in their utterly oppressed and ultra-cautious way, that June and Hilda Thompson discovered that Tommy would indeed let their mother out of the house during the daytime to join them at Courtaulds rayon works. Literally, for once in their lives Tommy was prepared to let his 'hostage' system break down simply because he desperately needed new money. Now installed in a derelict neighbourhood of what he took to be a fierce and dangerous new town, three good pay packets rather than two would enable him and June quickly to repair a damp and crumbling house again – the usual kind of house that was both his fort and his prison. Consequently, for just three or four hours on Monday, 1 June 1970, Mrs Thompson stood with her daughters among a cluster of new trainees in the Beaming Department of the Red Scar rayon works – together at last and safe from daytime beatings in the real and gregarious world of Lancashire factory life – the very life which had given her much-needed warmth and companionship as a teenage girl herself.

In all his married life, Tommy Thompson had never been left at home by himself and the Thompson women had frequently noted that he could not bear to be alone. Tommy was now aged thirty-nine and, it seems to me, he was beginning that dip into early middle-aged crisis when the worst pain of his own youth seemed to rise up in a newly violent and apparently insoluble way. That morning, with all three women out of the house together, I could just see him sitting dumb on the downstairs bed like a huge toddler who suddenly realizes that he has been abandoned. He had been made to stay somewhere utterly alone and he could not bear it. Tommy Thompson had always used the telephone as a kind of long arm of warning, and shortly after his daughters had begun working together in their first job at the laundry, he had occasionally rung them at work, as if to say, "I'm-still-here-and-thinking-about-you-so-don't-do-anything-stupid."

Now he fled to a public coin-box again and, within hours of working alongside her now smiling daughters on Monday 1 June 1970, Mrs Thompson found herself back on the bus which stopped outside the works, trundling on up Longridge Road, past the big gates of the cemetery, into Ribbleton – and then on home to Skeffington Road and Tommy.

After the family's move to Preston in 1970, Tommy Thompson's sexual needs also took a downward plunge. As if incest with his elder daughter and 'ordinary' sexual relations with his wife were not enough, he seemed driven on to some new twist. In a letter to me, Mrs Thompson wrote:

> *I used to dread June & Hilda being on 2 till 10 at Courtaulds. Tommy always went out drinking every afternoon and he was always in a queer angry mood when he came home . . . The problem I had was that he wasn't just satisfied with normal sex.*

One afternoon, when Mrs Thompson was safely back in the old way of always staying at home and Tommy had lurched back from the County Arms, a pub rather wittily situated within 100 yards of Preston Prison, he made it clear that his wife must begin to have sex with other men – in fact to prostitute herself – because the idea of her lying with other men in some odd way excited him. As usual, when it came to very intimate matters, Mrs Thompson preferred to write rather than talk about it face to face.

> *I have never refused anything but to go with other men like that just to satisfy his Lust made me very Unhappy.*

She point blank refused to do it. That afternoon, when she had again rejected the idea of even pretending to have been with other men, and June and Young Hilda were safely out of the way at Courtaulds, Tommy told her to strip naked. Then he lifted her up like a little doll on to the top of his crazy home-made sideboard, where she stood, utterly defenceless, a woman who had borne children, while he stood before her, fully clothed and lounging on the downstairs bed to laugh and mock.

> *He made me take all my clothes off and made me stand on the Sideboard. He then Ridiculed & Mocked me &, as I was rather slim, he called me Belsen.*

But strangely enough, and with her own characteristic touch of *amour propre*, Mrs Thompson added:

I was eight stone five stripped and I was only five feet tall. I wasn't that thin.

Some time during her early days in the Courtaulds job at Preston, June Thompson also found that her father's sexual needs seemed to alter. Although she could not frame this change in words, his deepening sado-masochism, presumably displaced from his mother to his wife, was now in turn directed at her.

He was still having sex with me, June wrote, *but he was violent with it, not because I wouldn't do anything he said, but he must have enjoyed doing it.*

Always a keen watcher of 'health news' in the press and on television, Tommy now dispatched June to the local family-planning clinic to get the Pill.

He said to me if ever I got pregnant I would have to have an abortion because he said, "There's no babies stopping in this house or anywhere else."

"Ye go with other men, don't ye – *don't ye!*" Tommy would hiss on to her face when physically engaged with her on Friday nights and the television blared on below. But although she had been used by him for as long as she could remember, June remained a perfect innocent. In what was now a normal feature of her daily life, she did not have the sophistication to play sado-masochistic word games with a middle-agd man.

"No!" was all the young woman could say in terrified bewilderment. "No! No!"

Then, just as Tommy sometimes had a stammer, of which he was deeply and bitterly ashamed, a kind of hesitancy also seemed to enter into the last moments of his sexual acts with her. No longer could June entirely float to the ceiling in detachment to separate her spirit and real being from the body below, because nowadays a sharp, hard blow from his fist on the side of her head always preceded the moment he could finally gain release.

It was a bright afternoon in late November when June

Thompson and I got off a bus and entered the gates of a vast industrial estate off Longridge Road – out at the very edge of Preston. What had once been the Courtaulds rayon mill now seemed to be something very different and a huge board at the foot of the drive stated the names of "companies on site". They seemed to be very 1980s-sounding company names, such as Assembly Line Recording Studio, Windowland North-West and Bodycare Toiletries Ltd. In the way of a brilliant winter afternoon which will almost instantly plunge like a theatre into darkness, the sun shot out warnings of dying light between hail showers, the blue moors seemed almost touchable and the sky was stacked with mountainous cloud, reflected back in silvery winter puddles. Beneath it all, there was no Courtaulds Red Scar rayon works any more – just smart, new, grey metal factories.

"I suppose Courtaulds was brick before?" I said to June, because it was over ten years since she had last seen it.

"Yeah," said June, looking about over the distant sea of chic new grey design. "The gate lodge is the same though." Then, from the place where a factory hooter sounded, June suddenly noticed the roofs of the old weaving sheds still tucked away in the distance and found that they were much the same as before. Taking in the brilliant wintry scene and perhaps thinking of the cemetery further up the road, where her father was buried, June said, "If we had to be buried where we had some good memories, I think it would be here in these grounds."

On days when their shifts at Courtaulds were from 6 a.m. to 2 p.m., the Thompson sisters rose at 5 in their damp upper bedroom and, standing on icy lino, quickly dressed in front of the makeshift wardrobe, where their other jumble-sale clothes crept with mildew like moss on a stagnant tree. Then, floating like ghosts past the downstairs bed, where Tommy and their mother were still sleeping, the sisters crept out to the kitchen to wash their faces at the kitchen sink, make a cup of tea and pass silently out to the street. Down at Preston Bus Station in the grey morning light, three works double-decker buses were waiting to convey them, and hundreds like them, on out to the Red Scar mill on Longridge Road.

"We didn't mind getting up early," Young Hilda had once told me, "because it were something nice to get to . . ."

On the dismal weekend mornings when, despite their utter cat-like silence, Tommy stirred in his bed beyond the kitchen door, that sometimes meant making toast for him – again in utter silence, because the slightest domestic noise instantly provoked his terrifying rages. At the very thought of lighting the grill and possibly clattering the grill-pan on its journey back under the flames, Hilda's hands shook with terror. Most frightening of all was the possibility that Tommy might call from his bed for a fried egg, which had to be cooked, yolk unbroken and with absolutely no trace of a brown fringe on the outer circumference of the egg. This was work which Young Hilda silently handed over to June's infinitely steadier hands.

"I hated doing that, because from being very young I was frightened of anything to do with heat. You understand . . .?" and I again recalled how Tommy had held her infant hand close to the flames of a coal fire in Chorley all those years ago.

When June had settled any of Tommy Thompson's breakfast needs on the unfortunate days when he stirred early, the sisters then cut themselves jam sandwiches on working-days for lunch, but in the meantime, there was always Courtaulds' big, wonderful, northern working breakfasts to look forward to. Unlike the minimal food that Tommy strictly doled out to them at home, here, from the largesse of a good employer, they could choose and choose and eat and eat the most delicious hot subsidized things they were denied at home. Remembering the works canteen at Courtaulds was the only time I ever heard June and Hilda Thompson describe some incident in their past lives with what amounted to sensual pleasure – the warmth of the vast room with windows steamy against a frosty northern day, committed cooks in absolutely spotless white aprons and caps, and the long, under-heated chrome counters, subtly lighting trays of crisply fried bacon, big round sausages, glistening fried eggs, kidneys, golden triangles of fried bread, hot buttery toast, well-grilled tomatoes so sweetly squidgy in the middle, and gallons and gallons of hot, sweet tea.

"Oh," said June, looking back on the vast hungers of youth, "the breakfasts at Courtaulds were *lovely*!"

Back in Maureen and Dennis Preston's sitting room, my eyes had settled on the big, horizontal, mock-stone fireplace, which had a slit cut out of it to hold the video, while they too extolled the virtues of Courtaulds' works canteen. Every surface on the fireplace was sprinkled with tiny brass objects – little glinting kettles, pairs of baby shoes, a cat with an arched back, rearing horses, horse brasses and miniature bellows. Supposed Old English country life made small and glittering.

"It was a canteen as big as this street – as big as a ballroom!" Dennis was saying, casting a hand in the air in his search for superlatives. But Maureen was thoughtfully bringing up an important subject – who sat with whom during meal-breaks, and ultimately, I supposed, some idea of the internal social groupings of the place. Even then a staid married woman, Maureen Preston had very definite ideas about good manners and general behaviour at work, and I was getting the impression that she found some women in the works a bit "clannish", or possibly a bit too rough to her way of thinking in speech and manner. Apparently, men and women in the canteen were segregated and she could not sit with Dennis.

"I usually ended up sitting with Jean, who was very fat, little Winnie, who was a bit . . ."

"A bit . . .?"

"A bit simple, love," said Dennis. "You know – two bars short of a picnic."

And then, of course, June and Hilda Thompson had almost invariably drawn close to sit with nice Maureen too.

"They were so well brought up and well mannered," said Maureen reflectively. "That's why you never suspected anything. That's why the others used to skit them – because they were so old-fashioned."

"*Skit them?*" I said in amazement and then, for the first

time, it began to dawn on me that, on top of all their other hidden woes, June and Hilda Thompson had been teased at work because they seemed to others to be different.

At first that afternoon, I had supposed that the Thompson sisters attracted comment at work because of the sheer difference marked out on them by poverty. With no money for nice clothes, shoes and make-up like other girls, they had to dress entirely from jumble sales on the pound or so which Tommy doled back to them at the end of each week, and out of which they had to buy subsidized meals at the Courtaulds' canteen too. Looking back, though, Maureen Preston seemed to find no real or striking fault with their appearance.

"They didn't have a *lot* of clothes, but they always looked very smart."

One day, she had seen Mrs Thompson waiting in the doorway of a second-hand clothes shop. Like many old-fashioned women, Maureen seemed to have eyes and ears everywhere in a neighbourhood, flying over space and time in the way that amazed local recipients of casual information once used to call 'The News of the World'.

"They – June and Hilda – were both inside looking for clothes. Minis, they wore then . . . June always used to go for minis. I used to think, 'Isn't she nice and slim?' And although Hilda were always eating – toasted cheese sandwiches *that* thick *and* with chips as well (and she were always eating toffees all afternoon, although she were a nice girl and would always give you one), she were nice and slim as well. I don't know *how* she could eat all that and still stay as thin as a lat. She were a funny one, Hilda. Every time she washed her hands, she always put handcream on – every single time. She were always very fussy."

But now, although Maureen kept going with her torrent of affectionate speech, she cast her eye back wider to the social scene at Courtaulds and, I thought, rather evasively. "They were always quizzing June and Hilda – them ones who live in the sky-scraper flats. Taking the mickey out of them, trying to find out what they were doing at nights and weekends . . . But, of course, June and Hilda never told them *anything*."

"This is the way people at work used to be," said Dennis quickly. "In the mill they were always proper nosy. Where did you go last night? Did you do this? Did you do that?"

"They were real Lancashire women, nosy and personal," continued Maureen. "They were always thinking about boy-friends. I think June and Hilda used to tell them, 'Oh, we go to bingo at the weekends, or we go shopping in Asda, but we don't like going out much at night.'"

But then June Thompson had begun to appear in the Beaming Department at Courtaulds with those small squalid bruises called 'love bites' on her neck, and soon the mill-girl hunt was on for the dark horse – her secret lover. The responsible Prestons took a perfectly reasonable view of this.

"As they'd just moved to Preston from Chorley, we thought they had boyfriends there . . ."

But one day, in her ubiquitous way, Maureen had seen Young Hilda walking into the County Arms pub, arm in arm with a man.

"He was a smart man – a good-looking man – you saw him going about. I thought, happen she's got a boyfriend, *but it was her and her Dad*, walking arm in arm! He were very crafty, always keeping one of them with him."

"My feeling is," said Dennis, firmly picking up a question which his wife had been charitably trying to set down. "My feeling is that the other girls at Courtaulds quizzed them that closely because they were trying to find out if they were a bit on the queer side . . ."

"The queer side?" I said, thinking of the perversion of family life which had run on unchecked, day by day, year by year, within the enclosed confines of Tommy Thompson's kingdom.

"You mean," I said, "that the Thompson sisters must have seemed rather odd?"

"Aye," said Dennis, toning down a bit. "That and the fact they always kept so close together and didn't seem much interested in men. I think the others thought they were lesbians, like."

"*What?*"

"Dennis is right," said Maureen quietly, "that's what was said."

And now, because the Prestons had been so open and free in telling me what they knew of the Thompson sisters' plight, I decided it was my turn to vouchsafe them a little story, so off we set again, all together up half-crazed zigzag avenue.

Ever since his youthful days in the army, Tommy Thompson liked to be very well turned out. During his spare time, which was now full-time on the dole with two grown-up daughters to support him, he often wandered into men's outfitters in Preston to pick up some item that might enhance his good looks. With trousers, for example, which he liked to hang just so, he would fling a new pair over to June in the evening so she could alter the lie of the back pockets to his taste, because her needlework was very fine and even in his worst moods he could rarely fault it.

One day in Preston, when Tommy was out cruising the streets as usual for new clothes, he spotted a man's second-hand gold ring in the window of a jeweller's shop. The ring was broad, shaped like a belt with a buckle on the front, and for some weeks after buying it, turning it over and over in his hand at home, Tommy Thompson found that it somehow sparked off a solution to the social quandary he now felt himself to be in. Even in the 1970s in Britain, when domestic violence and incest went largely unrecognized by public and officialdom alike, Tommy Thompson still struck me as being something of a genius in this hidden world – still continuing to dominate his wife and daughters utterly, as June and Hilda crept on half-way into their twenties. Unlike the vast majority of sexually abused children grown to adulthood, they had still not broken away. But now that his own life was slowly turning over in middle age, Tommy felt the urgent need to reassert his authority over the Thompson women in a new way. Even with his daughter-wives now 'safely' working together at Courtaulds and his real wife silent behind closed doors at home, he had begun to fear the day when his fists, shin-kicking and gun might not keep away a threat on his own front doorstep – that June and Hilda, meeting young men out there in the big wide world of work, might be wooed and won in the normal way, abandoning him in a publicly acceptable way while seeing a chance to reveal something of their past. Given the Thompson sisters' horrific sexual experiences with their father, the fact that June and Young Hilda might *not* be avid for the sexual company of young men did not occur to Tommy in his ignorance. He knew only that out there in the real world of work, the daughter-wives he claimed as his must be guarded and marked out as forbidden territory to other men while, at the same time, veiling June and Hilda's true sexual connection to him.

That November day on the bus back from the Red Scar industrial estate, June had wandered, for some reason, on to the subject of Tommy's fascination with rings and, as she spoke, I tried to avert my eyes from the big Gothic gates of the Victorian cemetery where, I could not forget, this dismembered and bizarre man was buried.

"When we were getting older," June said, as the bus rattled on, "I think he felt there was a chance probably of men – boyfriends – you know, saying to us, 'Do you want to go out tonight?' or something like that. He knew that when we were only children and at school that wouldn't happen, but now we were out working at Courtaulds, there were men . . ."

First of all, Tommy Thompson bought a few more rings for himself, bringing them home and and again turning them over in his hand and mind.

"And then he started on about how it would be a good idea for us to wear one – a wedding ring."

"And did he *really* say all that about keeping boys away?"

"That's right – yeah – I think that's where it came from. The gold rings sort of triggered his mind on to it."

In his strange way of combining old traditional values with the most extraordinary perversions, Tommy felt that wedding rings were indeed the way to keep his daughters for himself.

"At the time he said just a cheap one will do, just as long as it's gold and won't turn your finger black or anything."

So one Saturday afternoon Tommy took June and Young Hilda down to the Gold Bullion jeweller's shop in Church Street, Preston – a small, dark-panelled place specializing in second-hand trinkets, where gaudy trays of instant wedding and engagement rings glittered with impossible brilliance on royal-blue velvet trays under the lights. Already instructed by Tommy to buy something cheap, on pain of a hard thumping once they got home again, the young women gravely gave their attention to the padded trays while Tommy stood back, the very model of disinterested generosity. June chose a widish gold ring with ridges on it and Young Hilda chose a wide one too, but with a chamfered design.

"Like a piece of tin, you know, with the sharp ends turned over. But they were both *gold* – 9 carat gold," June observed.

"But, June," I said, my mind revolving lightly in disbelief, "you were working at Courtaulds for about ten years. All the girls there knew you, and yet you were able to go about wearing wedding rings . . . *Surely* they must have thought you'd secretly got married?"

But simply because it was the truth, and a true account of her own life, June pressed on with absolute patience, as if explaining something difficult to a child. She did not have the words to describe the golden wedding rings as a symbol of unavailability, but that is what she meant.

"Well, they knew we *hadn't* got married, because they knew we were very quiet and that it would have been impossible for us to be married, you know. But those girls we were quite friendly with – them we had our tea-breaks with – would say, 'Oh, you've got a wedding ring on!', and we would have to say, 'Oh, it's just that we're not interested in going out with any boyfriends.' You see, we *had* to tell them that, because we couldn't say, '*We are married!*'"

Maureen Preston was sitting absolutely rapt beside me on the sofa and, still in his comfortable place on the other side of the big mock-stone hearth, Dennis was sending smoke clouds up from his cigarette in higher and higher ejections of incredulity.

"And so you see," I concluded rather lamely to both of them, "Tommy did sort of marry them – in that shop."

Maureen then was suddenly back on form.

"A secret like that was *so* well kept!" and I now supposed that she was referring to Tommy's most unusual continuing sexual liaison with his daughters until their early middle age.

"The wonder to me," I said, "is that they didn't kill him twenty years before."

But then Dennis became rather wise. Throwing his mind over the changes in society since the 1970s, the greater insights we have nowadays into the secret world of the family and, with all its imperfections, the greater humanity that is today shown in court to victim-perpetrators of domestic violence, Dennis said, smiling, "If they'd done it twenty years ago, they wouldn't have got away with it . . ."

And then he rose to make us all a very welcome cup of tea.

They had plugged Mrs Thompson's nostrils with special gauze, wadded her nose on the outside, where two black eyes were closing, and passing nurses left more icecubes beside the bed for her to suck, because this time Tommy had broken her nose.

Tommy Thompson was now drinking something like a bottle of whisky a day and, in the evenings, his violence towards her seemed to worsen, if that were possible. He thought nothing of thumping, head-butting, kicking or dragging any of them round the room by the hair. Mrs Thompson flinched in agony when he hit Young Hilda or June as if he had struck her as well, and they in turn found having to stand by and watch him laying hard into her quite unbearable. June had begun to say that she couldn't watch, and that evening she had had to turn her head away.

But it was when he was cruel not to them but to animals that Mrs Thompson saw Tommy most clearly as a child – someone she had genuinely tried to understand as a man for over twenty-five years. If he could kill animals slowly and imaginatively time and time again, he could also, like some little master of life and death, cause them to breed frantically and desperately within a purlieu of his own. Even if blissful painkilling drugs had not made her woozy, she could scarcely remember in which dark back yard it had taken place, because there had been so many – but that time he had permitted rabbits by the score to breed and bob about like a sea of fur on filthy flag-stones strewn with rotting cabbage leaves. Then, from a back downstairs window she could only bear to watch for a few seconds as some new system of destruction went into operation. Tommy, towering out in the yard, legs apart like a colossus, had swung each rabbit up in turn by the ears, slicing the hard edge of his right hand into the back of each creature's neck and then flinging it down to add to a pleasurable stack of the dead. Only one rabbit of the silent multitude had uttered a thin, piercing shriek as he had swung it up to kill it, and the cry of the mute is unbearable.

These days, June and Young Hilda found that if either of them spoke or uttered one sound when Tommy was beating their mother in front of them, he would hit her more and harder as a punishment. And tonight, when he had directly punched her in the face and suddenly there had been blood everywhere, cascades of it, Tommy relied on his daughters as usual to clean up and cover up.

"Stop her nose from bleeding!" he had instructed through clenched teeth, "or I'll put *you* both in hospital!"

Then they had tried everything to stop the bleeding, but it wouldn't stop and she had had to keep spitting out blood because she couldn't swallow it – there was so much, she felt she was going to choke on it. Above her head and the red-soaked kitchen towels, June asked if they could send for an ambulance and he said "Yes", because he must have known it was more than just the usual nosebleed she sometimes got when he knocked her about.

Young Hilda had just gone, parting from her in casualty, and now she had been formally admitted and trundled into the sheltering depths of a hospital ward. As usual, Hilda had accompanied her to hospital and June stayed behind with Tommy to clear up the mess on the living-room carpet and furniture, while he sat by and watched. As usual, she had made up another story to tell the ambulance men and casualty staff, because, from a curious mixture of habit, hopelessness and shame, no way would she let them think that her own husband had done this to her.

Young Hilda always seemed to be detailed by Tommy to accompany her mother to hospital. On another evening when her daughters had tried to move silently as usual, one to each side of her to stop her falling so hard when Tommy was punching her, they had failed to save her from stumbling backwards through an internal glass door, but that time Tommy had deemed her fit enough to walk the twenty minutes or so to the old Preston Royal Infirmary in Deepdale Road. It was a cool summer night and on the way she had complained to Hilda of feeling pricked in the back, as if by needles ("Sometimes I've not felt the pain of something until afterwards . . .") and when Young Hilda had fearfully run a hand up inside her mother's coat, she had found splinters of glass sticking out of her back. Just as she had done tonight, Mrs Thompson was accustomed to lying about how she came by such injuries and, because living with men like Tommy seemed barely recognized or questioned by the outside world, the medical staff had efficiently and mechanically treated the injuries that presented themselves without attempting to look much further into what had repeatedly caused them. By now this was a situation that almost suited her – no questions asked, just treatment given – because going into hospital was her "holiday time". Even when she was going to have an operation or radiotherapy for cancer of the mouth, everyone was so nice. There was the peace and cleanliness of the bed, being able to lie quietly and unmolested, and then the simple but extraordinary fact that other people, staff and patients, treated her with politeness and even deference, just as if she were a real person. But when the ward doors on women's surgical eventually opened at visiting times to let in the busy stream and shaken-down umbrellas of the outside world, that dark, gleeful figure would stalk down the centre of the ward again – and it would be Tommy.

Sometimes, even as long ago as when the children were still at school and he had started the shameful business of abusing June, Tommy would lie down on the hearth-rug in front of the fire, saying that he could not go on any more, signalling to her to lie down beside him and to hold him until some inner bad time had passed to the point of being bearable. At other times, he would lie on the downstairs sofa-bed and she would sit on the floor, holding his hand until she knew "he felt better of himself". Very often (and it was something the girls had also noted for a long time) Tommy, when in one of his calamitously black moods, would reproach them with, "*You* never had Devil sent to ye!"

> *Tommy's mother said she would send the Devil to him if he were Bad. Tommy's mother told me he was strong-willed and very defiant as a Child. She used to say to him that if he wasn't a good Lad she would send DEVIL to him and he used to be afraid.*

Then, at the end of a black outburst which sometimes reduced Tommy and herself to the floor, he would say, "I'm not bothered about living" meaning that if only he could die, he wouldn't care, and sometimes, with what seemed to be genuine anguish and a kind of plea, as if they were the powerful ones able to dispense mercy to him, "I want out. *I want out!* If you were out there in the real world – you don't know what it's like . . ."

Tommy looked like such a model husband that other women in the ward often turned their heads to glimpse him. He was always so smartly turned out, so good-looking, alert and punctual. Whatever the visiting hours in Preston, he was always there on the dot, kissing her lightly on the cheek and then sitting down affectionately at the end of the bed (although sitting on patients' beds was supposed to be forbidden). He always kept up some sweet-talking flow of words for the benefit of women in neighbouring beds – We miss you so much at home, June and Hilda send their love, Get well soon, Arguing with a door, were we? Get well soon, love, We can't do without you. And then, when he had sat out the full hour or so, and had gone again with perfectly executed kisses and that penetrating look which made her remember exactly where reality lay, a woman in a neighbouring bed would almost always make some respectful remark about what a lovely husband, he was – "I wish I had a husband like that!" And, as if drawn into Tommy's compelling fiction, she would write letters to him from her hospital bed as if they were so deeply in love that they could not bear to be out of communication for forty-eight hours.

> *Darling Tommy, June & Hilda, Here's a few lines, love to let you know I arrived at Hospital Safe & sound*

or

> *Tommy Love, I have just had my Pre-Med at ten-past-one. I don't know what time I will be going to the theatre but I will think of you all the way love*

or

> *Dearest Sweetheart, It was so nice to hear your voice on the phone. You are a Big Love to phone me like that*

or

> *To my Dearest Sweetheart & Daughters, hello loves – thanks very much for your letters and phone calls you make. It's very good of you all. I miss you all so much . . .*

At first, when I had discovered these love letters stapled to the appropriate pages of June's diary, I was shocked and dismayed. Dear heaven, I thought, surely she doesn't love him as well? Mothers in incestuous families are like lightning rods, instantly conducting indignation from those who have never experienced domestic violence themselves. But unlike some perhaps more reprehensible women, Mrs Thompson had not herself been erotically involved in the abuse of her children. She was physically broken by Tommy to the point of regular hospitalization, ill, financially dependent on what he chose to dole out. She seemed merely to have done the deal which many women were once forced to do, hoping her children could endure their father's violence in return for food, shelter and, in her case, after the shotgun had entered their lives, in return for life itself.

Eventually, it turned out that throughout the 1970s, as Tommy became increasingly anxious that his adult daughters might blow the whistle, he demanded written evidence, bits of paper to hoard away, 'proving' that he was a good husband and father. By writing letters as he instructed from her hospital bed, maintaining Tommy's fiction to the outside world that they were an ideal family, Mrs Thompson hoped that he would not be too hard on June and Young Hilda, either sexually or in casual physical punishment, while she was away. She must write in her letters what Tommy wanted to read. But what Tommy was doing to June and Young Hilda when, say, she was away for longer times, "enjoying" herself at the Christie cancer hospital in Manchester, was a constant shadow at the edge of her relief in getting away from him ("I knew I could beat cancer but I couldn't beat him"). Then, from time to time (and she was always very courageous when faced with the needle) some blissful drugs would take her out of it altogther.

For a man not much given to reading, Tommy Thompson seems to have believed in the power of the written word and in family photographs almost as if they were forms of magic to ward off the intrusion of the outside world, while 'controlling' external appearances and inner reality. In the quite transparent way that he increasingly revealed his own inner stresses as an exceptionally successful abusing father, he once actually announced to the family, "Preston's a harder town. I'll have to keep a front on, especially with three women." Consequently, from Thursday, 30 April 1970, until the last entry on Friday, 11 March 1988 (the day before his murder), Tommy made June Thompson keep a daily diary, sometimes reading what she had written, to ensure that a 'proper' record was being kept in case any outsider should ever begin to seek the truth.

Sure enough, as I pored again over the scores of tiny pocket diaries, meticulously wrapped in brown-paper bundles by June Thompson for me to carry back to my room in Glasgow, many of her short, banal entries, day by day, year by year, began to make rather more sinister sense.

Wednesday 13th July 1977

Mam cut her wrist, bottom of back and cheek of her bottom on the glass vestibule door. Went to PRI [Preston Royal Infirmary] *had them stitched, had a tetanus injection and then came home. Has to have stitches out in 10 days.*

Wednesday 12th April 1978

Mam caught her finger of right hand. Has it checked at PRI in case it was broken. They said it wasn't broken but they have strapped it to the finger next to it. Has to keep it like this for a week and then go back to PRI . . . Mam also caught the back of her left leg.

Tuesday 16th June 1981

Mam went to PRI because her index finger of right hand was a purple colour. They didn't X-ray it. They taped it to the other finger so Mam wouldn't bend it. They said rest it. They couldn't tell her why it was like that.

"If anything happened to Mum when he was hitting her," June explained over the phone from Preston (because now we were able to hold short, long-distance telephone conversations), "I had to write in my diary that she had just fallen, or had a little accident or something. He was keeping a kind of false record."

Needless to say, June was also required to keep a record of her 'voluntary' visits to the local Family Planning Clinic, just as any mature woman keeps calendar jottings of her sexual activity.

Thursday 3rd November 1983

I went to clinic to tell them I want to come off the Pill because of news in papers about there being more women getting cancer that is on the Pill . . . I decided I wanted to come off it myself. It has been changed on my file to sheaths – lighter-weight Durex contraceptives . . . my last smear test was 2/6/83. Only allowed 30 Durex every 3 months.

And then, tracking back, I began to notice that, among hundreds of usually rather boring diary entries, June had been sometimes commanded by Tommy to write down 'proof' of her own happiness.

15th June 1977
It was my birthday today . . . I have everything that I could wish for.

One day, when casually left beside boxes of smiling family photographs, these fabricated records, diaries and love letters were intended by Tommy Thompson to stand as an officially acceptable account of the family. Tommy Thompson had long wanted to die and now the urge was becoming imperative. Very soon, when he could no longer bear the weight of his colossal deceit, all members of this enclosed branch of the Thompson family would be shot, and the truth would also die with them. As June recalled:

The year before he died, I used to think it was only a matter of time before it would be in the paper [local newspaper] *Family Found Shot Dead In Their Home & nobody would know what we all went through Physically and Mentally trying to cope and live with somebody who wouldn't let us leave him.*

It was Young Hilda, the most 'protected' member of the family, who mentally buckled under the strain of Tommy Thompson's game with the outside world and his own increasing mental illness. Day by day, leaking and oozing round the house like vapour, creeping insanity was the one thing that Tommy Thompson could not catch hold of or contain.

I was in a dark tunnel and I kept running and trying to get to the end of the tunnel but something or someone kept pulling me back.

It was such an effort getting up in the morning that sometimes June had to help her rise from the edge of the bed. Young Hilda could barely lift her arms up to her head to comb her hair and washing her hair seemed like a task of such heroic proportions that she could only weep at the idea of it. The tears that seemed to roll down a face belonging to a stranger were big, cold and effortless, yet somewhere in the darkness she still knew that Tommy could not stand crying.

"*Pull yourself together*. Don't be so soft. If you don't stop crying, I'll give ye something to cry about –" and the blow, when it came, seemed to arrive on her leaden body from nowhere.

Young Hilda had no appetite, was losing weight so that clothes hung loose and even her shoes seemed bigger, and she woke early in the morning, crushed by tingling fear that she could not remember exactly what to do to get through a day that stretched ahead as long and arduous as a month. She seemed to make more and more bad mistakes at home.

"Did anybody *make you* leave that drawer open?" Tommy would say sarcastically, when, entirely through her fault, some drawer in his crazy sideboard stuck out by a quarter of an inch.

"No, Dad. Nobody made me leave that drawer open."

"You've done it to cause bother?"

"No, Dad."

"*Don't quote me!*"

And then a swift movement across a room that she could no longer see very clearly meant that she would receive a punch on the side of the head, beneath her hair, where the marks would not show. At times June and her mother seemed to waver and sometimes vanish at the very edges of a pall of black. She felt she was going blind and sometimes tried gently shaking her head from side to side, to see if the darkness could be dispelled. They were there but out on the outside of it all, trying to help her perform her duties as usual, because now the House Rules seemed to be more than ever impossible to sustain.

Smile!

1. Every item of food, domestic hardware and medication must be logged in writing with date, price and place of purchase and put in the upstairs storeroom.
2. All ornaments in house must be always placed in *exactly* the same position. Little turquoise china cat on sideboard (left) must be always in exact same place to smash burglar with at night.
3. Small glass mug must always have its handle pointing exactly to the right. Must be always filled with clean water and placed *exactly* at edge of mantelpiece so Tommy can reach up from his downstairs bed to pick it up and drink from it.
4. When drinking at home or in pubs (*Smile*!), all used mugs and glasses must be pushed into centre of pub table, exactly five inches from edge of table so that no passer-by will "catch" the edge of them. Tommy is always warning against everything that can cause an accident – "If anything should happen – if anything should happen."
5. When holding glasses in pub (Tommy likes to be seen with us in County Arms, where, although he will have already told us beforehand what we must drink, we must pretend we are considering our fancy about what to order while he stands back normally). In pub he smiles and looks friendly, looking around. So, when holding our drinks' glasses in pubs, little fingers of me, June and Mum must be placed *underneath* pub glasses, "in case a wet glass should slip out of your hand . . . If anything should happen – if anything should happen."
6. Washed spoons must be turned downwards on draining board in case their metal bowls collect water.
7. Prongs of forks must always point upwards.
8. No clatter. There will be absolute silence when washing-up is being done (June, help me). There merest sound of one plate clashing against the next makes him boil with rage.

9. No click must be audible when electric light is being switched off but, on the other hand, all jobs must be done quickly and to order.
10. No drawer will be left open.
11. In morning, margarine must be spread on bread quickly and efficiently in one direction only and always fully to the absolute corners of the slice.
12. When out walking as a family up Skeffington Road, we all walk two abreast, Young Hilda and June in front, so that I can keep an eye on you.
13. When out walking as already described, pockets in all outdoor coats and jackets must not have anything in them to spoil line of garment.

And then he had bought all three women in the family cheap identical red jackets so that, although it was embarrassing in the outside world, they all looked like uniformed members of some little platoon.

In the evenings, the Thompson women would watch Tommy closely and keep an eye on the dying light outside to try to judge the exact psychological moment to draw the curtains. The right moment of balance between the outside and inside worlds had to be struck – so dark inside the house that, in front of the television set, all four heads of the Thompson family looked violet in the shadows, while the evening sky beyond the window still looked light.

"If it was too light outside," recalled Young Hilda, "he'd say, 'Get those curtains open', but on other nights he would demand, 'Why haven't ye got those curtains closed yet?'" Eventually, curtain-closing time was posted up on the wall in the manner of military orders.

In his ceaseless DIY way, once sending them out to scavenge useful bits of wood from derelict houses in the neighbourhood and then dragging them home, lashed together with old tights, Tommy had made a little wooden cabinet to keep his daily bottle of whisky in. It was locked and Tommy kept the key, but now Young Hilda longed and then needed to drink some alcohol. Occasionally in the past Tommy had given them all small measures of whisky, doling it out like medicine as if in some effort to keep the family going. Nowadays, because it floated her away, Young Hilda needed more and more, and craved a lovely amber bottle of her own. Holding back a little money from the housekeeping, she eventually had enough cash to buy and hide away her own first bottle of whisky. It took her away to sleep and darkness, and she loved it. Sometimes, when she ventured out with her mother, Mrs Thompson would wait, keeping a watch for Tommy in a shop doorway, while she slipped into an off-licence for a smaller bottle, hiding it in her pocket and swigging it in the lavatory or bedroom to keep her going.

To cope with the stress of living at home with Tommy, Young Hilda had begun to drink a little whisky on and off from the age of twenty. Although he had long since ceased to make sexual advances to her, fiercely concentrating his sexual needs on June, Tommy Thompson seems to have recognized that somehow Young Hilda was the one to watch. She seemed capable of mentally cracking up and, in his situation, her very vulnerability spelled danger. To quell her distress and to keep her going, he would increasingly administer whisky to her himself, measuring it out from an optic bottle he kept at home in the manner of medicine. Alcohol is known to figure very much in child sexual abuse. Sometimes a potential abuser will give it to a young girl as part of the 'grooming' process to loosen her inhibitions and make her feel special or 'grown-up'. More often it is used by the abuser to blur his own intolerable distress. By the early 1980s, though still able to work, Young Hilda had become heavily dependent on alcohol because all anti-depressants had failed.

The doctor and then the psychiatrists were so quiet with her in the daily shifts of colour, when things floating about in the room seemed blue and then the cycle altered to black. None of the anti-depressant drugs they gave her seemed to do any good but, coming in from the outside, their kind questions always sounded the same.

"Hilda, is there anything troubling you at home or at work?"

"No."

Or, "Hilda, are you *quite sure* there's nothing you can think of that might be causing your depression?"

"No."

And because she could not tell them anything for fear of what would happen to her mother and June, all she could do was to shake her head and say, time and time again, "No, nothing I can think of."

Then she had gone with June to Sharoe Green Hospital (a mental hospital, she knew) and all she had known of the first ECT day, 4 April 1984, when they were going to make her brain jerk with a big electric shock, was an injection which put her to sleep. After what seemed only seconds, she woke with a headache so deeply and drivingly bad that she wanted to be sick. The nice nurse had let her lie in the recovery room, given her painkillers, and brought in the first food of the day – a slice of toast and a cup of tea. She could remember nothing, knew nothing and merely seemed able to take in remote but familiar objects of the present time – a white china cup and saucer and her sister smiling at the side of the bed.

"Don't worry, love," the nurses always said, because, eventually, she was given four of these ECT things. "Sometimes people find they can't remember things for a little while, but then your memory comes back."

It was the terrible sound of his latch-key in the door after a night's drinking in the pub that still had the power to stir Young Hilda from her torpor of drugs, darkness and whisky. Suddenly hanging on to the frame of the living-room door, Tommy would yell in an agony of madness and drink, "I want out! *I want out!*" Reaching up to the crazy cupboard he had nailed together from two chests, one set on top of the other, he would pull it forwards, letting the thing crash down onto them in the room. If all three women did not rise to right the heavy piece of furniture instantly, Tommy sent for the gun and, lying with it beside him on the downstairs bed, he would make them all stand in different corners of the room, faces turned to the wall, for hours on end, until the television hummed blank and he fell into a drunken doze. Gauging the moment when he might be deeply enough asleep, June would sometimes silently take the gun away from his resting arm, restoring it to its proper place upstairs.

June Thompson now agreed that if their mother should die from this latest bout of cancer, and at last be out of it, she and Hilda would kill themselves together. But Young Hilda wondered if she could last that long. Around her the walls of the house seemed to close in, inch by inch. Every day, the ceiling came down an inch, with a little jerk. The walls moved in an inch. The floor rose by an inch, like a cell of little ease. To make one last effort to get through to her father, Young Hilda told him she wanted to kill herself – presumably he wouldn't mind? But, as if his long arm reached beyond the grave itself, all he said was that if anything happened to her, he would kill June and Mum, and she knew he meant it.

> *Dad knew that if I killed myself there would be enquiries into why I did kill myself, so he didn't want anybody asking this & that about everything. So I couldn't even kill myself because I loved Mum and June that much . . .*

All she could do now was lie down, pulling her knees up to her chin inside a kind of grey veil, and even if he kicked her to pulp, she would scarcely notice. Curled into a ball, with Tommy yelling at her, somewhere far away, to get up – "Get up, get up. *You're not pulling your weight in this house!*" – Young Hilda passed through the interior colours of withdrawal from blue to black and then on sometimes to a total inner raptness, almost white, of cataleptic depression. She couldn't live, couldn't die, couldn't bear it but, now aged thirty-five and turning on some kind of inner pivot, she would not go on any more.

8

In Sickness and in Health

It was Friday, 11 March 1988, the day before Tommy Thompson's murder. In the nearby Geoffrey Street group medical practice, Dr Andrew Mayor – a hard-pressed GP in his mid-thirties – added the name of one of the Thompson sisters (193 Skeffington Road) to his already swollen list of house-calls for the day. Over the years, each member of the Thompson family had contributed to medical records as long as your arm – heart disease, cancer, back pain, epilepsy, diabetes, sleeplessness, chronic this and that, depression. You name it, they had it, in the way that health calamities always seem to shower down on the simple and unemployed. The health of the Thompson sisters had more or less held up during their years of employment, but both had been made redundant in 1980 and then again in 1983. From what he could see, neither of them had worked since.

Back in June 1981, Tommy Thompson had suffered a 'mini-stroke' and was hospitalized for a month. June and Young Hilda had just begun work in their last job at John Barnes in Miller Road, Preston – a nearby purplish-brick Victorian mill with a mass of grey corrugated metal sheds tacked on to it. After Courtaulds, John Barnes had seemed to be rather an old-fashioned place, as if they had drifted back to some ancient way of textile working. But it was a gloriously hot summer and Tommy was away from home for a whole month. June wrote:

> *It was lovely to get up in the morning &* [the fact] *he wasn't there made life worth living. We were very careful with money but we managed to treat ourselves to some treats like buying fish in sauce that you boil in the bag, biscuits, ice-cream sometimes . . .*

Whatever June and Young Hilda's shifts, all three Thompson women contrived to visit Tommy twice a day in hospital, and they found at the beginning that he was a model invalid. Very patient, not a cross word and

> *us three thought, 'I wonder if having this Mini-Stroke has stopped him getting bad-tempered with us?' We prayed that he would be like this, if only some of the time. At least it would give us a break.*

Needless to say, once Tommy had regathered his physical strength, left the surveillance of hospital and returned home, *Our prayers weren't answered.*

Shortly after Tommy Thompson was discharged from hospital, he began to suffer from epileptic fits as a result of minor brain damage sustained during the stroke. On one occasion, he had as many as eight in one day, before they were largely brought under control by drugs. Like any ordinary person, Tommy Thompson found the idea that he could be randomly seized from consciousness and flung down, completely out of control, quite terrifying – the gaping blank in an otherwise ordinary day when he would not have known that anything at all had happened to him except for drowsiness, stiffening bruises where he had involuntarily lashed out, struck his head on the floor or bitten his tongue in the indignity of a major convulsion. For him in particular, a man whose life had been built around retaining control over others and walls around himself, this new lack of physical integrity seems to have become intolerable, and he began again to mention in a vague way that he hoped during one of these fits to die.

On 7 October 1982, after working at the John Barnes mill for just over a year, the Thompson sisters were made redundant once more and both of them began to have minor epileptic episodes themselves – in June's case no more than a momentary blackout. The first time it happened she was just reaching up to get hold of a tin from a shelf in the Asda supermarket. This was when Mrs Thompson was continuing her long battle with facial cancer and, with no more work to structure the Thompson sisters' day, all four members of the family seemed to sink entwined in a kind of invalid twilight.

Late that Friday afternoon, Dr Mayor entered the fiercely neat terraced house in Skeffington Road, toning down the briskness which a busy doctor always feels towards the end of a long house-call run. The elder daughter, June – a gem – led him into the downstairs room. With its two single beds, one on each side of the teak fireplace and the neatly arranged batteries of drugs set out at Mum's and Dad's separate ends of the mantelpiece, it had the air of a small, competently run hospital ward.

That day, June and Young Hilda had waited hour by hour for Dr Mayor as for the coming of a saviour, because this time, even in that family, there was a sense of something gliding out of control. In his younger daughter's damned blackness, Tommy Thompson also sensed an ultimate presence he could no longer cope with alone. Dr Mayor must take her away, *take her away*, because in her vagueness, wandering and slow horrible tears, there was something now encompassing them all that could not be destroyed by any physical means he knew.

As usual, in the small fiercely neat room, Dr Mayor had to speak to his patient in full view of everyone else in the family. Even if they had had the grace to withdraw, there was probably nowhere else for them to go.

"Hilda," he said, kneeling down to meet the blank young woman face to face. "How are you feeling?"

"Black . . . black. I'm in a tunnel. I can't get out."

"You don't think the anti-depressants are doing any good?"

"Black. It's the worst I've ever felt. I can't stop crying. I think I'm going to faint all the time."

"Listen, Hilda –"

"I can't go on, doctor."

"Hilda, listen. I'm going to admit you to the Avondale Unit at the PRH. Do you understand that? I'll get you in there on Monday."

Then Dr Mayor was conscious of Tommy Thompson back from the edges of the room and rather sharply at his side in an instant.

"Get her in there today!"

Jotting down the details, as if he had not heard, Dr Mayor rose to meet him.

"Look, Mr Thompson, I'll make the arrangements to admit Hilda as soon as I get back to the surgery. The weekend's just starting – not a good time for hospital admissions unless it's an emergency."

"You'd get 'er in there fast enough if she were a bloody drug addict!"

"That's a different thing altogether."

"*Get 'er out of 'ere!*"

Beginning to sense fear on the air, because witnessing mental illness often took people that way (and possibly the man was even crying?), the doctor minutely backed away. Mentally noting down Tommy Thompson as "over-protective", Dr Mayor glanced at June Thompson, so solid, silent and calm in the background. He knew with absolute confidence that as long as this sensible sister was in the house to look after her, there was no question of Hilda Thompson taking her own life for the next seventy-two hours.

Calm professional procedures produce the best outcome and now it was time to part on good terms with the family, having established that help had been properly set in train. Facing Tommy Thompson, Dr Mayor said in as reassuring a way as he could, "Your daughter is in no immediate danger. She has her sister here to look after her until she can be admitted to hospital on Monday morning."

"*If you're going to be like that, get out of my house!*"

"Mr Thompson, you're only making it worse for Hilda. I'm going back *now* to make the arrangements. Hilda will be admitted to the Avondale Unit on Monday morning."

Then, with a friendly nod towards June Thompson, her patient and their mother, who stood pale, deaf and faintly dribbling – for ever dabbing with a paper tissue at the corners of her collapsed eye and mouth – Dr Mayor was suddenly immensely relieved to put a perfectly painted front door between himself and the family at 193 Skeffington Road.

There were two whole days and three more nights to get through. On the night of Friday, 11 March 1988, tacitly recognizing crisis, the entire Thompson family slept together in the downstairs room, June and Young Hilda sharing one bed, Tommy and Mrs Thompson sharing the sofa-bed under the window. In the first hours of the night, when ITV had run its span, the light was off and, cooling, the electric fire twanged in contraction, Young Hilda got some sleep, knocked out by antidepressants, sleeping pills and whisky, while June lay awake on watch. Soon, giving point to the way that night hours both float and drag, June would sense the renewed consciousness of her sister, rigid at first and then whispering under their father's snores and their mother's delicate wheezing, "I can't go on any more. I'm really very bad."

Even when pressed down by this suffocating darkness, June Thompson could have stolen blind over the perfectly ordered room to put her hand immediately and silently upon any item in it – the big picture above them of three kittens looking up through pink spring boughs, the pink and blue His 'n' Hers plastic waste-bins perfectly set at the side of each bed. Apart from the drugs she had so carefully arranged at each end of the mantelpiece, there were still more pills and medicines arranged on a little table beside Tommy's bed, along with items he now liked close to hand – a policeman's whistle and a knife. Sometimes he would ask her to shave him in the morning as he lay on top of the bed, buzzing the warm chrome heel of the electric razor over a facial landscape she knew so hideously well until, in exasperation, he would seize the razor to complete the job himself ("*Give it 'ere!*"), or demand that she stand quite still beside the bed while he hit her. As if she could remember nothing, he had asked her to write out little notices in biro and to post them up inside the cupboard doors.

MORN TABLETS

DAD (Fits)
4 Phenytion
1 Sun
1 Royal Jelly
1 Vitamin

JUNE
1 Epelim
1 Sun
1 Royal Jelly

HILDA
1 Epelim
1 Sun
2 Vitamins
1 Nortripyline

MAMS
1 Sun
1 Royal Jelly
1 Vitamin
1 Blood Pressure
1 Anti-Sickness

Then, as if animals and even day-to-day shopping could be controlled only by writing it down and putting it up for all to read, came another notice inside Tommy's home-made cupboard door: BUDGIES LOSE THEIR FEATHERS (MOULTING) IN SEPTEMBER.

STARTED TO USE NEW SOAP-DISH (FROM 'CHOICE') ON 26.11.87. £3.99. Meanwhile, to spare their evening quizzing of the skies, June's new notice on the wall read: CURTAIN CLOSING TIME 21.00hrs.

Next morning, by the seam of light round the curtains, Young Hilda's blank eyes were visible, staring only at the ceiling. With anxiety churning in her own stomach, June Thompson sat bolt upright in bed and quite formally wished her parents, "Good morning."

That day, helping Young Hilda to lift her arms to dress and to rise from the side of the bed was very hard work. As if to spite his seriously depressed daughter and her continuing foul presence in the house, Tommy Thompson demanded that she and she alone should be the one to cook his egg on toast for breakfast. But her head again gravitated to the bed, because she felt drawn downwards remorselessly and must lie.

"Get the fucking thing. Go on! There's fuck-all wrong with you."

There must be no tears, but they reamed down like rain as, willed by her sister's eyes, Young Hilda made it up and across the few daunting yards to the kitchen.

Behind her, through the open kitchen door, the same voice went on and on, but with some new note in it, to June and her mother.

"You lot have everything you want. She should be able to carry on doing ordinary things in the house, whatever she feels . . ."

This time, June could not help with the terrible task of frying the egg. But somehow, beginning to do the thing that she must do, Young Hilda held the box of matches in her left hand and took one out. The gas of the unlit grill quietly hissed on as she struck the match time and time again – holding at arms' length the possibility of that sudden sulphurous flare engulfing her and her smooth white hands. When it came, the sudden sheet of flame made her want to scream, but at least the fire was lit to make Tommy's toast. Level with her blank eyes, the purple tongues withdrew, settling into a steady square of fire.

Tommy Thompson's fried egg needed to be perfection. When cooked, there must be no brown fringe round the circumference of the white. The yolk must be runny, enclosed on top by the faintest film of white but sufficiently well cooked beneath to let it slide without breaking from pan to plate. Tommy had already counted the eggs in the box and none must be wasted. Breaking the egg perfectly was a hard thing to do. He must not hear the cracking of the shell, but the hard oval thing in her unsteady hand seemed quite impenetrable. Somewhere down in the darkness she tapped the egg again on the edge of a thick-rimmed basin, passed her thumb into the dent in the shell, but still felt the thin white membrane resisting. What if the yolk should break, spewing out yellow to whiten hard in the babbling fat of the pan? But then the whole yolk went free, safely and quite whole on its gluey float. The spoon that lapped a little hot fat over the dome of yellow was held at arms' length and soon the ghost of white also rose. With June and her mother willing her to be careful, Young Hilda now had an eye to the slice of toast, turning it over – not a sound – letting it take colour on the underside before drawing it away from the red-hot square.

House Rule 11. In morning, margarine must be spread on bread quickly and efficiently in one direction only and always fully to the absolute corners of the slice.

Then, perfectly centred on the Teflon slice, the fragile white and yellow thing in all its perfection travelled over to the bread. Passed over from darkness with a knife (handle presented to his hand to avoid injury) and fork (*House Rule 7. Prongs of forks must always point upwards*), the last food she would ever cook for Tommy was in his hands.

Young Hilda felt the breath of the outside world that afternoon but saw nothing as, like a blind woman, she stumbled beside her mother a few yards to the shops to get in what was necessary for the next few days' survival. Because it was Saturday afternoon, jolly time, June had gone to the County Arms with Tommy. Already instructed to ask him casually for cider, she set her glass down on the damp towelling beer mat exactly five inches from the edge of the pub table, while Tommy looked round smiling but distracted at the landlord, Brian Atkinson. June always kept the little finger of her right hand very carefully under a glass each time she raised it to her smiling lips in a pub, but this time she did it with extra care and precision, because this was a day on which nothing must go wrong. She raised her cider glass, looked pretty and smiled. Tommy drank whisky and beer and then, as if he did not really want to go, they walked home arm in arm.

There was one more evening, one more night, a whole day and one last night to go before Young Hilda could be taken away to a place of safety. To spare her sister further bother June Thompson sat on a chair for the rest of the day beside her father's bed, utterly alert to every wish he might express, waiting for the clock to crawl forwards. At 5 that evening, ITV was switched on again and June tried to adjust the volume of sound, almost minute by minute, to Tommy's liking – silently moving to turn it down when loud music blared up at dramatic moments; then equally deftly raising it again when there was nothing on but speech. At last, Tommy permitted Young Hilda to lie down fully on the second bed and, under the soothing flicker of TV twilight, she wept silently and unmolested, waiting for Monday, the Avondale Unit and the utter freedom of lying at peace among the mad.

At about 8.30 that evening (still half-an-hour before curtain-closing time) June Thompson noticed that her father's bright, dark eyes were fixed but quivering slightly. Blank as an ancient statue, the whites of his eyes then slid up to the ceiling. His body was becoming rigid, fists clenched and legs drawn up, as if gathering strength for some terrible purpose. Breathing had stopped and he was turning faintly blue.

From the kitchen came the sound of running water as Mrs Thompson, far away in a deaf, sick, fragile world of her own, fiddled about at the sink.

"Hilda," said June very quietly, rising to her feet at Tommy's side.

Since Tommy's fits had begun, the Thompson sisters had always drawn close to their father's side, placing a clean, folded handkerchief between his teeth to stop him biting his tongue and saying from habit kind words he could not hear. But this time June Thompson found that she had no words. Instead, the ancient gurgling cry of the *grand mal* epileptic hit the ceiling as Tommy entered the so-called 'tonic' phase of his fit. Trapped air in the seized man's lungs involuntarily shot out, as if a spiteful child had jumped on a thrown-down squeeze-box.

Rising like a spectre from her mother's bed, Young Hilda looked at June across her father's body and her voice was hollow as if it belonged to someone else far, far away.

"June," she said, "I can't stand any more of this life we're living."

Out in the kitchen, the tap ran on and on, splashing and drivelling, and grappling with his bucking pelvis, June Thompson began to loosen Tommy's leather belt to give him ease. Jumping and lashing from side to side in the twilight, the man had now been fully seized, as if thrown down in a crazy dance gleefully instigated in a world they could not see – come dance with *me*!

Young Hilda had been so well brought up – right from wrong, obeying always, cheerful in adversity, fending off despair. But now, as if walking quite calmly from one room to another, like the shadow of a new person, she said quite simply, "We have to do something. We'll have to shoot him."

This time, even June Thompson had not been able to say, "It's all right, Dad – you'll be all right soon."

"Hilda, I'm too frightened."

But very denial set her legs in motion, jelly joints pulled on metal wires up the stairs to the place where the gun was kept. He had sent her for it so often before (*don't let him come to yet*) and, as if in a dream, it was loaded, snapped back into one rigid whole and she was at his side in an instant. Tommy's chest was being flung about so violently that June put the muzzle of the gun directly to it because all she knew was that she must not miss.

At the first shot, her mother stood aghast in the kitchen doorway while the tap ran on and on behind her.

Young Hilda merely said, "You'll have to do it again. To make sure."

But Tommy's thrashing and jerking had stopped, although his eyes still seemed alive and still looked up to the very same place on the ceiling.

"We *can't*!"

"But," reasoned Young Hilda to her elder sister, speaking words she did not know she could speak, "he always said he wanted to die – never wanted to come round from a fit. He wants to die."

Remembering the howls and screams of all the animals that he had later tried to square with her in an almost kindly way, she repeated his words, "We can't let him suffer."

Truly believing that at any moment Tommy would breathe naturally again, regain facial colour, stir, turn his head and say, "Am I still alive?", June reloaded the gun (because only she knew how) and passed it over her father's body to her sister who, quite calmly and with no hesitation whatever, shot him again at point-blank range in the chest, barely a quarter of an inch away from the shot June had just administered. Two wounds – my pain and yours.

Mrs Thompson collapsed into a chair. They cannot remember how – but the key was found to Tommy's DIY cabinet which held the whisky. It was opened and, getting glasses from the kitchen – they all held them with the little finger of each right hand carefully placed beneath – they drank and drank and drank the quantity they needed. Then, spread about the room, prostrate in agonies of fear and grief, the Thompson women wailed around the bed of Tommy Thompson as if at the wake of a great man. Some time later, in a state of slurred, automatic lightness, June Thompson rose to her feet and dialled 999. At 9 p.m. a police constable in the communications room of Lawson Street police station took a call from a woman who sounded distressed and whose speech roved a bit as if in drink:

"Someone has shot my husband in the head and I think he is dead."

She was so tiny, pale and shaking, and her daughters had

already been taken away together. To make conversation as the woman lowered her head to get into the police car, the Detective Sergeant said all he could think of to personalize, in a kindly way, her removal from the house.

"What's your name?"

"Hilda."

She looked out of the window like a child suddenly seeing familiar streets unfamiliar from the back of a strange car, and now began to speak like one.

"Is he dead?"

Technically speaking, the Detective Sergeant did not know. It seemed to him that the man in the house was dead all right but, as it was his place to seek information rather than give it, it was best to change the subject.

"How long have you lived there?"

"Eighteen years."

"Do you all live there?"

"Yes."

The three women in the house seemed so odd in speech and manner – remote and rather too staidly dressed, like poor dafties from an institution. Thinking the elderly woman was a bit simple, the Detective Sergeant said, "Are you looked after?"

"No. Do you think he's dead?"

"Does anybody come and visit you?"

"No. Do you think he's dead? Who's in the house with him? He shouldn't be on his own."

The driver of the car was a young police constable, who said, to quell her agitation, "He's not on his own. Don't worry, love. There's somebody with him."

"*Who's* with him?"

The Detective Sergeant resumed control and the younger man returned his eyes to the road.

"A policeman will be with him."

"Is he dead?"

"I'm not a doctor but it looks like it."

Again and again on this short ride she insisted, "But is he

dead?" because having known what was to her his demonic brilliance and power since the day she had first been drawn into his eyes as a lonely girl, she no longer believed that he could die.

"*But is he dead*?"

Eventually, to quell approaching exasperation, the policeman in the front passenger seat just said, "I think so," but still it seemed she could not quite believe it.

The Detective Sergeant noted that, even when waiting with Mrs Thompson that evening in the custody office of Preston police station, the frail elderly woman still demanded more and more confirmation that Tommy Thompson had truly died an hour before.

"Is he dead?"

"Yes."

"*Is he*?"

"Yes, yes, he is!" And then, for the sake of saying anything to deflect her from this repeated and passionate questioning of him, Detective Sergeant Mallaby asked her something merely to test her sanity.

"What's your last name?"

"Thompson."

Since Saturday evening, the three women had been in custody. As usual, they had been put into white-paper boiler-suits while their own clothing was being examined. Barefoot, they had then been separately placed in the warm, almost cosy, police cells downstairs. The youngest of the three, Miss Hilda Thompson, had begun to shake from alcohol withdrawal and had begged not be locked in. She was also an epileptic, a diabetic and was accustomed to anti-depressants. To avoid distress, her cell door had been unlocked and left partially open, with a policewoman seated outside. A doctor had been summoned.

Having read through the statements that had been garnered in the previous forty-eight hours, it was now down to Detective Chief Inspector Donald Biscombe to finally sort out the position of the elder sister, June. First she claimed to have shot her father alone. Then, in a second interview – perhaps as the reality of a new institution closed round her – she claimed that her sister had both instigated the murder and committed it. Now that alcohol and the confusion of the moment of killing had passed away, Mr Biscombe merely needed to peel away the last layer of what he knew, from long experience, was going to be a sordid story to which those in Preston police station were the first close listeners in the outside world.

The weekend was over. It was 10.40 on Monday morning and, in the arid quiet of an interview room, Mr Biscombe ran, priest-like, through the formalities of introduction and caution as he looked in a direct but friendly way at the young woman seated opposite. She was a local lass, polite and deferential, with short dark hair, a pale oval face and the curiously staid, old-fashioned manner of one who seemed much older than her years.

"June," he began, "since you were last interviewed by Inspector Hooper, your sister Hilda has also been interviewed and she is saying that she shot your father. What *we* want to do is just to get to the bottom of what really happened on Saturday night. Can you tell us?"

Having done it for years, June Thompson moved quite automatically to cover Young Hilda's position.

"Yeah, I can tell you. It was my sister who shot my Dad."

"Can you carry on from there?"

"I didn't want her to get in trouble so I took the blame for her. She was that bad with her health."

Mr Biscombe now had to test this version of the story move by move.

"What were you doing when she went and got the shotgun?"

"I was attending to my Dad then. He was in a fit. He was dressed and lying on top of the bed. We have a bed downstairs."

"And the shotgun was upstairs?"

"Yes."

"Where were the cartridges?"

"Same place."

"So," said Mr Biscombe, arranging events anew in the very strange house he had visited, "Hilda goes upstairs for the shotgun, comes down into the front room . . ."

The young woman spoke quite blankly and quietly, as if she were somewhere else entirely.

"As you come downstairs it is in the front room . . ."

"What did you say? It's only a small room?"

"I was near the window. I said she couldn't do anything like that, but he kept saying that when he went into a fit, he didn't want to come round."

"Did you try to stop your sister?"

"Not at the beginning, no. Not until she did it a second time. He couldn't cope. He wasn't depressed all the time, but he couldn't cope with my Mum's bad health and my sister's health as well as his own."

Then Mr Biscombe said, rather matter-of-factly, "You appear to be a very close-knit family . . ."

"Yes. We are."

"Were you frightened of him?"

"Of his temper."

"Was he a violent man towards you and your sister?"

"When he was in a temper he was. He used to be worse when he'd been out drinking."

"Did he knock you about?"

"My Mum mostly – but me and my sister as well."

"All three of you?"

"Yes."

Mr Biscombe leaned across the table and looked very straight at June in a kind of firm but friendly way.

"June, I've got to ask you. Did you *and* your sister each fire one shot into your father?"

"No!"

"Did you both hold the gun when it was being discharged? There were two shots fired into him and the first would no doubt have killed him. Why reload and fire another one into him?"

June Thompson lowered her eyes and began to feel the mood in the room deepen in a way she could no longer control.

"To make sure . . . She said so that he didn't suffer and didn't come round from the fit."

"Initially, you said that you pulled the trigger and then Hilda said that she pulled the trigger. We've got to be sure where the truth lies. Do you understand that?"

"Yes."

"Are you sure it wasn't both of you that shot him?"

"It wasn't both of us."

The next question took June faintly by surprise, as if Mr Biscombe had suddenly started talking about something else entirely.

"Have you ever had a boyfriend, June?"

"No."

"Has your sister?"

"No. We've been very close as sisters."

"Has your father ever tried to . . . *interfere* with you, sexually or indecently?"

"No."

"Are you sure, June?"

"Yes. I'm sure."

"June, your sister, Hilda, is being interviewed now. If what you are saying is the truth, she will be telling the same story. Do you agree?"

Mr Biscombe rose from his chair and disappeared out to the busy neon-lit corridor. When he returned a few minutes later, his face had changed and he spoke very gently.

"June, I've just spoken to my colleague who is interviewing your sister. Hilda says that over the years, Dad has had sexual intercourse with you and that he has also had sexual intercourse with her – that that's one of the reasons why you were both so frightened of him. Is that true, June?"

For the first time since, as a child, she had learned never to weep but only to endure, June Thompson felt her true life begin to groan to the surface, like an ancient wreck gushing and spewing up horrors of the past. The interview room and Mr Biscombe's broad, concerned face began to waver behind tears so hot they seemed to boil from her eyes and she could not stand the pain. All three quiet witnesses in the room moved back slightly, as tension broke and the truth was close to telling.

"*Yes!*"

As paper tissues were produced and Mr Biscombe lowered his eyes to let this first storm of feeling subside, he said quite quietly, "Why didn't you tell us that in the first place?"

"I didn't want to make things any worse. It wasn't just *that* – it was his temper as well."

"Has he been having intercourse on a regular basis with you?"

Still she could not bring herself to admit it.

"No!"

"How long then?"

"It's – it's been going on for some years now."

"Can you remember how old you were when it first happened?" But June found that she no longer had any real landmarks in her sexual life at all.

"About sixteen, I think. I can't remember."

"When was the last time? Is it recent?"

"No. About six weeks ago."

"Did Mother know what was happening?"

"Yes."

"What was her attitude?"

"She didn't want it to happen, but she was too frightened."

"Where did all this take place?"

"Sometimes upstairs. Sometimes downstairs."

"When Mum and sister were out?"

June Thompson now began to realize the full shame of how all this would appear to the outside world.

"Not . . . always."

And Mr Biscombe quietly pressed on.

"Did that cause rows between Dad and Mother?"

"Not always. Sometimes it was other things."

"Did you know he was having intercourse with your sister?"

"When she was younger. But she always knew what was going on with me."

"Would you have any objections to being medically examined?"

"I wouldn't want to be."

Then, in the quaint and euphemistic way that an English policeman moves on to other sexual practices, Mr Biscombe asked rather gruffly, "Has he ever done anything unnatural?"

Wondering what else could be 'unnatural' in her situation, but also sort of knowing, June Thompson had barely said, "No" when Mr Biscombe broke the news from Young Hilda, further up the corridor. It was information he had been holding back but that, in a way, June Thompson now wanted to hear.

"June, your sister has also said that you were *both* involved in the killing on Saturday night."

"*Both* involved!"

"Yes. And that you went and got the gun. Is that true?"

Mrs Thompson had been talking too and, rather vaguely, it was emerging that all three of the Thompson women had discussed murdering Tommy once or twice before. At last June Thompson felt on top of something – that something approaching real life was being reached.

"Yes," she said quite simply with her head bowed.

"Would you like to tell me what really happened?"

Confident now that the truth of the Thompson sisters' last hours with Tommy lay within his grasp, Detective Chief Inspector Biscombe suggested that before June Thompson finally began her story, they should all break off for another cup of tea.

Later that day, Mrs Hilda Thompson was formally charged with conspiracy to murder and the Thompson sisters with conspiracy to murder and with murder. But when a policewoman accompanied them back to Skeffington Road to pick up a change of clothes and they found, so oddly, that Tommy had vanished from the house, the Thompson women sensed a kind of lightness in the air. Like getting up from bed after a great fever has passed, they went light-headed and on shaky legs back into the police-car with the feeling of a new beginning. Even if they all should be found guilty and sent to prison for the rest of their lives, it was the first true freedom they had known in forty years. Few former inmates of Risley Remand Centre, Cheshire, can be said to have truly enjoyed their stay there, but that afternoon, as the sharp spring light closed down and the police-van halted to be checked in, the Thompson women felt that they were passing through the gates of heaven.

Winckley Square sits at the very heart of Preston and, since the 1920s, as I have said, it has been a legal quarter. Grander than many Georgian squares in London, its elegant white houses tilt and settle towards the River Ribble, enclosing vast leafy gardens.

Over the course of two years I came to know these gardens well, reading back my notes there in the hour before a train, puzzling over apparently trivial things the Thompsons had done or tried to explain, glancing for lighter relief at the *Lancashire Evening Post* ("Angry Man Stole 500 Bin-Liners"), and generally idling through the seasons. One summer afternoon, bunked off from school, an Asian youth lay beneath trees becalmed by summer, kissing and kissing someone in the grass and longing to do more. In winter, walking briskly in dark-clad pairs after a good lunch nearby, legal men and women crossed and criss-crossed the frosty paths back to their comfortable rooms beyond the lighted windows of the square. In the clattering front office of No. 17, some time in the spring of 1988 machines had begun to feed through sheets of paper bearing strange words the Thompson women did not fully understand:

REGINA V. JUNE THOMPSON
ADVICE TO COUNSEL

This is a most tragic case in which the defendant and her sister are charged with the murder of her father. It is a case in which there will be every sympathy for the defendant

> because of the terrible life which she has been forced to lead but in which there is, as yet, no evidence of diminished responsibility and great difficulties in relation to her defence of provocation . . .

As defence lawyers began to wrestle with the new legal problems caused by women who finally turn against domestic violence – that in English and Scottish law, killing by stealth cannot be technically classified as acting in 'self-defence' – Mrs Thompson and her daughters were experimenting with life on bail. Deeply ashamed of what they had done (to this day, still able only to refer to Tommy Thompson's murder as "It"), the Thompson sisters fully expected to go to prison for the rest of their lives but, in the meantime, in the strangely calm and accepting atmosphere of the Eastcliffe bail hostel, they became as energetic as children.

Take a narrow, promising entry on a corner of Winckley Square and you pass into Eastcliffe, an ancient, steeply descending lane closed in by high, mossy walls of mellow English brick. If you stand back to see what rises up behind these walls, you will find brooding gables, ochre twisted chimney-pots and the hidden presence of massive trees, stepping and terracing down in tangled gardens to the hidden river. What is now the Eastcliffe bail hostel has the appearance of a mid-Victorian rectory – serene light grey, steep steps leading up to a Gothic porch and a gable topped by a Celtic cross. Inside, in a well-ordered kitchen, the Thompson sisters each morning peeled and steeped the potatoes they might expect to eat as part of dinner that evening and then found themselves curiously free to explore the town for the rest of the day.

That summer, prison still stretched away in the distance, like going back to school after the warmth and excitement of playing on holiday streets. They looked in shop windows to see what they could buy if they had the money – sweets, colourful little ornaments in the shape of animals, bars of sweet-scented soap – and noted nice soft things to eat which their mother could have managed with her dismembered mouth. Month by month, parts of an invisible legal mechanism fell away, leaving behind the strangeness of first freedom. In a magistrate's court, their mother was acquitted of conspiracy to murder and returned alone to their old home in Skeffington Road. They also had the charge of conspiracy to murder dropped, but knew that the charge of murder still stood. One day, after Tommy had been interred for some months in Preston cemetery, they bought Mrs Thompson a puppy – a white Yorkshire terrier – to keep her company during the long years they expected to be away in prison.

The Thompson sisters did not understand the ins and outs of it all, but on the day of their trial at Liverpool Crown Court, although it was back to the old days of being racked with nerves (and they hated having their handbags taken away as they were led into the dock), somehow the legal people in Winckley Square were struggling to make everything all right. They pleaded not guilty to murder but guilty to manslaughter and when, in a matter of thirty minutes, the judge sentenced them to two years' imprisonment, suspended for two years, and said, "Go home and look after your mother", June and Hilda Thompson wept in the dock with joy, noticing that Brian Atkinson, landlord of the County Arms, was giving them a cheery thumbs-up sign from his seat in court. As June wrote:

I wanted to thank the judge that day in court but everything went by that quickly and I didn't know what to say.

A man from the council housing department said, "It's yours now," as they marvelled at the first-floor maisonette they were going to live in together – a place with no bad memories of the past and where, in middle life, they could start afresh. It was a few weeks before they could move into it,

but in that time we managed to get the painting and decorating done. There was a lot to be done. It was lovely for us to choose the colours that we wanted in paint and wall-paper & not to have him behind you when you were buying it.

On the day they had new rose-coloured carpets fitted everywhere and as sunshine flooded in through picture windows, making the rooms seem huge,

It was like we were on Holiday & this was our accommodation.

After forty years, this still seemed to be the thing that Mrs Thompson had wanted most in life – a beautiful home in which to bring up children. Although they were both nearly forty, children was what June and Hilda Thompson seemed to have become. In middle life they went back to the interior place where childhood had been frozen, becoming for a while young teenage girls of the 1960s, delighting in skating at Blackburn ice rink. Older girls at the rink soon told them that the skating boots available for hire had coarse, blunt blades which did not glide so freely and so they bought their own – new gloriously white boots on which the blades were as keen as knives.

Mrs Thompson, in her early days of freedom, used to sit and watch her daughters skating. It was a nice place, she said, rather cold if you were not actually moving, but with music and a bar overlooking the scene. At this stage, Tommy had not begun to visit her again; she felt free, while out there in the throng – aged what would you say? – her daughters seemed to fly.

With her latest bout of mouth cancer again in remission, Mrs Thompson too picked up the strands of an earlier youthful existence. As if she had never been away she resumed church-going, usually afternoon meetings at the local Methodist church in Ribbleton Road, where the minister "accepted me although he knew about us and I could not put my teeth in". Then, feeling wonderfully strong and energetic, she took Young Hilda ballroom dancing in Preston, reliving the excitement of getting ready to go out, the prospect of music and then both of them leaving the new maisonette, beautifully dressed and coiffed at last. Quite dazzled by their novel freedom – the fact they could do anything they wished with the hours of each day – all three women also went to afternoon sessions at the Buckingham bingo hall, a place which made Mrs Thompson particularly happy. Despite her exceptional misfortune in the lottery of marriage (to put it mildly), the idea of *chance* in life still had the power to excite her – not knowing what *might* happen in the concentrating balloon-decorated room, and the possibility, if they won, of extra money of their own, cash straight into your hand, at the end of a lucky afternoon.

It was December. Just about the end of my second year in trying to get as close as any outsider might be able to get to the inner track of the Thompson family story. That morning, with Christmas only ten days away, my elder child was ill, lying in our bed next door to my typing room and sleeping in the deep random way that feverish children heal themselves. Free for a short while, I was literally writing the word 'Preston' on the envelope of a Christmas card to the Thompsons when the telephone rang and there at the other end of the line was the warm, attractive voice of Detective Chief Inspector Donald Biscombe. I had not seen him for two years.

"Mr Biscombe," I said with real pleasure. "It's lovely to hear from you!"

"You wrote to me, Alexandra," he said, "a long time ago. I was too busy, I never replied. You mentioned something about Brian Atkinson, but I'm wondering if you ever did speak to him?"

Brian Atkinson was, and still is, the landlord of Tommy Thompson's favourite pub (he has been the publican there for twenty-five years). It is an old-fashioned, pastel-washed pub, standing at a curious angle within a few yards of the gates of Preston Prison. In the staging-post manner of ancient pubs in England, it was, I supposed, something of a major information exchange for people travelling in and out of the shopping centre of Preston.

Brian Atkinson had been present at the Thompson sisters' trial in Liverpool Crown Court and he was one of the few people who had seen Tommy Thompson and his family day after day for many years, though admittedly only from the other side of a bar. Because I was very nervous of contacting him out of the blue, I had written to Mr Biscombe just to ask if he knew anything about him – particularly whether he might be easy of approach. For some reason, I had imagined that Brian Atkinson might be a bit like Tommy Thompson's brother Cyril – rather tough, with little time for women journalists. He was such an important witness that I was afraid of losing possibly my one and only shot at him by fluffing it.

As usual, I could not speak *directly* on the telephone as one is supposed to do and now, with Mr Biscombe, I was at it again.

"Is it the County Hotel or the County Arms?"

"County Hotel."

"I suddenly thought it might be the County Arms."

"County Hotel."

"I mean, I must have passed it thirty times in the past two years but I was too nervous to go in. I thought of telephoning Mr Atkinson, but I thought he might do a Cyril Thompson on me. I mean, *I sympathize* with Cyril Thompson, *entirely*. I mean, if I were closely related to a notorious man who had been murdered, I wouldn't want my family held up for all and sundry to poke into either. To be honest, I was afraid of being rebuffed on the phone."

Mr Biscombe was amazingly jolly about all this.

"Old Brian's a good sort. You'd have had no problems with him."

"Well, if I *did* ring him, I suppose a good time to call a publican would be about 10.30 in the morning. Not in the evening, that's for sure."

Mr Biscombe was very patient. In the background other telephones had started to ring and it seemed to be down to him to answer them.

"Alexandra, would it be any use to you if *I* tell Brian Atkinson that you're going to ring him? What time would you like?"

"Ten-thirty in the morning? Tomorrow morning?"

"That sounds like a good time."

And then Mr Biscombe was gone.

Next day, when Brian Atkinson in turn picked up a telephone receiver, his voice was so broadly welcoming – he had a nice, enveloping, deep voice – that I wondered why I had not attempted to speak to him two years before. I had first seen his name in the *Lancashire Evening Post* shortly after Tommy Thompson's death. At that time, he had been quoted as saying that Tommy Thompson was "a very worried man" who seemed to have something preying on his mind. There was also an implication that Tommy Thompson might have taken his own life. At that time, I had only the haziest notion of the ever-mounting and concealed emotional stresses of the male incest-perpetrator. Like the public and, indeed, his own family, I was still at the stage of seeing Tommy Thompson as an overwhelmingly powerful and confident man. Far from making a very perceptive statement about Tommy Thompson's mental health, Brian Atkinson seemed to me just to be saying bland, supportive things about a regular customer out of local loyalty or, perhaps, a natural distrust of the Press.

"Well, now I realize how right you were about Tommy Thompson, although I half dismissed what you said at the time."

Brian Atkinson gave a kind of appreciative chuckle, the comfortable sound of one who has been overlooked but who was, in general, quite right all along.

"He *was* a very worried man and from what's come out since, now we know why!"

"I suppose I should have come to you first but I – I thought you might be the sort of person who wouldn't want to be bothered by journalists."

"No, you're all right, Alexandra," said Brian Atkinson very cheerfully. "I can handle 'em. Just after the trial, you should have seen what went on in 'ere – Italian television, the lot. I've been in a book before, you know –" and here I quietly gasped, as if I had just accidentally telephoned a character in a 'novel' who said, 'I'm not fiction, you know, I'm real' – "You've been in a book before?" I said rather weakly.

"Aye. It were called *The Butler* – sometime in the late 1970s. It were about a house-breaker who used to pose as a butler in all the big mansions before he robbed them. Then there was a murder – he was called Archibald Hall, I think – he's still doing time somewhere up in Cumberland."

Now totally relaxed with Brian Atkinson, I got on to the subject of Tommy Thompson's last days.

"You're so important a witness," I said, "because you probably are the only person who saw Tommy and possibly the rest of the Thompson family in the days immediately before the murder. Did you *ever* see the whole family together? Just looking on from the outside, what did you think of them?"

Brian Atkinson recalled the four members of the Thompson family walking towards his pub.

"They had to walk after him –"

"After him?"

"Yeah, they had to walk after him along the street like Indians, like Pakis – no disrespect to them – but just like them, when they walked along the street."

"Did you ever notice what Mrs Thompson was like?"

"She was in a world of her own when she came into my pub. I expect the tablets took her like that."

"And June and Hilda?"

"June might sometimes say just one sentence to me if she passed on her way to the toilet. But he were very possessive, by the way –"

"Possessive . . ."

"He was a very jealous person. He came into my pub seven days a week like a family man with them, but if another regular put his arm around June's shoulders and might just say, 'How are you, love?' he would go mad. He used to put his *own* arm round the girls when he was playing pool in here at 11 in the morning. He came in about 11 often, because he didn't like a crowd. When people came in later and the place filled up, he would drink up and go out."

As with me, the psychiatrists and doubtless anyone else who had attempted to know her, Young Hilda seemed to have passed like a ghost through Brian Atkinson's consciousness, but of one thing he was sure, and that was the day when June Thompson had risen from the pub table and disappeared into the ladies' lavatory, asserting in the most banal way some kind of freedom of movement and physical integrity.

"She said something in passing to me on her way there – I forget what – but then she was in there quite a long time, a quarter of an hour . . ."

"Go on," I said.

". . . and then Tommy Thompson came up to the bar and, as it was quiet, he said, 'June's been in there a long time. Can I see what my daughter's doing?' It was quiet in the pub and he flew in!"

Brian Atkinson's voice altered a little as voices do when the owner is called upon to look back on events not fully comprehended at the time.

"When she came out, she was shaking. She must have been going home to a good hiding, because she was absolutely terrified."

"Did you not think," I said, "that something unusual was going on in the Thompson household?" I tried not to make this sound accusatory, as one is sometimes tempted to do when talking to people who have glancingly witnessed the outer shape of suffering but somehow felt constrained from acting to ameliorate it in any way – to be socially shocking, to dare to be wrong, to *intervene*.

Brian Atkinson then recalled the thing which had seemed to him unusual and which to me seemed the most staggering of all Tommy's acts – a gesture of utter social defiance – in the open air, in broad daylight where all could see it.

"One or two regulars said they had seen Tommy Thompson kiss June – here, outside the pub – on the street."

"On the cheek . . . or on the mouth?"

Brian Atkinson seemed amazed that I needed further clarification.

"On the mouth!"

"You mean that Tommy Thompson was actually kissing his elder daughter, June, full on the mouth in broad daylight on the street and nobody thought that was odd?"

"Well, if she'd been a *child* . . ." Brian Atkinson was trying to explain. "But she was a fully grown woman in her late thirties. We just thought that, at that age, the Thompson girls could look after themselves."

This kiss, wild, full and in the open air beside the cream side wall of Brian Atkinson's pub, now seemed to me to be the final unsought touch to my necessarily halting portrait of Tommy Thompson as possibly the most successful male child abuser so far discovered in Britain. Like the conclusion of some hyperactive romantic film of the 1940s which Mrs Thompson had watched long ago as a lonely child seeking comfort in a Chorley cinema, it was The Kiss, Il Baccio, Der Kuss – The Sunset and The End. It was the ultimate act of a type of man sexual therapists nowadays say would make the perfect subject for a novel – a man with no friends, no accepting family, alone, terrified, frustrated, alcoholic and yet, in his deceit, capable, handsome, powerful and full of pride – a kind of Vautrin (Balzac's master criminal) of sexual deviancy and, at the same time, just a child in agony grown to manhood.

Over the telephone from Preston, Brian Atkinson was continuing to give the bewildered point of view of those pub regulars who had not known what to make of Tommy and June so blatantly kissing in the street; in the conservative British way, not wishing to interfere in a neighbour's affairs or to inform.

"They were big girls and *not* children. I suppose it was thought that they *could* look after themselves, like . . ."

I then saw the purpose of what was, in fact, Tommy Thompson's double-bluff. With incredible audacity, this man had worked things so well that he was now able to kiss his elder daughter fully on the mouth in public and forever keep his hold on her by publicly passing any 'blame' on to June, as one who should have known better but who was content to play the seductress with her own father.

I could just see a couple of Brian Atkinson's regulars giving each other the nod as they passed by the rapt pair.

"Oh well, a little of what you fancy, eh?"

A genius, thought I, and some brass neck.

This now brought me on to what was the most cruel and painful newspaper account of the Thompson sisters' trial, the report in the *Sun*, which headlined Mrs Thompson and her daughters as "The Family They Called The Munsters". In a way, although this presentation of the Thompson women's story was vile, the *Sun* had hit on one strand in child sexual abuse quite by accident. This is the fact that when such abuse is technically incest (that is, contained between an adult and children who would be prohibited by blood connection from marrying), society is much more tolerant of it than one would like to suppose. Few people see humour in such a weighty taboo as parricide, but incest in many cultures is both absorbed and defused by jokes, as in this North American stand-up comic turn about supposed hillbilly incest:

> "Gawsh, Jack," says Jill to her brother. "You're much better than Paw."
>
> "Yep," says Jack. "That's what Maw always says."

"Brian," I said, because I really wanted to know, and anyway, from what he had said earlier, Brian Atkinson did indeed seem to be very confident in dealing with newspaper reporters. "Can you tell me, did people round here *really* call the Thompsons 'The Munsters', like it said in the *Sun*?"

Brian Atkinson suppressed a kind of chuckle and then said quite firmly, "No. They didn't. That's just what was said in the papers."

"Because I can assure you that what came out in court really was only the tip of the iceberg."

"Well, now we *know*," said Brian Atkinson, seeming to see in his mind's eye the pale image of the Thompson sisters nowadays still occasionally passing his pub in their new time of freedom. "They are two young ladies – two *beautiful* girls. I often say 'hello' when I pass them in the street, but I always let them just pass by me – I don't say any more in case it brings back tragic memories."

He seemed to voice the reaction of a good many ordinary men in Preston when he rounded up by saying, "When I finally heard in court what he had done to all three of them over the years, if I'd had a gun, I would have shot him myself."

During this initial period of freedom, Mrs Thompson had been distracted by the sheer lightness of life brought about by Tommy's absence, but then he began to return to her at night, stalking the hours of darkness with authentic ferocity – the sound of his voice roaring in through her deafness, his swift and direct movement towards her just before delivering a blow, the old threats about pulling down the interior of the house and making them all live in a wreckage of blood and terror once more. Now she was seeking professional counselling for night terrors and had begun to realize that although killing Tommy had removed his physical presence, who he was and what he had done to them would continue to live with them after all. Living with him had been desperate, but living without him was forcing in new terrors of its own. Having passed through the phase of skating and sometimes dancing ('catching up' with lost time), June and Young Hilda also returned to a fragile state of mind. Young Hilda, in particular, sank once more into deep and terrifying troughs of depression, at one time being hospitalized for over three weeks. Nowadays the three Thompson women sat together with the remote vagueness of hospital patients in the new home they had at first taken such extraordinary delight in fixing up, but during their better spells they still took passive pleasure in just looking at the daily things of domestic life they had never had before. New Hygena melamine units in grey and white made the kitchen look long and sleek, like something gleaming in a DIY brochure. They had chosen textured kitchen wallpaper in primrose and had hung on it a red plastic clock shaped like an old-fashioned kettle and a china plaque saying "Mothers Are The Most Beautiful People In The World", and beside the real electric kettle they had placed a small china cat with a dip in its back in which to neatly rest a teaspoon after silently making a considered cup. On the sitting-room wall, two colour photographs of June and Hilda taken during their schooldays had been reframed and now had pride of place above the television set – a big one fitted with some new device whereby Mrs Thompson could now command subtitles on the screen for all TV programmes. Up on the landing of the yacht-like wooden stairs, new videos were housed in a row of gilt-tooled 'books' and upstairs on her single bed lay new Sony headphones for Young Hilda's "Beat Depression" tapes with which she tried to go to sleep.

Beyond the second bedroom, that left the third, which housed the replica of Tommy Thompson's store room. This time, grey metal industrial racking, the items of siege life – old pots and pans, boxes of dried food, cartons of tights, ropes, spare clothing, patent medicines, DIY tools – remained the same as before, except that June and Young Hilda had tried to personalize the stores by sticking up, at the end of each bay, brightly coloured posters of kittens and dogs and the occasional greetings card. As usual, on what they continued to call "the spare items", June had done all the painstaking work of labelling each thing in biro, printing neatly on white sticky paper.

Once or twice I had tried to bring up what the future might hold for the Thompson women and, as far back as that day in Preston cemetery, June Thompson herself had caught a glimmer of a future in which her mother might no longer be with them. But that was as far as it went. She merely assumed that for the rest of their lives, she and Young Hilda would continue to live very quietly together. The possibility of the sisters at some time leading separate lives seemed to be out of the question.

In many ways, this continuing simplicity of life runs counter to what many therapists describe as the 'emotional fall-out' which takes place after an abuser has been removed from a home. If a father has been the abuser, it is often said that a 'honeymoon period' then takes place between a mother and her abused daughter. Mother and daughter suddenly come very close together (and here I thought of June and Mrs Thompson sleeping together) to sink or gloss over what has hitherto been the painful reversal of their roles in the family. According to these clinical observations, the daughter feels intense anger at having been betrayed and left unprotected by her mother, while the mother feels deep anger at having been sexually supplanted in the family by her own daughter. Although many abused girls grown to adulthood quite rationally 'understand' that the mother was, in fact, in a powerless situation at the time, the child within continues to 'feel' the mother as an omnipotent figure who merely seemed at the time to turn away from her appalling suffering. Eventually, so the theory goes, mother and daughter part on poor terms and the death of the mother is particularly fraught for the daughter because bereavement in any situation is always very difficult when the survivor feels ambivalent about the deceased. As June Thompson had borne the brunt of exceptionally brutal sexual abuse in the family for almost thirty years and, by doing so, seems to have shielded Young Hilda from the worst of it, I also wondered from time to time whether, after Mrs Thompson's death, June might begin to assert, in turn, greater independence from her sister. This would be on the lines of, I carried the can for you for thirty years and I'm carrying it no more.

Instead, I can only say from what I know of these strangely heroic women that these well-based theories do not seem to apply. Instead, perhaps because they witnessed almost from birth the extreme violence done to their mother, the Thompson sisters truly know *and* feel that she could not save them but only continue to suffer with them. I feel that rather unusually, the Thompson women will always continue to stick together, because Mrs Thompson actually was a very good mother in appalling circumstances. In their case there is also the other factor which resists rational analysis: their sheer simplicity and goodness.

On one of the better days that I was with them, June Thompson had just bought a Polaroid camera and, turning to me, full of happy anticipation like a child, she said, "Would you mind, Alex, if we took a photograph of you and Mum together? We've known you all this time and never had one of you."

Mrs Thompson and I stood together in front of the gleaming fireplace and then, when June had pressed the shutter, there came the satisfying rolling click and whizz of a Polaroid camera delivering its instant opinion of the scene. For some reason, I felt immensely pleased that June was taking a photograph all by herself. Like using a telephone, a pen and, I suppose, a gun, it was another small sign of personal integrity being restored at last.

With a kind of simple merriment, Young Hilda came forward in her fluffy slippers to warm the Polaroid picture between her hands and, gradually, from a bloom of under-developed confusion, emerged the image of Mrs Thompson and myself, side by side in the pink velvet glow of the afternoon maisonette.

"It's come up really well!" declared June with genuine pleasure as she and Young Hilda pored, heads together over the newly minted snap, like two primary-school children at a desk. "I didn't think it would."

Having been photographed by Tommy Thompson for years and forced to pose to his liking as happy and smiling members of a 'normal' family, now June and Young Hilda would be able to make a record of this part of their lives themselves and to see that it was truthful.

June was a novice in photography and, merely because I had come in from the outside world, they assumed as usual that I must know about everything, including photography. In fact, I have little time for photography because I rarely believe what I see. But then I began to say that, for them, photography would be a very good thing to do in future and as in the writing of their story, it probably just depends on the careful positioning of subjects and, after that, mostly on the light of the day.

Sources

This book is closely based on nine notebooks written by Mrs Hilda Thompson and her daughters, June and Hilda, in 1990, on family letters, photographs and documents, and on diaries kept by June Thompson at the instigation of her father from 30 April 1970 to 11 March 1988. These were developed by interviews carried out by me with members of the Thompson family and with other people in central Lancashire between 1990 and 1992. I also looked at legal files. Real names have been omitted or changed in the book in three places.

Background research, of course, played a major part in priming what I hoped to learn from interviews. As every conversation, description and speculation can be supported, the book could have been footnoted, almost line by line, in the conventional way of a non-fiction study. On editorial advice I chose not to do this because it might clog the narrative flow for the reader. That being the case, the sources given below are more of a general guide to some of the more important background material that proved helpful in this book rather than an exhaustive list of all the material I actually consulted.

Child abuse (physical, emotional and sexual) and neglect, plus marital and co-habitee violence

The literature on domestic violence and child abuse is vast, including specialist journals solely devoted to it. For a modest fee, the NSPCC Headley Library, 67 Saffron Hill, London EC1N 8RS, will run a computer search on any aspect of physical or psychological violence as it affects children and supply a bibliographical print-out. For the general reader, the very best introduction to child sexual abuse of all kinds – utterly objective, wide-ranging and readable – is Jean La Fontaine, *Child Sexual Abuse*, Polity Press, Cambridge, 1990. Any book involving the work of David Finkelhor is also very perceptive in this field. I looked at: David Finkelhor, *Sexually Victimized Children*, The Free Press, New York, 1979; David Finkelhor, *A Sourcebook on Child Sexual Abuse*, Sage Publications, London, 1984; David Finkelhor, Richard J. Gelles, Gerald T. Hotaling and Murray A. Strauss (eds.), *The Dark Side of Families,* Sage Publications, London, 1983. Others were: D. S. Trepper & Mary Jo Barrett, *Treating Incest: A Multiple Systems Perspective*, The Haworth Press, New York, 1986; Arnon Bentovim, Anne Elton, Judy Hildebrand, Marianne Tranter, Eileen Vizard, *Child Sexual Abuse Within the Family*, Wright, London, 1990.

You may have noticed that the publishing firm Sage Publications (6 Bonhill Street, London EC2A 4PU), which is also based in Newbury Park, California, and New Delhi, has a particularly good list on these and related subjects. (It also publishes the excellent *Journal of Interpersonal Violence*). From that imprint I also read: Peter G. Jaffe, David A. Wolfe and Susan Kaye Wilson, *Children of Battered Women*, London, 1990.

Whether Tommy Thompson was himself sexually abused as a child, I was never able to confirm but I strongly suspect that he was. When they reach adulthood, males less often disclose that they have been sexually abused as children because of cultural pressure on men to be 'tough' and to be able to defend themselves. (They also wrongly fear that such abuse indicates latent homosexuality in them). Other hazy areas in the field of child abuse include just how many children have been sexually abused by women. The previous lack of research into this area is now known as 'the over-extension of the feminist case'. A pioneering attempt to draw a 'personality profile' of the male child abuser is Anne L. Horton, Barry L. Johnson, Lynn M. T. Roundy and Doran Williams (eds.), *The Incest Perpetrator: A Family Member No-One Wants to Treat*, Sage Publications,

London, 1990. Try also: Jane F. Gigun, 'Self-Centeredness and the Adult Male Perpetrator of Child Sexual Abuse' in *Contemporary Family Therapy*, 10 (4), Winter, 1988.

In my book I occasionally experienced private flashes of anger against Mrs Thompson when, in uncovering the family story, I felt she had not 'protected' her daughters against their father's assaults. I hope I very obviously atoned for this as the story went on, but society at large still holds the mothers of sexually abused children to exceptional account for their supposed 'collusion'. Calmer light is thrown on this very difficult subject by Carol-Ann Hooper, *Alternatives to Collusion: The Responses of Mothers to Child Sexual Abuse in the Family* (paper presented at the Annual Conference of the British Psychological Society, University of Leeds, April 1988).

The numbers of child sexual victims (both female and male) who, when they have reached adulthood, murder or do violence to the abuser have still not been collated to my knowledge in Britain. But the lasting psychological effects of such abuse (however slight it seemed at the time) are understood, and many child sexual victims, particularly women, feel it helps to write about their experiences (the NSPCC library can provide a list). More objectively, try: Denise J. Gelinas, 'The Persisting Negative Effects of Incest' in *Psychiatry*, vol. 46, November 1983.

Domestic violence and child sexual abuse are, as we know, far from being new things in society – it is just that we nowadays attempt to understand them rationally in the hope of ultimately preventing them. For a general twentieth-century introduction to wife-beating, Erin Pizzey's pioneering book, *Scream Quietly or the Neighbours Will Hear* (Penguin, London, 1974) remains startlingly fresh and applicable even today. A very unusual but well-observed side-light on this painful theme is Rhian Ellis, 'The Way to a Man's Heart' in Anne Murcott (ed.), *The Sociology of Food and Eating*, Gower Publishing, Aldershot, 1983. An early and very interesting attempt to understand child sexual abuse is: S. Ferenczi, 'Confusion of

Tongues Between the Adult and the Child (The Language of Tenderness and Passion)' in *International Journal of Psycho-analysis*, vol. 30, 1949.

Local history

George Birtill, OBE, is Chorley's Honorary Town Historian and he has written a three-volume history of the town and its surrounding villages. *Chorley & District Between the Wars*, Guardian Press, Chorley, 1975, was particularly useful to me. Also vital was a tape-recording of childhood reminiscences of life in Lyons Lane, Chorley, during the Depression, made by Mr John Gilgum and kept in the collection of the North-West Sound Archive, Clitheroe Castle, Clitheroe, Lancashire BB7 1AZ. Essential reading for anyone wanting to understand the techniques of oral history (and debates about veracity between oral historians) is Paul Thompson (ed.), *The Voice of the Past: Oral History*, OUP (2nd ed.), 1988, and Raphael Samuel and Paul Thompson, *The Myths We Live By*, Routledge, London, 1990.

The verses of John Wilson (1859–1918), Chorley's 'town poet' and antiquarian postman, can be found in various local editions in the Harris Library, Preston. His life and samples of his verses recently appeared in Kenneth Hodkinson, *Old Chorley: In the Footsteps of Wilson*, CKD Publications, Chorley, 1988. Joan Pomfret's poem 'Untilled Land', which I used to set the mood of this book, won the Scholes Cup for the best Lancashire dialect poem in 1982. Joan Pomfret (who is Deputy Resident of the Lancashire Authors' Association) has broadcast 'Untilled Land' on local radio several times and has recorded it for the North-West Sound Archive, Clitheroe. As it has never been printed, I give it here:

Untilled Land

Eawr farm wor just up t'slope o't fell
Ah'd lots of room to play,
But when Ah grew to nine or ten
Mi Mother used to say:
"Think on, eawr Kath! Yo've t'run o't place,
Pray God yo allus will! –
But dorned set foot eawtside t-top field!
Thad's part o' Pendle Hill!"

"Id's *Untilled Land* – id's '*Witch Country*'*!*
An' nobdi's safe up theer!
At Lammas or at Midsummer,
Or ony time o't'year!
Ah've yeard o' children vanishing –
An' young lambs lekkin ill;
An (well, ne'er heed!) *Just keep away*
Fro' harm – an' Pendle Hill!"

At seventeen, Ah went wi Jim,
We used to meet i't lane –
"*Think on! Dorn'd goo up theer wi him!*"
Mi mothyer ud complain:
"I'd's Untilled Land, id's Witch Country,
Id's dark an' drear an' chill –
Love him i't fowd ort' bluebell wood,
But nod o' Pendle Hill!"

Appen ah should ha' minded her –
But th'Harvest moon wor breet,
An' "*Owd Wives' Tales*" sez Jim – "Come on!
Id's grand up yon toneet!"
Id *wor!* T'wend's song were cowd an' sweet

An't' kissin' sweeter still,
When *Owd Nick laughed and plucked mi sleeve*
At t'top o' Pendle Hill!

A lot o' watter's come deawn t'clough –
Neaw mi own childer play
I't fowd, and t'fields an't Bluebell Wood
But when Ah see's 'em stray
Ah skrikes, "*Torn Back!*" (Ah wonder if
Mi mother co'ed as shrill?)
"*Id's Untilled Land – id's Witch Country*
Id's part o' Pendle Hill!"

I also looked at Joseph Wright, *The English Dialect Dictionary* (8 vols.), London, 1896–1905.

A great deal has been published on the technical, economic and social history of the Lancashire cotton industry. For local living voices describing what it was like to work in a cotton mill, I relied on Sally Coleman and Nigel Morgan, *Old Yarns Respun: The Story of Preston and the Cotton Industry 1791–1991* (exhibition catalogue), Harris Museum & Art Gallery, Preston 1991. For some idea of the beauty and strange psychological power of cotton mills see Marcus Binney, Randolph Langenbach, Ron Fitzgerald and Ken Powell, *Satanic Mills: Industrial Architecture in the Pennines*, SAVE Britain's Heritage, London, 1979. With the usual SAVE aplomb, this gives a brief economic history of Lancashire's cotton mills and is remarkable for the beautiful plate-camera photographs of mill architecture taken by Randolph Langenbach. In the 1970s before the mass demolition of mill chimneys, the Pennine mill towns were still aesthetically admired as the most romantic industrial landscape in Europe (a fact not lost on early nineteenth-century German travellers like Schinkel). Mill buildings have such emotional power because in architectural terms they conform in every particular to Edmund Burke's definition of the Sublime.

General background

C. L. Mowat, *Britain Between the Wars*, London, 1955, remains a good starting point for any study of Britain in the 1920s and 1930s. The way the very poor in Britain attempted to house themselves in makeshift accommodation during the same period was brilliantly revealed in Dennis Hardy and Colin Ward, *Arcadia for All: The Legacy of a Makeshift Landscape*, Mansell, London & New York, 1984. (As Britain's leading anarchist social commentator, Colin Ward's understanding of the almost perpetual British housing crisis is unparalleled in this and many other publications on housing.) See also David Crouch and Colin Ward, *The Allotment: Its Landscape and Culture*, Faber, London, 1988. For the day-to-day thraldom of being a pre-war working-class mother without any state support whatever, Eleanor Rathbone's classic study of the way the free market decimates families is a classic of first-hand social and economic analysis. See: Eleanor Rathbone, *The Disinherited Family: A Plea for the Endowment of the Family*, E. Arnold, London, 1924. Later, as Eleanor Rathbone's long campaign for family allowances (child benefit) reached political fruition, this book was reissued as *The Disinherited Family: Family Allowances* (with a new chapter by Eva M. Hubback), Allen & Unwin, London, 1949.

As with Roman Catholicism, many rather bad books have been written about spiritualism, often, alas, by spiritualists themselves. For the insights of a good sociologist into the history of this attempt to create a 'scientific religion' for modern men and women, see Geoffrey K. Nelson, *Spiritualism and Society* (The International Library of Sociology and Social Reconstruction), Routledge & Kegan Paul, London, 1969. Finally, for the cultural rather than medical nuances of epilepsy, I read O. Temkin, *The Falling Sickness: A History of Epilepsy*, Johns Hopkins Press, Baltimore, 1974. It is an absolutely fascinating account of attitudes to the so-called 'sacred disease' from

Ancient Greece to Fyodor Dostoyevsky (who incorporated many of his own psychological experiences as an epileptic into his fictional characters).